Cultural Revolution in China's Schools, May 1966–April 1969

Julia Kwong _____

Hoover Institution Press
Stanford University, Stanford, California

Hoover Press Publication 364

First printing, 1988
Manufactured in the United States of America

92 91 90 89 88   9 8 7 6 5 4 3 2 1

Library of Congress Cataloging in Publication Data
Kwong, Julia.
    Cultural revolution in China's schools, May 1966–April 1969/Julia Kwong.
        p.   cm.—(Hoover Press publication; 364)
(Education and society)
    Bibliography: p.
    Includes index.
    ISBN 0-8179-8641-3
    ISBN 0-8179-8642-1 (pbk.)
        1. Education—China—History—1949–1976. 2. China—History—Cultural
Revolution, 1966–1969. 1. Title. II. Series.
III. Series: Education and society.
LA1131.82.K93 1988
370' .951—dc19   87-21750
                              CIP

Design by P. Kelley Baker

Cultural Revolution
in China's Schools,
May 1966–April 1969

26-1038 LA1131.82 87-21750 CIP
Kwong, Julia. **Cultural revolution in China's schools, May 1966-April 1969**. Hoover Institution, 1988. 200p bibl index **ISBN 0-8179-8641-3, $24.95; ISBN 0-8179-8642-1 pbk, $16.95**
A readable yet scholarly discussion of China's most disruptive period. The Cultural Revolution (1966-69) in China is one of the most important and dramatic events of China's postrevolutionary history. It involved millions of students throughout China and eventually spilled over to the entire society. With the approval of Mao Zedong and a faction of the Communist leadership, the nation was mobilized into several years of revolutionary fervor—and disruption. The movement started on the university campuses and spread to the schools, and then outward. In considerable detail Kwong describes how the Cultural Revolution affected the schools. Her research is based on interviews with participants as well as on documentary evidence. Kwong describes the factional struggles and the violence that accompanied the movement. She quotes from her interviews and brings the events to life. The mixture of analysis of events and graphic portrayal of specific instances is effective. The book does not provide an analysis of Chinese educational developments or even the broader impact of the Cultural Revolution. It is a detailed treatment of the 1966-69 period from the perspective of the educational system and will be a lasting contribution to our understanding of this dramatic period in Chinese history. While an excellent scholarly contribution, this book is understandable to the general reader. It will be useful to graduate students and upper-division undergraduates.—P. G. Altbach, SUNY at Buffalo

Education and Society

Paul R. Hanna and Gerald A. Dorfman, series editors

Publications in the Education and Society series, a research project of the Hoover Institution on War, Revolution and Peace, address issues of education's role in social, economic, and political affairs. It is hoped that insight into the relationship between inculcated values and behavior and a society's approach to development will contribute to more effective education for the establishment and preservation of justice, freedom, and peace.

To my parents

Contents

Foreword

Recent Chinese history demonstrates as powerfully as any other example the vital link between education and development. This is a major concern of the Paul and Jean Hanna Collection on the Role of Education in the Twentieth Century at the Hoover Institution of Stanford University. It is also the major concern of Julia Kwong's study, which examines one important aspect of recent Chinese history, the Great Proletarian Cultural Revolution, from May 1966 to April 1969.

The relationship between education and development has been demonstrated repeatedly during this century. The intense efforts by Nazi Germany to indoctrinate its citizens; the re-education of Germany and Japan after World War II, leading to their prominence in the contemporary world; and the impact of student protest movements on the stability of regimes in many countries are clear examples. None of them, however, exceeds in its explicit relationship the example of the Chinese Cultural Revolution that Professor Kwong has researched.

Kwong points out in this volume that education was much more than a part of the Cultural Revolution: it was the centerpiece of that upheaval. The Cultural Revolution was a revolution sponsored and produced by a communist Chinese political elite that acted as the strong and highly centralized Chinese government. Fully understanding the power of education, that elite explicitly used China's schools as the vehicle for the turmoil it wrought. The elite's purpose was to displace what it regarded as pre-revolutionary feudal-capitalist values and norms and to replace them with proletarian ones. It did not know exactly what forms and structures Chinese society should have, but it did believe passionately that the old values, norms, structures, and processes needed to be destroyed. The elite also knew that the students could ignite and press this process and that it was in the schools that the future would be built and transmitted. But the student leadership degenerated into internecine warfare and fell victim to a takeover of the schools by peasants and workers, who headed in a very different direction from that of the Chinese political leadership and their student activists. It is the story of this revolutionary process that Julia Kwong insightfully presents in this volume.

Paul R. Hanna   Gerald A. Dorfman

Introduction

A revolution is a telescoping of social changes. It occurs when the participants are dissatisfied with the existing system and cannot find a means to
change it within the current institutional arrangements, so that extralegal
means—including physical force—have to be used. The movement
spreads throughout the society, and such concerted efforts result in the
overthrow of the old regime. Aside from the radical structural changes
that separate the new society from the old one, a revolution is distin-
guished from other social movements by the changeover in the class
background of those who hold power.

This book is a record of the Great Proletarian Cultural Revolution in
the People's Republic of China from 1966 through 1969; the focus is on
the role of schools in that revolution. It was triggered by students' dissatisfaction with the school system, and the movement soon involved the
800 million people in Chinese society; it surpassed the French and Russian revolutions, and even the 1949 Chinese revolution, in scale and
scope, if not in the importance of their ramifications. Despite the Cultural Revolution's scale, however, the definition of it as a revolution is still
debated. Of the many objections raised to such a definition, the main one
is that there were insignificant changes in the political power structure at
the end of the movement, which resulted only in greater participation of
the military and representatives of the mass organizations.[1] The picture,
however, was different within the educational system: workers and peasants replaced intellectuals as the decisionmakers in the schools. The irony
was that this was not exactly what the revolutionary student vanguard

had intended. How these goals were compromised in the schools is the focus of this work.

The Cultural Revolution was a national movement involving every factory, farm, business, and government department. It would therefore be impossible to describe all its complexities and variations in the various regions and sectors of the society. The choice of the schools as the focus of this study is fitting because, as the term Cultural Revolution implies, culture was the focus of change. The aim was to replace, in the jargon of the hegemonic ideology in China, the feudal-capitalist values and norms of the precommunist period with proletarian ones. Feudal-capitalist values and norms took different forms and were articulated in different ways in different social contexts; the school, as the transmitter of knowledge, values, and definitions of reality to the next generation, was a principal battleground in determining whether the new ideology could be successfully sown in society.

The communist government was not slow in effecting changes in the schools once it took power in 1949. However, it faced tremendous difficulties. Traditionally, the state did not provide education for its populace; that task was left to the philanthropy of the rich and to community efforts. The state's role was largely confined to administering the civil-service examination and rewarding successful candidates with lucrative and prestigious official positions, thus indirectly sanctioning the legitimate knowledge that was to be acquired. The formal educational system as we know it in the West was introduced in China at the end of the nineteenth century by missionaries, who saw the establishment of schools as part of their social services and a way to proselytize the people. *Sishu,* schools operated by the villages or rich families, coexisted with these Western schools, which were primarily located in the treaty ports open to foreign trade. It was only in 1902 that the Qing government endorsed the Western three-tiered system of elementary, secondary, and university levels of education as a way to strengthen the country; in 1906, the government abolished the civil-service examination system to pave the way for the expansion of public education.[2] State noninvolvement in education remained, however, and initiatives were left to the local level. The Qing government fell in 1911, after which the country was engulfed in political turmoil. The republican government established in 1911 was racked with internecine struggles of power between the different military contenders. As of the 1920s, it was also faced with the invasion of the Japanese and a growing threat from the Communist Party. Since the government was preoccupied with meeting these political challenges, little attention was devoted to public education.

The communist government took a more active role in the control and provision of education. The three-tiered division in education was retained, but in 1950 higher education was restructured in accordance with the Soviet model. That is, comprehensive universities (a combination of liberal arts and sciences colleges with professional schools) were subdivided into specialized institutes and professional schools. Missionary and private schools came under direct official supervision, and the government expanded the provisions for secondary education more than eleven times and of primary education five times between 1949 and 1965.[3] More important, new curricula were drafted for the nation's primary and secondary schools to conform to the hegemonic ideology of communism. The written language was simplified to facilitate the acquisition of literacy by the population, of which more than 90 percent were illiterate. The Young Pioneers and the communist leagues in the schools replaced the youth organizations of the ousted Nationalist Party.[4]

These changes removed the more salient and formal aspects of the Western capitalist influences in education. As with education in other countries, there was a decoupling between procedural regulations and the activities in the schools.[5] Given the autonomy and seclusion of the classroom, teaching—that is, the interaction between students and teachers—was an activity difficult to regulate. Since the socialization of the young rested as much on the written curriculum as on the organization of activities in the classroom, an important part of the socialization responsibility rested with the teachers. Yet all of the 935,000 teachers in 1949, and even the majority of the 3.5 million pedagogues in 1960,[6] had received their education prior to the communist takeover. It would therefore be logical to conclude that they were socialized in the traditional Chinese—if not Western—traditions, which were not entirely compatible with the ideology of the new government. As a result, the greater the gap between the new principles of education and the traditional philosophy, the more difficult it would be to enforce the program. Teachers ignored, where possible, central regulations incompatible with their own outlook or followed them formally and mechanically if the situation required them to comply. Such attitudes reduced the implementation of central directives to procedural rituals and undermined or even thwarted the original intentions of those regulations. The introduction of political education as a subject in school was a good example. Since not all the teachers were committed to communism, students' commitment to the hegemonic ideology that was the goal of political education was reduced to their ability to memorize political tracts.[7]

Even school administrators did not necessarily understand central government intentions. The government's efforts to encourage student participation in labor (in order to integrate theory with practice) and to augment their love of the proletariat during the Great Leap Forward in 1958–1959 were not part of the traditional concept of education. Consequently, student involvement in work as a pedagogical measure was transformed into a primarily money-saving device for the schools, with students used as a cheap source of labor.[8] What went on in the schools was the same as those in traditional China: rote learning, strict discipline, and strong authority of the teachers. The influence of traditional concepts of education shaped the actions of the teachers and administrators, and the central government faced inertia and strong resistance to the introduction of new educational programs. The problems, of course, were not confined to the schools. As Harry Harding points out, the Cultural Revolution was an attempt to shake up the bureaucracy, "to indoctrinate officials in a coherent set of philosophical principles, so that they would pursue the goals set by the policymakers in a unified and reliable manner" and, in so doing, realize the communist social programs and ideals.[9] The opportunity came on May 28, 1966, when Nie Yuanzi, the party secretary of the philosophy department at Beijing University, put up a big wall poster criticizing the university administration, and the Cultural Revolution began.

Sinologists have offered many interpretations of the origins of the Cultural Revolution. Ahn Byung-joon sees it as a master plan of Mao Zedong to seize power; to others, like Harding, it was a campaign of reform gone astray.[10] The origin of the movement was complex, an amalgam of different causes, and it is not my purpose here to weigh the relative importance of each interpretation. My interest is in the *process* of the revolutionary movement. The foregoing description of the communist government's efforts to reform education provides the background for understanding what was to take place in the schools and why the different constituents took the positions they did on educational reforms. The Cultural Revolution was the concerted attempt of the central government and the students to bypass school administrators and teachers to effect changes and create an educational reality closer to the communist ideal, embodied in slogans like "to create intellectuals of the working class," and to unify "theory and practice, mental and manual labor, city and countryside."

The lack of consensus on the causes of the movement among sinologists should not be surprising, since there is no agreement even on its temporal demarcations. Some scholars, such as Craig Deitrich, date the Cultural Revolution back to the Great Leap Forward and see it as a sequel to the earlier reform efforts.[11] Others, like Lowell Dittmer, see the movement as beginning with the publication of Yao Wenyuan's article in early 1966 criticizing the play *Hai Rui's Dismissal from Office,* a satire of Peng

Dehuai's dismissal in 1960 for criticizing Mao Zedong's policies in the Great Leap Forward.[12] There are also inconsistencies in the official Chinese position identifying the end of the movement. At the Ninth Congress of the Chinese Communist Party in April 1968, Lin Biao declared that the Cultural Revolution was coming to a successful end.[13] However, the current government identifies 1966–1976 as the decade of the Cultural Revolution, with the epoch coming to a close only when the Gang of Four (Jiang Qing, Yao Wenyuan, Wang Hungwen, and Zhang Chunqiao) fell from power.[14] My dating of the Cultural Revolution in China's schools from May 1966 to April 1969 is not entirely arbitrary. May 1966 marked the beginning of student initiation of the movement. Then, in the period up to April 1969, students took an active part in the struggle for educational changes, and a radical restructuring did occur in the schools. By mid-1969, the direction of the reforms had been set.

The central government played an important role in all these developments; however, students were the primary actors in the drama. Despite the significant role and manipulations of the different levels of the government, the revolution in China's schools was a mass movement, and hence we must focus on the students to understand the Cultural Revolution in general. There is also a practical reason for this decision. Culling information from the respondents and documents to map out the development in the schools was difficult, but data on the machinations at the central level were much more fragmented and harder to get. Therefore, references are made to the central government and other sectors of society only as they impinge on the movement in the schools.

The Cultural Revolution in the schools was not a simple phenomenon. As one respondent said, "Who was not a Red Guard at the time?" The movement affected 534,000 students in 434 universities, 6.4 million students in 56,000 high schools, and 100 million students in China's one million primary schools, totaling 107 million youths.[15] Although the schools shared a more or less similar pattern of development, the experience of each was a little different from the next; schools in one region underwent the revolution a little differently from those in another, and what happened in schools in one level of education was not identical with events in the next. For the sake of clarity, however, I have traced only the general trend of the movement, reminding readers now and again of the range of experiences that might have occurred.

This work examines how the students took part in the Cultural Revolution, how the different factions formed and fought each other, how the leadership was wrested from their hands, and how the new educational program was introduced. Most important, it examines the dynamics of the movement, that is, why the movement developed the way it did. To give coherence to the analysis, one particular theme is highlighted: the compromise of revolutionary goals. It is a theme common to all revolutions.

If the aim of the central leaders in launching the Cultural Revolution consisted of no more than shaking up the educational bureaucracy, the students' reasons for participating in the movement were even more amorphous. Their goals were couched in general ideological terms such as purging the educational system of its authoritarian, capitalistic traits and to bring it closer to communist ideals. These included the participation of the proletariat in schools, the unity of intellectual and physical labor, and greater emphasis on egalitarianism throughout the entire system. Although students were critical of existing arrangements, they had no concrete suggestions for change beyond such vague reformist sentiments. In short, they knew what they were against, but were not sure what they were for. Consequently, when the Cultural Revolution ended in 1969—after the intellectuals had been replaced by the proletariat in the administration of schools, academic courses eliminated, and examinations replaced with recommendations in evaluation—many students who had earlier supported such proposed changes in theory felt betrayed. In practice, the reforms were too radical for them. The outcome of the Cultural Revolution in China's schools was not what the vanguard anticipated. To explain how this came about is the purpose of the analysis.

A high point of the revolution in China's schools was the dismantling of the school administrations and creation of a power vacuum. One important cause among the many for the students' initial success was their unity. In fact the very vagueness of their goals worked for them in the beginning, submerging the cleavages within their ranks. Once the common enemy was removed, however, and they attended to the specifics, their differences surfaced, with each group deeply committed to its position. By that time, the students had developed their own organizations, but there was no one group strong enough to take control. The institutionalized channels of arbitration had been dismantled, and there was no mechanism for peaceful settlement of their disputes. In any case, these revolutionaries did not consider the established channel legitimate and acceptable, or a revolution would not have occurred in the first place.

Violent disputes occurred among the student groups. Their earlier successes in using rhetoric and sometimes physical force in overthrowing the school administration convinced them of the efficacy of these measures, and they used them in the new situation. Differences of opinion were often resolved through a test of physical strength. Once these fights started, they developed their own dynamics. Settlement of personal grudges intermingled with the defense of revolutionary goals. No group could afford to compromise or refrain from the use of violence, because to do so would mean undermining the prestige or even spell the demise of their organization, and so the revolutionaries became mired in internal fights. Such prolonged fighting alienated groups that formerly supported them.

In response to the chaos and violence, a countermovement developed. Different sectors of society—the peasants, the workers, the military, and the government—joined forces to isolate the revolutionaries. The workers and peasants, groups originally involved though they did not take a leadership role in the movement, emerged as leaders in the countermovement. Together they overwhelmed the students and took control of the schools. Thus, with the leadership falling into the hands of another group, the changes introduced at the end of the revolution were different from those anticipated by the vanguards.

Factionalism, or group rivalry, was at the root of the compromise of goals of the Cultural Revolution, just as it may be a cause of failure in other revolutionary movements. A revolution can be seen as having occurred only when the existing power structure is dismantled. This creates a power vacuum and, when there are also different groups with different ideas who are willing to use physical force, such conditions are favorable to the development of factionalism. Once the vanguard of the Cultural Revolution was trapped in internecine fights, constructive efforts to realize its revolutionary ideals were pushed into the background, opening the way for the ascendancy of other groups. The revolutionaries were not fanatics but were caught in a vicious cycle that they themselves created. The risk of a revolution degenerating into such chaos is greater than for other social movements because of a revolution's scale and because the ousted dominant group has usually held pervasive control, thus making it difficult for any one group to be strong enough to fill the power vacuum in a short period of time. The Chinese revolutionaries' preoccupation with a struggle for power drained their strength and alienated their former support, thus opening the way for a countermovement to develop and for another group to bring the revolution to a close.

Effecting educational change is a particularly difficult process, especially in a society that has recently experienced a radical change in its political ideology and power structure. Even in a peaceful process of change, policymakers' attempts to reform a system are encumbered by the resistance and recalcitrance of dissident school administrators and teachers on whom their reform measures depend for implementation.

The following chapters describe in detail how the process of educational change unfolded in the case of the Cultural Revolution. The book is divided into four sections. Part I looks at the way in which students were mobilized and a power vacuum created in the schools. Part II examines the manner in which the Red Guards attempted to fill this void and became involved in internecine fights. Part III analyzes how the chaos generated a countermovement that replaced the students with workers and peasants as leaders in the movement. The final section situates observations made on the different stages of the Cultural Revolution within the literature on revolution—that is, on the process of effecting abrupt changes.

Unlike existing works on the Cultural Revolution, this is neither a documentary of the politics of the Cultural Revolution nor personal accounts of the participants' experiences. Instead, I incorporated the macro and micro perspectives and examined how the larger structures and developments in society impinged on the actions of the participants. To achieve this, information was collected from different sources (documents and interviews), different perspectives (individual and official), different geographic regions (in and outside of China), and different periods (documents released at the time and after 1976) to provide a more comprehensive and, I hope, a more objective understanding of the processes of the Cultural Revolution than would otherwise be possible. In 1980, I read the large holdings of published works on the topic at the Fairbank Center, Harvard University, consulted the *People's Daily* (1966–1969) and collections of English translations of the Chinese media that offered a reliable outline to the occurrences of the period, and read recent news releases that provided an alternative interpretation of the events. The following year, I spent the summer at the University Services Center in Hong Kong perusing their *Guangming Daily* and the 21 volumes of *Red Guard Publications*, which provided valuable information on the reactions and perceptions of the Red Guards at the time. In the spring of 1981, I spent three months in China talking with participants in 59 educational institutes about their experiences in the schools, and during the summer I interviewed nineteen former Red Guards residing in Hong Kong. In 1983, I returned to China for a month to talk further with some of the respondents. Throughout this time, I was also helped by Chinese scholars in North America who generously shared with me their experiences and feelings and who commented on the analysis.

A piece of work is always a collective achievement accomplished with the collaboration of others, and this one is no exception. I am grateful to the Fairbank Center for East Asian Research, Harvard University, and the University Services Center in Hong Kong for providing me with facilities and an intellectually stimulating environment in preparing this work. I am also indebted to the Social Sciences and Humanities Research

Council of Canada and the University of Manitoba for their continuing financial support, which has made it possible for me to collect the data and draft the manuscript. Colleagues, both Chinese and North American, whose suggestions and comments clarified my thinking, are too numerous to name individually. The former shall remain anonymous; among the latter, I am especially grateful to Paul Cohen, Lawrence Douglas, Philip Kuhn, Hong Yung Lee, David Livingstone, George Rude, Mark Selden, Peter Seybolt, and Nicholas Tavuchis. I am also grateful to my editors, Martin Robbin and—at the Hoover Institution Press—Julia Johnson Zafferano, who helped me turn this manuscript into a readable text. Finally, I am most appreciative of my husband, Victor, who put up with me through the tortuous process of preparing this book.

PART I

Mobilization

CHAPTER I

The Beginning of the Revolution

On June 27, 1981, at the sixth session of the eleventh Central Committee meeting, the Chinese Communist Party adopted a resolution on the evaluation of the Cultural Revolution. According to the resolution, the Great Proletarian Cultural Revolution was a disaster that led to "domestic turmoil and brought catastrophe to the party, the state, and the whole people." The official Chinese position holds that the Cultural Revolution was initiated by Mao Zedong based on his misconceived ideas of the Marxist-Leninist theory of continuous revolution and his erroneous view of Chinese reality. Lin Biao, Chen Boda, and the "counter-revolutionary cliques" of the Gang of Four—Jiang Qing, Yao Wenyuan, Wang Hungwen, and Zhang Chunqiao—took advantage of Mao's mistakes and conspired to satisfy their personal ambitions. But the people in their "heightened political consciousness" boycotted the revolution; some even resisted.[1] In short, the official view is that the Cultural Revolution was purely the concoction of several powerful government leaders, and so all others are absolved of responsibility. This interpretation appears simplistic, but it is probably a political move to stabilize the country and avoid ill-feeling among the population in the current period of a turnover of power. In reality, the mobilization for revolution was a much more complex process.

Nie Yuanzi's Big Wall Poster

At 2 P.M. on May 25, 1966, outside the dining hall of Beijing University, Nie Yuanzi and six other members of the philosophy department put up a big wall poster questioning the university administration's handling of the cultural revolution. That cultural revolution was not the Great Proletarian Cultural Revolution for which we use capital *C* and *R*. No one in May 1966 anticipated the scale and duration of the latter movement. Instead, cultural revolution in the wall poster referred to the government-sponsored campaign that began in 1963 to criticize Yang Xianzhen's theory of "two combined into one" (which overemphasized compromise), Xia Yen's association of self-interest with happiness, and Wu Han's play, *Hai Rui's Dismissal from Office*. The play depicted an official in the Ming dynasty who lost his position after pointing out the mistakes of the emperor's land program. The parallel was clear: during the Great Leap Forward, Peng Dehuai was dismissed for criticizing Mao's agricultural policy. The purpose of the cultural revolution was to highlight for the younger generation the extensive "bourgeois" influences in society. According to the government's interpretation, anything that did not accommodate communist ideals was considered bourgeois, including advocating the pursuit of individual happiness, attacking Mao's attempts to implement socialist policies, or promoting compromise with traditional society.

Nie's wall poster was titled, "What have Song Shuo, Lu Ping, and Peng Peiyun done to the cultural revolution?":

> Now the people of the whole country in their great love of the party and of Chairman Mao, and in their extreme hatred for the antisocialist gang, have risen up in the cultural revolution. . . but the administration of Beida [Beijing University] has not moved. The campus is quiet. The teachers' and students' request to revolt was suppressed. What is the matter? What is the reason?[2]

Lu Ping was the president of the university; Peng, its vice party secretary; and Song, deputy director of the municipal department of education. The three administrators were accused of prohibiting public meetings and large wall posters and of tightening the administration's control over the students. They were charged with glossing over the political significance of the campaign and turning it into a "purely academic and theoretical" one, even commissioning the law faculty to produce a fifteen-volume case study of Hai Rui's dismissal.

Since 1958, Nie had fought with the university administration under Lu Ping over the policy of integrating theory with practice, study with labor. According to the policy, students were to work in factories and farms as part of the regular curriculum. During the Great Leap Forward in 1958, this became an integral part of the government's programs of grass-roots involvement in promoting economic development. Nie supported the government program, but Lu was critical because labor participation might lower academic standards. In the early 1960s, Nie had also clashed with Lu when he backed a promising young academic as the candidate for party secretary of the philosophy department against Nie. In 1964, disagreements again flared up over the Socialist Education Movement when Nie and other radicals criticized Lu and others in the university administration as bourgeois intellectuals. In 1965, just before the Cultural Revolution, a meeting was held at the International Hotel at which Nie had to make her self-criticism.[3]

These disagreements paralleled those in the central government between Mao and Liu Shaoqi, although their personal conflicts were shrouded in secrecy. Among other things, the two disagreed on how the educational system was to be run. Mao emphasized the power of ideology in transforming the individual as well as modernizing the country, and he believed that modernization could be achieved by the concerted efforts of the people. With determination and ingenuity, difficulties could be overcome without undue dependence on the intellectuals. Hence, he emphasized the role of education in transmitting socialist values and generating ideological commitment. To do this, he experimented with increased student participation in labor during the school term to inculcate the young with the love of labor and to give them the chance to understand working-class lives. In contrast, Liu had greater faith in technology's role in modernization, and consequently he gave more weight to transmitting conventional knowledge within the schools. Even though "Seventeen Years of Two-Line Struggle," a pamphlet published during the Cultural Revolution, supported Mao's position, it did reveal clear differences of opinion, power struggles, and major policy changes. These different views had tremendous implications for the part played by intellectuals and teachers in Chinese society. If greater emphasis was given to technology and expertise, then a greater role would be assumed by the intellectuals. Compromise and a more liberal attitude toward those intellectuals would be required. In the 1960s, the majority of intellectuals were still those educated before 1949 and, according to Mao, in the "feudal-capitalist tradition." They were therefore not completely trustworthy and had to be re-educated. To counteract their unhealthy influence in the schools, Mao launched the Socialist Education Movement in 1962 in the city and the ssu-qing movement in 1964, whereby university students—the new generation of intellectuals—were sent to work on the farms and investigate corruption among the rural cadres as part of their education.[4]

Nie's personal grudges might have prompted her to criticize Lu, but it was unlikely that a departmental party secretary would take on the university president alone without assurances of support from other quarters. Two informants, whose major task during the Cultural Revolution was to gather information and assess the situation for their rebel groups, concurred that Nie had the backing of Cao Yiou, the wife of Kang Sheng, a member of the Politburo. According to them, Cao was aware of the differences between Nie and Lu, sought Nie out, and even helped her to write the wall poster criticizing the "bourgeois intellectuals" in Beijing University. The details of Kang's and Cao's involvement could not be authenticated, but Chinese official sources in 1980 did accuse them of opportunism during the Cultural Revolution. My informants speculated that they promoted the cultural revolution in Beijing University to court Mao's favor. Whatever their motives, their involvement marked the beginning of interference from high-level government leaders, and the Cultural Revolution, like social movements in North America, escalated at the urging of government provocateurs.[5]

As a party secretary, however, Nie would be familiar with developments in the party. As early as November 11, 1965, Yao Wenyuan's article criticizing *Hai Rui's Dismissal from Office* was published in Shanghai's newspaper, *Wen Hui Bao*. Despite Mao's wishes, the article was rejected in Beijing, which showed his weak position in the capital. Ten days later it was published in the *People's Liberation Army Daily* and the *Beijing Daily* as Mao gradually enlisted support.

On May 16, 1966, the *People's Daily* editorial criticized the articles by "Three-Family Village," the pen name used by Wu Han, Liao Mosha, and Deng Tao. In a series of 27 articles published between 1960 and 1962 in *Frontline*, the *People's Daily*, and *Peking Evening News*, they had used allegories and historical events to criticize Mao's dismissal of Peng Dehuai, authoritarianism in the party, and weaknesses in the government.[6] The *People's Daily* editorial labeled these articles as the work of bourgeois intellectuals trying to usurp cultural leadership. On the same day, a memo from the party Central Committee that reflected Mao's position was distributed to county party committees, party committees in the cultural organizations, and regiments in the army. This was later known as the May 16 Directive. It denounced a report on the cultural revolution by the mayor of Beijing, Peng Zhen, on February 12, 1966, and accused Peng of downplaying class struggle and relegating it to an academic debate. The committee members were asked to compare Peng's report with the memo and to "expose the reactionary bourgeois stand of those so-called academic authorities who oppose the party and socialism, to thoroughly criticize and repudiate reactionary bourgeois ideas in the spheres of academic work, education, journalism, literature, art, and publishing, and to seize the leadership in the cultural spheres." The memo continued with language that made Mao's position unmistakable: "To achieve this, it is at the same time necessary to criticize and repudiate those representatives of the bourgeoisie who have sneaked into the party, government, army, and all spheres of culture."[7]

Nie knew about these developments. The editorial and the May 16 Directive were assurances that the situation was favorable; perhaps the prodding from Cao, if it did take place, gave her more confidence. This linkage between factions of the central government and local groups was a characteristic of the Great Proletarian Cultural Revolution; the movement was an interplay of spontaneity and manipulation. Local participants carefully watched the trends in central government policies and rode with the tide. This is not to suggest that the student revolutionaries went along with government policies solely because the government was behind them. Human action, especially that of intellectuals, was complex, prompted by a mixture of consideration of personal gains and convictions, evaluation of the situation and the possibility of success, and the show of government support.

Registering grievances on wall posters was not new. Issues had often been debated on bulletin boards in universities, schools, and work units, though few posters directly challenged the power and legitimacy of the authorities. Nie's bold action resulted in swift retaliation. The administration immediately called a meeting of the philosophy department, putting Nie on the defensive. Despite the allegedly high level of support, Nie and her followers were a minority, and the administration overwhelmed them with sheer numbers and forced them to engage in continuous debates. A research associate who defended Nie, for example, was taken to a dining hall to defend his position after he finished his speech in the main auditorium, and then again to the office of the Communist Youth League to argue his case.[8] In the ensuing heated exchanges, the administration convinced most of the students that Nie was wrong. The Chinese have an exceptionally clear sense of hierarchical social order. Until 1966, many students had never questioned the school authority. Neither were they aware of the central government's internal division, position, or involvement, and they felt that the university administration, as representative of authority, had to be correct. They felt that Nie and her supporters had overextended their prerogatives. For the moment, the students followed the school administration. This trust in authority and conformity to the hierarchical nature of the society would play an important role throughout the Cultural Revolution: when the central government's pronouncements went against the school administration, the students would have no qualms about abandoning the latter, which stood lower within the authority structure.

When Mao ordered Nie's large wall poster to be publicized in the national media, the central government's position became clear to the students and they reversed their stand. Kang Sheng, a member of the Politburo, had briefed Mao on the situation in Beida, which was not unusual because Beida had remained the key institute of higher learning in China. On June 1, Mao phoned Kang and told him to publicize the poster. On June 2, the entire text was read over the national radio and published in the daily papers. Such coverage by government-controlled media meant that something important was happening, and its significance was clear to the students. For example, a group of Beida students, returning after a three-day train ride from their participation in the ssu-qing movement to root out corruption in the Sichuan province countryside, immediately set out for the campus after hearing the broadcast to join in the revolution.[9]

Mobilization in the Schools

The publicizing of Nie's wall poster in the national media signaled the beginning of the Cultural Revolution in schools across the country. The schools in China provided excellent infrastructures for mobilization because they were efficient machines of social control. Each school class had its own class committee, of which everyone was a member. Paralleling this organization were the Young Pioneers at the primary level and the Communist Youth League at the secondary and university levels, all of which were extensions of the communist party. The class committees were supervised by the homeroom teachers, and the political organizations were overseen by party members acting as "counselors." The functions of these two organizations overlapped. Both groups organized picnics, games, and outings for the students, and both monitored students' behavior, but the class committees stressed cultivation of skills and hobbies and helping the slower students with their schoolwork, whereas the party organizations emphasized values and attitudes. Each organization had its weekly and biweekly meeting, and students who belonged to the political organizations took part in both. An executive of the class committee at Beida described the "group life" (meetings) just before the Cultural Revolution:

> We had class meetings once every two weeks when I helped students
> with their school work or reported to the teachers if there was anything

they did not understand. Then there was the weekly political study session when everyone had to attend. Besides, as a member of the Communist Youth League, I had to take part in "group life" every week.

Through these weekly meetings and activities, the schools communicated current government directives in addition to the fundamentals of communist morality to the students.

The administration also had a dual structure. The teaching and administrative staff had class, department, faculty, and university or school committees, although schools and professional colleges (for example, agriculture or engineering institutes) did not have faculty committees. The incumbents held their positions mainly through their educational qualifications. Paralleling this structure was the political one, whereby party members formed cells at the department, faculty, and school/university levels. Each level had a weekly study session in which party documents, reports from the *People's Daily*, or other pertinent issues were discussed. Party members had separate meetings to study the documents and issues before the rest of the group. Theoretically, the party and the administrative structures were to remain autonomous, but in practice it was difficult to draw a line between politics and "business," especially when one of the tasks of education was to transmit values and the memberships in the two groups overlapped. Often party opinion overrode that of the administration. Regardless of who exerted more influence, this principle of dual command penetrated every level of the educational institutions and facilitated the communication of central directives and control of members.

In such a highly centralized system, a local movement would usually have little success if the center were against it. However, with the central government on its side, success was virtually guaranteed. An efficient organization for social control was also an effective one for mobilization, depending on how it was to be used. Such mobilization required only a change of agenda in the weekly meetings.

The agenda of these meetings and the government directives in 1966 are not available. The activities on campus, however, certainly indicated that the government sanctioned the Cultural Revolution. Regular instruction was interrupted; teachers disseminated news of the movement in class, and they assigned readings on reports of the Cultural Revolution to their students. Indeed, one respondent recalled that she first heard of the movement from her Chinese-language teacher when he assigned readings from the *People's Daily*. Young Pioneers, Communist Youth Leagues, and class committees suspended their activities to schedule the study and discussion of party documents and *People's Daily* commentaries on the Cultural Revolution for their weekly meetings. Writing wall posters to criticize bourgeois education became another privileged activity. Class meetings, and often large ones involving the whole school, were also convened to criticize so-called bourgeois intellectuals. A student from Yunnan University recalled how a group of students examined the linguistics text written by an "old intellectual" for evidence of his bourgeois or antirevolutionary crimes. Her classmates picked the sentence, "The sun is setting behind the hill," as proof of his antirevolutionary intentions: the "sun" being a reference to Chairman Mao, and the setting sun, his fall. She disagreed even at the time, thinking it was ridiculous, but she never voiced her opinion. These activities in school exerted strong influence on the students. Many complied with enthusiasm, and those who disagreed kept their reservations to themselves.

University students in China lived on campus, and Chinese universities, unlike those in other parts of the world, were insulated, self-sufficient units. The students, faculty members, and support staff all lived within the university compound. The institutes provided not only education but also food, lodging, medical care, recreational activities, nurseries, and primary and secondary schools. Every activity was scheduled by the administration. It was the power of the administration over the individual that made it possible for the Cultural Revolution to be launched in such a short period of time and develop to such a massive scale. This intimacy and the sharing of a schedule created a campus atmosphere difficult for members to resist. No one could stay out of a movement. Even the noncommitted had to go through the rituals of the campaign. If students or teachers in high school or primary school spent six to eight hours per day on the Cultural Revolution, the university students or professors spent all of their waking hours on the movement. The hold of the university administration on campus facilitated the launching of the Cultural Revolution.

Once the movement started in one institute, it quickly spread elsewhere. Universities in China were clustered in cities and usually in the same neighborhoods. Of the 50 universities located in Beijing, ten were in the Haidian area. In Xian, Xian Normal University and the institutes of political law, foreign language, art, and communication were neighbors in the city's southern suburbs. Students visited each other's campuses, read wall posters, shared opinions and new strategies, and emulated one another. They did not have to wait for information to be filtered through newspaper reports. Consequently, the Cultural Revolution spread faster in the universities than among the secondary and primary schools; of the latter, those in the cities picked up the movement faster than those in the rural areas.

In the isolated schools or in schools where the administration disagreed and ignored central directives to promote the revolution, mobilization was achieved through personal contacts. Students in a university came from all over the country, and university students had friends studying in other universities or siblings still in high school or primary school. They had contacts across the country, and these networks helped to spread the movement. According to a lecturer at the University of Inner Mongolia, the university administration was slow to organize students for the Cultural Revolution, but students did so after one of them obtained a report from a friend about student activism in Beijing over the phone. In Guangzhou South China Engineering Institute, the students attacked the administration after one of them received a letter from Beijing describing similar developments.[10] Once a small number in the schools were mobilized, the other factors—such as social pressure and geographic proximity—came into play, and the movement spread inside and outside the school walls.

Theda Skocpol has suggested that revolutions occur when the ruling group is ineffective.[11] This may have been true at a later stage of the Cultural Revolution, but initially, many schools themselves mobilized students and disseminated ideas of a revolution. This did not mean that the school administration intentionally plotted its own overthrow. It was subjected to pressure from above and had to use its efficient and effective machinery to initiate the movement. Some administrators abided willingly, and even the unwilling ones did not see the movement as a threat to their security, so they encouraged student criticism. The school administrators thus gave the movement its first lease on life and let loose a force they later could not control.

The Students' Readiness to Revolt

Mobilization, it has been argued, will not occur unless a movement articulates an ideology that arouses enthusiasm and creates commitment.[12] The enthusiasm of almost 100 million students in China cannot be explained simply by the pressure of an authoritarian school system. Students were receptive to government suggestions to "revolt against the bourgeois intellectuals." There were two salient elements at work here: the students' tendency to obey authority and their faith in socialist ideology.

There was truth in the Chinese leaders' 1981 evaluation of the Cultural Revolution: the people had still been influenced by feudalistic (paternalistic) practices.[13] Under strong, lingering influences of Confucianism, with its emphases on the harmony of the hierarchical structures and the duty of those at the top to govern and those below to obey, the students were generally pliant and obedient. To many, their trust in the party and the government had not been misplaced. In 1949, the Communist Party had brought China out of chaos and had established a unified state. The Japanese and other imperialist powers were driven out, peace was restored, the corrupt Guomindang officials were punished, land was redistributed, new industries were set up, and the country began to recover. The people were secure and better off than before the communist rule. Most of the people—not just the young—trusted the government and were unaware of the discord within the party. When the government, like the emperor and government officials before them, called on the people for service (by asking the students to revolt), they obeyed.

In retrospect, the bad harvests of 1960–1963 could in part be attributed to the failure of the policies of the Great Leap Forward, which overemphasized mass mobilization, and could have undermined the people's trust in the government. Mao's resignation from his position as chairman of the state administration in favor of Liu Shaoqi might have alerted the people to the rift in the center. However, my informants confessed that they did not see it that way in the early 1960s. Their trust in the party was still unshaken, and they regarded the policies of setting up backyard furnaces and communal eating facilities as temporary oversights that were soon corrected. To them, the "three bad years" of 1960–1963 were the result of a bad harvest and the sudden withdrawal of Soviet aid in 1960; indeed, the Soviet action only underscored the necessity of being self-sufficient, which was one of the principles behind the policies of the Great Leap.

The Confucian emphases on passivity and compliance, interacting with the communist ideology, helped the movement to gather strength. In Chinese traditional culture, the individual found social identity and security through group interdependence. A person's social position could only be appreciated within the hierarchical structures of that society, such as emperor-servant, father-son, brother-brother, husband-wife, and friend-friend. Failure to fulfill these social obligations would lead to ostracism or even stronger sanction. The students in 1966 may have been educated in the values and outlooks of communism, which undermined certain Confucian values, such as the hierarchical conception of the social order; however, Marxist emphasis on the subordination of individual interest to the collective fit well with the Confucian tradition that required the individual to fulfill the roles of his or her social position in the hierarchy. These two diverse traditions (unlike the antithesis between the individualism of capitalism and the collectivism of communism) ironically reinforced each other, at least in the respect of demanding conformity from the individual. This demand was a powerful form of social control, yet under certain circumstances it was an equally strong mobilizing force in the close communal organization of Chinese society. Nobody wanted to be left out, and so they did what the others did. They joined the Cultural Revolution.

Many who first joined the movement participated because they wanted to serve society. They were committed to the communist ideals and wanted to see those ideals become reality. Susan Shirk found that even students who had left China wanted to be "morally good" and serve the people.[14] If such a commitment was still present among this group, we could expect those remaining behind to be even more faithful to these values. Indeed, my respondents throughout China showed a strong commitment to communism, especially to serving the people. One respondent in Xian confided:

> My nephew wrote me asking if he should go to Inner Mongolia. His parents objected, but I advised him to do it. I was brought up in Shanghai, but when I graduated, I obeyed the party's command and went wherever my skills were required. Here I am, for example, thousands of miles away from home.

Another confirmed that this willingness to serve the country had motivated her to choose physics as her specialty: "I chose physics because I thought that that was what the country needed and the best way I could serve it." Of her participation in the Cultural Revolution, she said, "I was listening to the teachings of Mao Zedong" and trying to save the country from bourgeois influences.

At least in the beginning, then, the students did not join the movement simply because they saw something to be gained. This contradicts James C. Davis's and Ted Gurr's predictions that revolutions result when the population feels deprived.[15] The Cultural Revolution did not occur initially among the dispossessed or the disenchanted thwarted in their personal ambitions. The university students were the elite of Chinese society, and yet revolution first started among this group. Only one out of a hundred high school students could enter the university, and since less than 1 percent of the population were university graduates, the future of these students was almost guaranteed.[16] They might not have anticipated the drastic developments later on, but even so, they had little to gain from any change in the status quo. A change in the educational system, and subsequently a change in the selection system for upward mobility, would only jeopardize their positions. Even the high school vanguards in

the Cultural Revolution were those from the better schools or were political activists who could be assured of a comfortable future. Certainly,
among the ranks there were opportunists and disgruntled youths without a job or sent down to the countryside, but these joined later when it
became clear that the government was behind the movement and they
had something to gain from the change in the status quo. The initial leaders in the revolution were those who were better socialized and integrated into the system, and they responded more quickly and more
wholeheartedly to the central government's call than those who were
not.[17]

These students, educated after 1949, had been nurtured by the values
and outlooks of communism and had internalized the communist ideology. In Jacques Ellul's terminology, the students had all the prepropa-
ganda necessary to prepare them for the call to revolt,[18] and so they
responded. Furthermore, reality seemed to confirm what the government said. No system is perfect, and China's educational system had
weaknesses. Liu Shaoqi was in control of the government in the 1960s;
partly as a response to the economic disasters between 1960 and 1963,
and partly because of Liu's educational philosophy, many schools were
closed, especially the locally financed, half-work half-study schools of
poor quality. Student enrollment in primary schools and universities
dropped by 14 percent and enrollment in high schools by 20 percent between 1960 and 1963.[19] Educational opportunities shrank and competition was keen, with academic performance considered the most
important criterion for admission and promotion in 1962, 1963, and
1964. The number of courses proliferated, and the curriculum often included materials students considered irrelevant to later job requirements.
The students' workload was heavy. In this unsympathetic atmosphere,
many workers' and peasants' children did badly and were expelled. To
these students, the schools, especially the good ones, were "little pago-
das" (ivory towers) nurturing the lucky few. They sympathized with
their cohorts from poor family backgrounds. As one graduate from
Beida told me with some emotion: "To be expelled from school is not
like dropping out in the West. It is a very traumatic experience in China.
It means ruining your whole life and a great humiliation."

Students might not have been aware of these inequities or bureaucratic abuses earlier, but once the government stressed the bourgeois
domination of the educational system, the students began to notice
things. They discovered that their experiences confirmed what the government was saying, and they interpreted Liu's policies of adjusting educational facilities to economic priorities as the preservation of bourgeois
dominance over the proletariat. For the moment, they held teachers and

administrators responsible. A student explained one way this could happen: "The older teachers were somewhat prejudiced against working-class students and preferred students who were studious, polite, and well dressed...Older teachers often criticized students with torn, dirty clothes, who were usually children of workers or peasants."[20] They resented these teachers' attitudes and the administrators' arrogance and aloofness; indeed, as one respondent in Ann Thurstone's study said, the revolution was sparked by the irregularities and pompous behavior of the administration.[21] In their idealism and concern for equality so central to the communist ideology, the young felt the school authorities had failed to create the "good" society, and they were there to improve it. The students were striving for a better society, not for their self-interest.

The Revolution Accelerates

The government call to revolt came at an opportune time. Examinations for the academic term were drawing near, and tension was high among the students. The government appeal represented a welcome break from mundane life and obligations, and many people complied enthusiastically. There was a flurry of activities in schools. Beida campus took on a festive mood:

> In front of the big mess hall which displayed the big wall poster, revolutionary students and teachers in groups gave speeches, read the big character posters, and denounced the "anti-black gang" for days without interruption. The entire campus of Beijing University resounded with stirring speeches, angry slogans, and revolutionary songs. The gathering of students and teachers raised their arms and shouted, "Smash the Three-Family Village to smithereens and wage revolution in a thoroughgoing manner," "Strike down the anti-party black gang and carry through the Cultural Revolution to the end," and "Long live the thoughts of Chairman Mao."[22]

Thoughts of examinations were easily pushed to the background.

Although the Cultural Revolution was something out of the ordinary, a movement of this nature was not entirely new to the students. Many were too young to have taken part in the numerous campaigns launched since 1949, but they knew about the land reform movement in 1949, the Three-anti Five-anti Movement against corruption in 1952, the Hundred Flowers Movement of intellectual liberalization in 1956, the antirightist campaign against bourgeois intellectuals in 1957, the

Great Leap Forward to increase production in 1958, and the Socialist Education Movement in 1962.[23] These campaigns might conjure up images of suffering to Westerners, but to the students at the time, these movements—especially the land reform movement—to change society had a romantic aura around them. Some of the older students had even participated in several of the campaigns. Many university students had just returned from the ssu-qing campaign in the countryside, and even secondary school students had taken part in the critique of *Hai Rui's Dismissal from Office* and Xia Yen's "theory of happiness." Such exposures prepared the students to participate in the Cultural Revolution and disarmed the administrators' suspicions. To many students and administrators, the Cultural Revolution was just another campaign, and no one could predict the scale and duration of the movement.

In July 1966, regular classes were suspended on school campuses. Class and school meetings were held to discuss central party documents and the local situation. The educational system was studied, and abuses by the school administrators were exposed. The publications and behavior of the teachers were reviewed for evidence to be used against them. Administrators and teachers considered to be tainted by bourgeois thoughts were attacked; their merits and demerits were discussed in class meetings, and when a guilty verdict was reached, the accused would be exposed to criticism meetings at the next level and finally to the whole school or university. An eyewitness described the activities in the schools in this way: "In every room there were turbulent meetings and arguments; people would be disputing something passionately, trying to outshout and outgesture others. Some would be busy with Indian ink and brush writing big character posters."[24]

Writing wall posters to expose bourgeois individuals and weaknesses in the system was a major student preoccupation throughout the Cultural Revolution. One wall poster triggered another, one poster invited criticism from another, and so the debate continued. The regular bulletin boards were no longer adequate, and posters began appearing on walls in dining halls, dormitories, and wherever there was free space. Clothes lines and mats were put up on playgrounds to hang wall posters, turning those spaces into alleyways of fluttering yellow, white, and pink paper. In one week at Beida, 100,000 criticisms were written, and in two weeks at the Zhongshan Medical School, 20,000 were written.[25] These numbers showed that the activities had gone beyond passive reactions to earlier mobilizations sponsored by the school administrations. The movement had clearly generated its own momentum, and students were acting on their own.

Opinions were not circulated solely within the students' own schools; many students wrote to the local and national newspapers. Two days after the publication of Nie's wall poster, students of Beijing University, Beijing Political Law Institute, Anhui University, and Fudan University wrote letters of support to the *People's Daily*. On June 6, students from Beijing Number 1 Girls' School criticized the educational system for perpetuating the "three differences" between manual and mental labor, workers and peasants, and the rural and urban areas. On June 10, students of Number 4 Middle School denounced the examination system. These criticisms were well received by readers, and on June 12, "inspired by these letters, students of People's University proposed a five-point program to reform education: (1) arts students were to integrate with the proletarians; (2) the arts program was to be shortened to two years; (3) the new curriculum was to focus on class struggle; (4) teaching methods were to be improved; [and] (5) workers' children were to be given priority in admission."[26] The students turned their attention to looking for bourgeois influences in their schools, and examples were not lacking. Criticism of education was more relevant and interesting to the students than philosophical discussions of the writings of "Three-Family Village," and so they pursued the former with enthusiasm. They were also familiar with what went on in the schools, and therefore the letters were likely to be written by the students and not necessarily penned by the government. However, the government's readiness to publish them in the national papers, such as the *People's Daily*, focused attention on educational reform and encouraged others to follow suit.

Other developments at the center also promoted the student movement. On June 3, the Beijing municipal committee, headed by Peng Zhen, was reorganized. That night, Wu De, the second secretary of the newly organized municipal committee, came to Beida campus to announce the dismissal of Lu Ping, the president.[27] On June 6, the front page headline of *People's Daily* exhorted the country "to carry the Cultural Revolution to the end" and "raise the great flag of Mao Zedong's thoughts." The next day, *Frontline*, the paper under the control of the former municipal committee, stopped publication and the editors of *Beijing Daily* and *Beijing Evening News* were replaced. On June 13, the central government suspended the examination system, giving the impression that this action was taken after considering the letters from the middle school students. On June 18, the government announced that the university entrance examination would be stopped until a suitable alternative was found.[28]

The outside observer might recognize the intense political maneuverings behind these events, but the students were too involved to realize it. They were delighted with developments, especially the suspension of examinations, which freed them from the drudgery of studying. This simple act removed any reservation students had about participating in the Cultural Revolution and swelled the revolutionary rank. On the day of the announcement, the *People's Daily* received 81 telegrams of support.[29] In Shanghai, over 100 students gathered outside the office of *Frontline War Gazette* to present letters to Mao.

> All over the country, there were outbursts of joy: when the exhilarating news reached all parts of the country, middle school and university students and teachers, and, in particular, those from the proletarian origin, shouted, "Long live the Chinese Communist Party. Long live Mao Zedong" and sang revolutionary songs. For the last two days, the teachers and students of the different regions and ethnic groups held discussions, wrote big wall posters, and telegrammed Chairman Mao.[30]

Their enthusiasm spilled into the streets. On the next day, "the revolutionary students of the middle schools and universities steadily streamed to the doors of the State Council and the Central Party Committee office, and to Tienanmen [Square] to express their support."[31] Such expression of support was part of China's tradition. Whenever new directives had come from the central government, the people beat drums and cymbals in street parades to announce the good news. These parades, in addition to wall posters and criticism meetings, became another feature of the Cultural Revolution.

The situation was changing rapidly, and the Cultural Revolution gained momentum across the country. It would be impossible to document exactly the scope of the movement, but newspaper reports indicated that, as early as June 9, middle schools in Guangdong province on the southern edge of the country were taking part in the movement. It had also spread to the major urban areas of Shanghai, Tienjin, Guangzhou, Shengyang, and Xian. By June 20, even the smaller urban centers had become involved. More dramatic changes were occurring in the universities. In the following two months, at least sixteen university presidents and party secretaries were overthrown. On June 3, Lu Ping was dismissed as president of Beida. On June 15, members of the party committee of Lanzhou University "stood aside"—a euphemism for being suspended. On June 16, Kuang Yaming, president of Nanjing University, was toppled. On June 26, Li Da, president of Wuhan University, and Zhu Shaotian, its party secretary, were discharged.[32] The power of the school administration weakened.

The Workteams Intervene

These rapid developments frightened some factions in the central government. Even though in mid-1966 the central government as a collective endorsed the Cultural Revolution, the members could not agree on its meaning, scale, or form. In June, Mao was in Shanghai and Liu Shaoqi was in the capital to implement the May 16 Directive on the Cultural Revolution. The reason for Mao's absence from the capital was not clear, but some scholars, like Ahn, interpret this as Mao's test of Liu's loyalty to him and of Liu's ability to carry out collective decisions.[33] Whatever the case, Liu preferred a more orderly approach in executing the Cultural Revolution, and he commissioned workteams (that is, ad hoc committees used by the Communist Party to monitor the implementation of new policies or campaigns) to take charge of the movement. The school authority might have weakened, but that of the central government was still intact. To Liu, the students had overstepped their limits. The workteams were a form of social control, imposed after these infractions, to redirect the movement.

The workteams were not sent to all the universities and schools; in all, the party Central Committee sent out only 400 workteams. On June 7, a workteam of 300 members arrived at Beida, and on June 10, one of 500 reached Qinghua University. Some universities in China were under provincial jurisdiction and others were directly responsible to the ministry to which they supplied personnel, and these government departments also had their own workteams. The Ministry of Foreign Affairs, for example, dispatched seven workteams to fifteen foreign-language institutes under its jurisdiction. In Shanghai, only six of the 24 universities were visited.[34] Many of my respondents, especially those from primary and high schools in the provinces, were unaware of their existence. This lack of coordination in dispatching workteams to the schools only further drove home the lack of consensus among the central leaders. They could not agree on the acceptable level of activism among the students or on the appropriate measures to deal with it.

The workteams were sent mainly at the request of school administrators uneasy with the developments on campus. Many administrators had complied with the central directive to organize cultural revolution in their schools, but now the students were getting out of control. School officials appealed to their superiors for help. In some odd cases, these requests even came from the students, who felt the school administrations were not supporting the Cultural Revolution. For example, some students in Guangzhou Number 45 Middle School thought their principal was stalling. They bypassed the school administration and asked the municipal bureau of education to intervene.[35] A respondent from Beijing described a similar situation. The principal in her school moved the examination date to ten days earlier, and she interpreted this as a ploy to control the students and suppress the revolution. Even though only a sixth-grade student, she was bold enough to report this to the local office of education, and the bureau intervened in her favor.

Initially, the students welcomed the workteams. As mentioned earlier, the students trusted the government and saw it as a monolith solidly backing the Cultural Revolution. Only the school administrators were the culprits. Even though the students at Qinghua and Beida did not invite the workteams into their schools, they too thought the teams were sent by the government to support the revolution and so welcomed them. This attitude reflected the students' initial political naiveté, a sharp contrast to their sophistication in the latter part of the movement.

The students were sadly disappointed. There were some workteams who supported the revolution, but the majority were conservative and shared outlooks with the school administration. They felt that students, given their young age and lowly position in the school hierarchy, were overstepping their prerogatives. Some workteams, as members of the establishment, also supported the school administration because their interests overlapped. They recognized that, if the movement spread, other civil servants in the government administration could also become targets.

Because the workteams were sent by the government to carry out the Cultural Revolution in the schools—in whatever way they chose to define it—they did not openly oppose the movement but channeled it in directions acceptable to them. Because of the novelty and immediacy of the situation, their role was not clearly delineated, and each workteam was relatively autonomous. Some workteams went along with the movement, hoping it would lose momentum. Liu Shaoqi, who supported the workteams, was later criticized for this attitude. He was quoted as saying, "When the majority of the junior high students want a holiday, give them a holiday; if those in junior two or three want to revolt, let them stay in school. When does the junior high school close? When they want a holiday."[36] This passive connivance characterized the approach of many workteams.

Workteams contained the scope of student activities. They allowed class meetings and small criticism sessions but not large gatherings. They permitted wall posters within certain school buildings, but prohibited them from being distributed outside the schools. Parades could be held within the school compound but not outside. Sometimes they even identified criticism targets for the students. The targets were usually older academics with "historical problems," that is, those who were from capitalist families, had worked under the Guomindang, had overseas connections (trained abroad or with relatives abroad), or had been identified as rightists in past rectification campaigns. The workteams did not openly order the criticism of particular teachers, because such tactlessness would only alienate students; instead, they simply slipped the names in passing or released these teachers' dossiers to students supporting the workteams. The students had a "high sense of moral and political purity," and the suggestion that someone was working against the communist policies or the teaching of Chairman Mao often provoked "a flurry of imagination" and action.[37]

The singling out of older intellectuals had historical roots. Party members distrusted intellectuals, especially the older ones and those educated abroad, and viewed them as recalcitrants who refused to submit to party rule. Intellectuals, in return, considered the party members ignorant outsiders meddling with professional matters. They disliked party cadres in their role of ideological police. In the 1950s and 1960s, the government had promoted a united front with these intellectuals in national reconstruction, but with the heightened emphasis on political purity during the Cultural Revolution, this temporary alliance was broken. The many incidents of criticizing the academic administration were not entirely opportunistic; some merely epitomized this gulf between the party and the intellectuals as well as the history of acrimonious relationships among colleagues in some schools.

These moves did not always satisfy the students. As the daily criticism sessions dragged on and the so-called crimes of the intellectuals lost their novelty, students in some schools looked for other undesirables in their midst. To placate the students, other teachers and administrators were singled out by the leaders, and the circle widened. This policy was later called "protect the minority, attack the majority." At Qinghua, 800 of its 10,000 teachers and students were implicated as counter-revolutionary.[38] But in Beijing Number 55 Middle School, the workteam criticized and quarantined all of the teachers and administrators in physical education, history, and geography, 90 percent of those in foreign languages, mathematics, and politics, and 80 percent of those in biological science and administration.[39] These figures, released after the withdrawal of the workteams, are probably exaggerated, but they do show the extent of opposition to the workteams and their failure to restrain the movement.

Sending in the workteams, however, had an important impact on the movement. Their tactics split student ranks and contributed to the factionalism to be discussed in Part II. To many students, the targets of criticisms were still the teachers, and the workteams as representatives of the central government could not be wrong. They supported the workteams, copied down wall posters criticizing the team members, and took pictures of students who opposed them. But some students thought otherwise. They resented the measures used by the workteams and recognized that teachers in the inner circle or with power were safe and that good teachers or innocent ones were sometimes falsely or unnecessarily accused. To them, students copying wall posters and taking pictures were traitors and spies.

For the first time, the students' confidence in authority was shaken. The authority was no longer infallible, nor was it monolithic. They felt that first the school administration, now the workteams, were wrong. Teachers opposing the workteams were, to many students, mistreated, and students opposing the workteams were themselves criticized and punished. They were accused of being antiparty and antirevolutionary. This was justified within the existing hierarchical structure of Chinese society. The rationale went as follows: since the workteams and the administration represented the communist party in the school, to defy them would be to defy the party; and since the party was revolutionary, to be against the party was antirevolutionary. For example, a student who opposed the president of Nanjing University was branded as an "antiparty, antisocialist commanding general and mastermind. . . hatching plots to oppose the party."[40]

Threats were used to cow such students into passivity. For example, the workteam members at Nanjing University warned a young rebel, "You are 23, you are young and yet not young. If you insist on your opinion, you will be guilty of opposing the workteam. . . Even if you want to die [to get out of this situation], it is not that easy. If you die, we'll settle accounts with your brother and sister."[41] When threats failed, the students' personal freedom was suspended. According to the regulations published in the August 11 issue of *People's Daily*, these students' movements were restricted and they were not even allowed to talk or laugh. They had to line up for work, seek permission to go to the washroom, and stay in the conference room even during breaks and Sundays to reflect on their mistakes and write their confessions. They swept the conference room twice a day and changed Mao's quotations on how to deal with the enemies every two days. But above all, they were forbidden to take part in the revolution in the schools.

These injustices turned students against the workteams and made passive observers into active participants. One student rebel leader described his initiation into the movement this way:

At first I did not really care. But the workteam came, the number of teachers attacked increased, including the literature teacher. I had worked with him as editor on the student paper. He wasn't bad like what they said he was. I disagreed with their accusations. But they locked him up and refused to let him see his family, they wouldn't even give him the medicine he needed.

The workteams' repressive measures, as in other movements, created martyrs and sympathizers. The movement might be momentarily pushed underground, but there were strong undercurrents of student dissatisfaction. Opposition grew and rebel following increased. But at that time, the opposing students could not match the concerted efforts of the workteams, the school administration, and sometimes even the public security bureau. Given the opportunity, however, discontent would surface.

CHAPTER 2

The Movement Gains Strength

As we have seen, the Cultural Revolution was a mass movement instigated by the government that found its initial momentum in the favorable environment of the schools. The schools were efficient machines of mobilization, and the students were committed to the ideals of the Cultural Revolution. The revolution in its early stage, however, required continuous external support. The workteams, by curtailing public meetings, parades, and the circulation of wall posters, dealt a severe blow to the movement. Their actions may have increased the ranks of the revolutionaries and support for the movement, but their power was too strong for the students to resist. However, as we shall see in this chapter, the triumph of the Maoists, who favored a more radical interpretation of the Cultural Revolution, over the Liuists at the center brought renewed support to the students and, once more, the revolution gained momentum.

The Students Are Vindicated

Even during the ascendancy of the workteam, the Maoists remained strong. In July 1966, the *People's Daily* carried editorials exhorting party members to trust the people and censuring administrators who restrained the students.[1] On July 27, the *People's Daily* carried Mao's article on the internal contradictions among the people, which was perhaps another appeal to the administration to moderate its treatment of the students. These conflicting messages, all sent in the name of the central government but at once promoting and suppressing the Cultural Revolution, reflected the different opinions among the central leaders and the power struggle going on behind the scenes. However, it is not my purpose to document these developments, but to show how these changes affected the movement in the schools.

The outcome of this power struggle became clear in late July. Mao returned to Beijing from Shanghai on July 18 and questioned Liu's handling of the Cultural Revolution. The next day, workteams in many schools were quietly withdrawn. On July 26, the *People's Daily* reported Mao's swim on the Yangtze River. It was a symbolic act, for in the next four days the newspaper carried articles urging the young to defy conventions and "swim against the tide." In the following three days, central leaders such as Liu Shaoqi, Jiang Qing, and Chen Boda visited the Qinghua and Beida campuses to learn from the students' "revolutionary experiences." This whipped up excitement among the students; even the national leaders were on campus to learn from them. On August 5, Mao wrote his own big wall poster, "Bombard the Headquarters," to show his support for the students. He attacked a "group in the government" who sided with the capitalists curbing the Cultural Revolution, "confusing right with wrong, black with white," and starting a reign of "white terror." Jiang Qing's exhortation to "kick away the party and make revolution" was promoted.[2]

It became clear to the students that the central government (even though in reality it might only be the dominant faction in government) was once more behind the Cultural Revolution and, moreover, that the revolution's scope extended beyond the teachers and administrators to the party. The Cultural Revolution had broadened from a movement against the intellectuals to one against the bureaucracy in general. First the intellectuals, now the party, lost its authority. The students' suspicion of the school administration's (and party's) fallacy in blocking the revolution was confirmed by a higher authority, the central government. It was at this juncture that Skocpol's explanation of revolutionary movements is applicable to the development of the Cultural Revolution in China's schools.[3] The movement surged ahead because the school administration was weakened.

On August 8, with the closing of the eleventh plenum of the eighth Chinese Communist Party Central Committee, the direction was set. The dominant faction under Mao, who controlled the committee, was in favor of the Cultural Revolution. The sixteen-point communiqué coming from the plenum defined the scope and strategy of the Great Proletarian Cultural Revolution. Point 10 reaffirmed the charge that education had been in the hands of the bourgeois intellectuals, and it stressed the necessity of creating a new system based on Mao's teachings to train students "morally, intellectually, and physically" to become "laborers with social consciousness and culture." Point 4 inveighed against "any method of doing things on the masses' behalf" and reaffirmed the correctness of mass mobilization. It called on the administration to "trust the masses, rely on them, and respect their initiatives. Cast out fear. Don't be afraid of disorder. Chairman Mao has often told us that a revolution cannot be so refined, so gentle, so temperate, kind, courteous, restraint, and magnanimous."[4]

This document essentially gave the students a free hand in the movement, and they reacted enthusiastically to the announcement:

> [A]fter listening to the broadcast, many revolutionary university students organized. They carried Chairman Mao's pictures and quotations, beat their drums and cymbals, sang revolutionary songs, and carried the good news to their sister schools even in the rain. The universities in Beijing instantly became a sea of joy. People gathered in the squares and the streets to discuss the matter with great zest and expressed their determination and support. Many revolutionary teachers and students talked through the night and rushed to report the happy news on wall posters and to post them on walls of buildings and dormitories. The revolutionary little generals were especially excited.[5]

The next day, the *People's Daily* published seven letters from students in Beijing schools and universities applauding the communiqué. One letter from Number 12 Middle School emotionally compared the sixteen points to "timely rain" and the "compass of the Cultural Revolution":

> When the central party's voice came, our hearts jumped, our heart boiled. How can we not be excited in these stormy days, in these changing conditions of class revolution? We long for the red light of Zhongnanhai [top government leaders' residence], and for the party to tell us "You are right."[6]

Their joy was understandable because some students, as described in Chapter 1, had been under attack; many were accused of being counterrevolutionary and antiparty and even of conspiring with the Guomindang. Many were criticized and others were interrogated, put into solitary confinement, or exiled to work in the countryside. The communiqué gave them timely support. With one stroke, Mao released them from their enemies, cleared them of their crimes, and confirmed that they had been right, endearing himself in the hearts of the student rebels. All the expressions of central government support allayed the fears of many students. Those who had been hesitant in the beginning now joined the movement. Some joined because others did. Once this process began, the movement could only gather greater momentum.

On August 9, the *People's Daily* reported for the first time that even workers and residents were involved in the movement. At the party's Central Committee office in Beijing, a reception center was set up for workers, peasants, students, and cadres of the different organizations to deliver their letters of support. This was carried out amidst the sound of fire crackers, cymbals, and drums. The capital was not alone: similar scenes were enacted in other urban centers, such as Shanghai, Guangzhou, Shengyang, Chengdu, and Xian.[7] The movement spread nationwide, affecting every sector of Chinese society, including government departments, farms, factories, shops, and schools.

A Power Vacuum in the Schools

Beginning in late July 1966, the school administrators were on the defensive and, in many cases, even defenseless. The school administration was one of the lowest echelons in the authority structure, and its legitimacy rested on the mandate of the central government. Once the central government withheld support, the administrators were powerless against the students. Even if they still had the sympathy of municipal and provincial leaders, support was not forthcoming. The Cultural Revolution had spread to government departments. Many mid-level cadres were themselves in trouble, and with the central government behind the students, local officials could not openly oppose them.

In Beijing, Wuhan, and other cities, the students dismissed the school administrators and sometimes criticized, interrogated, imprisoned, or even physically punished them. In some places, they set up cultural revolution committees or provisional cultural revolution committees to replace the school administration. These committees were named, if not modeled, after the Beijing Cultural Revolution Group, which had replaced Peng Zhen's municipal committee. Student rebels viewed these as models of democracy, with members elected from the schools at large and decisions made after consultation with the committee.

Some of the cultural revolution committees were formed on a democratic basis. One Red Guard of a Guangzhou high school recounted, "This was the only democratic election we had. The workteam left, and the school administration was weakened. We had a big meeting where the students of the whole school attended. At that meeting, we chose the

leaders, there was no coercion or manipulation. Everyone had a voice."
But in other schools, the members of the provisional cultural revolution
committees were the administration's staunch supporters. The administrators could see the trend coming and handpicked their successors on
these committees before they left. In Qinghua, for example, the provisional committee was dominated by Liu Tao and He Binghui, children of
top government leaders Liu Shaoqi and He Long. The other three members were children of regional party secretaries in the Southwest, South
Central, and Central China party bureaus.[8] Most of the students could
not be fooled, however, and the political good fortunes of such protégés
were shortlived. Even provisional revolutionary committees elected
democratically had a difficult time, because in many schools, factions had
formed over the evaluation of administrators and teachers and over how
to carry out the movement. Dissension among members of the committee obviously weakened its effectiveness. Even if the leaders of one faction dominated the committee, accusations of bias undermined the
committee's power. In other schools, disagreements among the student
rebels could block the election of committee members.

Even when cultural revolution committees were formed, they did
not replace the school administration's control within the schools. The
committees did not have a clear mandate, nor did they have the institutional backing of their predecessors. Their power and prerogatives were
not well defined and were subject to personal interpretations. Their generally accepted function was coordinating the movement, something difficult to define in the first place. In many cases, their major preoccupation
was the distribution of supplies to the student rebels, which was perhaps
their only hold on the students. A teacher elected to the committee explained his role to me in this way:

> We would be taking care of the distribution of moneys and supplies,
> like giving out paper, pens, and ink for the writing of big wall posters
> and handbills. We made sure we would not favor one group or another
> and open ourselves to criticism. But in essence, we gave everything the
> students asked for as much as we could. Who would dare to go against
> them? You would be accused of "holding up the revolution."

Fairness prompted by fear meant giving in to every request from those
below. Such an attitude could not have made the committee a strong authority, nor could it win students' respect.

The new members on the revolutionary committees were usually
student leaders or popular teachers, but the new body never commanded
the same prestige once enjoyed by the school personnel ousted from

power. They did not have their predecessors' abilities or experiences to administer and to teach. The implementation of their decisions rested on the students' goodwill. But times had changed; the slogan "To rebel is justified" was then in vogue, and those sitting on the committee did not have the school administrators' aura of authority and command of confidence.

The cultural revolution committees may, in fact, have been dispensable in running the schools. In some schools where the administrators were deprived of their power, revolutionary committees were never formed. Yet these schools were not especially different from those where committees were struck, and they continued to provide essential services with a small support staff. Running water, food, and accommodations were available for those on campus. The different departments loaned loudspeakers, trucks, ditto machines, and other propaganda equipment to the student groups and kept them in working order. Teachers reported to work though they did not teach, and the accounts department paid them salaries.

Many schools were not holding classes, and the campuses had become just gathering places for students and teachers to hold criticism meetings, plan strategies, write wall posters, and promote the revolution. The well-regimented mobilization campaign in June was replaced by a confusing—but nevertheless spontaneous—mass movement. The authority of the schools was shattered. A power void had been created. The situation in these schools is best summarized by a popular phrase describing the Cultural Revolution: "No one is in charge." The breakdown of the authority structure was requisite for a successful revolution, but, as we shall see in Chapter 3, it also provided fertile ground for the contest of power among the different groups.

Mao and the Emergence of the Red Guards

On August 11, 1966, Mao's brief visit to the reception center in Beijing generated enthusiasm far exceeding that given to political leaders in the West. The excitement lasted for a number of days. A man who shook hands with Mao was asked by his fellow workers not to wash his hand again.[9] This marked the beginning of Mao's public appearances.

On August 18, Mao appeared with other central government leaders in Beijing's Tienanmen Square before 50,000 student representatives from across the country. At that time, some students did not have their own formal organization, and their representatives were still chosen by the half-defunct party administration and flown to Beijing. Like students handpicked by the workteams to sit on the revolutionary committees, these students were usually of "good" class background—that is, children of high-level cadres. The continued existence of the party in some of these schools showed the variations in the movements across the country.

The August 18 rally was important not only because it was the first of eight such appearances, but also because it marked the first reference to the Red Guards in the mass media. The *People's Daily* took pains to explain the organization:

> Several tens of thousands of Red Guards with their red arm bands were brave as dragons. They were the center of attention of today's meeting. The Red Guards were started by middle school students in Beijing during the Cultural Revolution. They expressed their determination to stand by Mao Zedong's thoughts and defend the Communist Party for their whole life. They were the shocktroops in the defense of the country.[10]

The Red Guards were first formed on May 29, 1966, by 40 students in the secondary school attached to Qinghua when they were persecuted by the principal, Wang Pangyu, in the early days of the Cultural Revolution. They wrote to Mao and received an encouraging letter in reply.[11] At their first public appearance, Mao wore a green military uniform—which became the Red Guard uniform and fashion during the Cultural Revolution—and a young Red Guard, Song Binbin, placed a red arm band—their insignia—on his sleeves. This was Mao's ultimate sign of approval of the rebel organization.

There were eight rallies between August 19 and November 26, and each review gave the Red Guards greater prestige and publicity. Mao did not speak on these occasions, but speaking in his stead were Lin Biao, the chief of staff, and Zhou Enlai, the premier. On Tienanmen Square, crowds gathered, carrying their organizational pennants, Mao's pictures and slogans, and the little red book of Mao's quotations that became the symbol of the Cultural Revolution. At the second rally, on August 31, Zhou invited "all college students and representatives of middle school students from other parts of the country to come to Beijing, group by group, at different times." The crowds increased from 50,000 at this rally to 150,000 at the third rally on September 15 and to 250,000 at the last one. To cope with the increasing numbers, the order of review changed: at the first rally, Mao stood on Tienanmen; at the third, he rode in an open truck through the crowd; and at the final rally, 6,000 open trucks packed with Red Guards passed in front of him.[12]

The central government continued to mobilize the students for the Cultural Revolution. With the school administration disintegrating and the institutional linkage between the center and the grass roots broken, the central government increasingly used noninstitutionalized methods of mobilization, such as mass rallies and publicity in the media. The rallies in Tienanmen generated great excitement in the capital and throughout the country. Many students remained in the capital for several days. Some took the opportunity to visit vanguard institutions, like Qinghua and Beida; others went sightseeing; and still others simply reminisced over the excitement of having seen Chairman Mao. The day after the review, groups of students lingered around the square; some sat writing in their diaries, while others wrote letters home conveying their "happiness." Some waited in long lines to take pictures under Mao's picture on Tienanmen or to swear allegiance in front of it. One of the oaths was as follows: "Our most respected leader, Chairman Mao, you can rest assured, we will always listen to your teachings, resolutely defend and carry out what you represent—the proletarian revolutionary line. We shall resolutely defeat those who oppose the revolutionary line and the thoughts of Mao Zedong."[13] These actions and their reports helped to sustain the revolutionary zeal of the students despite the breakdown of institutional control.

The excitement was not confined to the capital. There were live broadcasts of these rallies to all the major centers of every province, as far as Guangzhou in the south, Urumchi in the north, and Nanning in the west.[14] Loudspeakers were hooked up in the streets, factories, schools, and universities. Crowds gathered on campuses to listen to Zhou Enlai and other central-government leaders. They shouted slogans together with people in the capital. Huge rallies were also organized the next day, and these were attended and probably organized by the highest level in the local government. Zhao Ziyang, the first party secretary of Guangdong, Wei Guoqing of Guangxi, and Zhang Texue of Hubei were present at their provincial rallies.[15] Even the local authorities who had once sided with the school administrations to curb the movement had to come out on the side of the Cultural Revolution. In major urban centers like Shanghai, 10 million people took part; in Guangzhou, Chongqing, Wuhan, and Nanjing, 50,000 showed up at each rally.[16] The rallies evoked images of fanaticism that intrigued the West, but in China they created a revolutionary atmosphere that generated enthusiasm within the population and kept the movement alive.

The Tienanmen reviews gave the Red Guards prestige. It was the organization Chairman Mao chose to become a member of, and his participation legitimized it as the grass-root organization fit for student revolutionaries. Mao's motives were hard to fathom. Most likely, he encouraged the forming of Red Guards to extend his influence and fill the power vacuum in the schools, to avoid a resurgence of opposition from the schools, and to create a dependable counterforce. Despite Mao's victory in the Central Committee, there was still opposition to the movement at the local level, and he needed the students' support if the movement was to continue. Besides, the students had received most of their education after 1949, and, despite accusations of bourgeois control in the school system, the young would still be the most trustworthy. However, they had no experience in hardships or revolutions and were leading a pampered life. What better way to prepare them for the important role as revolutionary leaders of a socialist country than to take part in the Cultural Revolution? By wearing the arm band and endorsing the organizations, he encouraged them to revolt.

Mao's actions also encouraged the formation of Red Guard units. The frequent rallies in Beijing and across the country, and the publicity given to the Red Guards in the national media, created strong social pressures on the populace to take part in the movement and on the young to form or join such units. The tight, institutionalized control of the schools on the students may have been destroyed, but pressure once exerted by the schools was replaced by a more diffuse though equally effective one generated by the rallies, wall posters, broadcasts, and news reports.

Large numbers of Red Guard groups were formed all over the country, and by December 1966, 17 of 116 million students in China had become Red Guards. There were only 13 million university and high school students in the country; the rest were primary school students.[17] Since classes were suspended and since most primary school students, especially those at the junior grades, were kept home, it can be safely assumed that the majority of these Red Guards were from the high schools and universities. As one informant who was a university student during the Cultural Revolution commented, "Who wasn't a Red Guard at that time?"

The basis for the Red Guard formation was already in place. Even before the official sanctioning of the Red Guards, students had banded together to criticize the administration and resist the workteams, even though they were sometimes forced to exist clandestinely. Others had existed informally as groups of friends from the same class or same faculty, sharing similar interests and views. They had frequently met to discuss their views. The formation of Red Guard groups only meant coming into the open, formalizing these networks, and assuming a new name.

With the enemies gone, the practical reason for forming into Red

Guard groups diminished, but the strong social pressure generated by Mao's Tienanmen appearances more than compensated for this. Students formed Red Guard groups because Mao approved and supported them. Their actions, in turn, generated pressure on others to follow. Some joined because others were doing it; others, for self-protection. A person's reasons for becoming a Red Guard were often mixed. As a teacher who had "historical problems" explained it, "Who would not form a Red Guard unit those days? Everyone around you was doing it. If you did not, you would be criticized for being not revolutionary. This is something I could not afford. Besides, with numbers come strength."

At the time, the "bloodline theory" dominated—that is, cadres' children were revolutionary, and bourgeois children, naturally, were not. Only the "five red categories"—revolutionary martyrs, revolutionary cadres, soldiers, workers, and peasants—could join. In some schools, there was even a special category of associate members, that is, those who were acceptable and yet not revolutionary enough to deserve membership.[18] My informant, the high school teacher, confided that she was rejected by many Red Guard groups. In her eagerness to be considered as revolutionary as the others, and for her own protection, she formed a Red Guard unit with two other teachers of "not-so-good family background." It was perhaps at this stage that opportunists infiltrated the movement. People saw that the central government was solidly behind the movement and that joining the movement would not only give its participants security, but they might also gain something from doing it. Yet even these opportunists were not as cool and calculating as they portray themselves in the 1980s. In all my interviews, these informants from "not-so-good family backgrounds" had a history of trying to please the party administration, and they were often hurt and bitter because their efforts were not given full credit by the authorities.

By the time the Cultural Revolution ended in 1969, it was difficult to find a school with only one Red Guard regiment. In the provinces of Hubei, Hunan, and Guangxi and the cities of Beijing, Guangzhou, and Shanghai alone, 1,417 groups were known to exist.[19] In 1966, Foreign Minister Chen Yi commented on this phenomenon in the Beijing Foreign Language Institute: "The Foreign Language Institute is divided into two sections. Originally 21 units were formed. A week later, there were over 50, and a week after that, more than 70. Seventy units for under 4,000 students. In other words, 70 schools of thought."[20] In Beida, there were over 70 groups besides the major contending groups of New Beida Commune and Jingganshan.[21] These organizations all had militant names, such as Mao Zedong Combat Troop or Fight to the End Combat Group, or they used the date of their formation or a major event, such as August 1 Combat Group, May 16 Combat Group, or April 14 Combat Group.

Smaller Red Guard units consisted of informal groups of friends sharing similar views, class background, or fates during the movement. Some groups had just two or three members, but larger ones numbered in the hundreds and adopted army organization with platoons, squads, and battalions. Others, like the Communist Youth League, had cells in every faculty and department. They edited their own handbills and newspapers and, at times, their own bulletins. Zhongshan University Red Flag Group had their own publication, *Zhongda Red Flag*; Beijing Geological Institute had *East Is Red*; and Beijing August 1 School had *Spring Thunder*. By the end of 1966, 200 such publications could be bought in Beijing alone.[22]

These grass-roots organizations became the basis for larger groups. The geographic proximity of campuses and the informal networks among students that helped to mobilize the students in mid-1966 now facilitated the formation of larger Red Guard units. With classes suspended, Red Guards visited each others' campuses and read each others' wall posters; for more distant campuses, they communicated by letter or telephone. Such actions, which at first had helped the movement spread, now led to the forming of umbrella organizations that gave the movement further impetus. The First Headquarters was a conglomerate of Red Guard groups in Beijing formed on September 13, 1966,[23] though it soon split into the Second Headquarters and then the Third Headquarters within the following two months. On October 1, high school Red Guards in Beijing joined to become United Action. Other Red Guards had also seen that combining forces augmented group strength; it had become a national phenomenon. On August 23, 18,000 representatives from the universities and high schools in Wuhan met at the Hungshan Auditorium to get organized; on September 3, twenty high schools in Guangzhou set up the Red Guard Disciplinary Corps; and two days later, the half-work half-study schools in the city also established their own headquarters in Guangzhou Municipal Workers' Cultural Palace.[24] The membership of these amalgamated groups numbered in the thousands. They had their own regular bulletins and sometimes fighting forces. They had committees to look after general administration, supplies, information gathering, strategy planning, security, interrogation of enemies, liaison, combat, and propaganda.

Soon the umbrella organizations developed contacts not only with local groups but also with those across the nation. Some larger organizations had permanent liaisons stationed in the major urban centers. Beijing had 120 liaison stations representing Red Guard groups from the provinces.[25] Qinghua University's Jingganshan had 47 stations outside Beijing.[26] When these outside representatives felt their forces were weak, they joined. In Chongqing, Red Guards from Beijing—Beijing Third Headquarters, Jingganshan of Qinghua, East Is Red of Beijing Geology Institute, and New Beida Commune—formed the Chongqing Bound Fighting Corps. The proliferation of groups of this nature increased the Red Guards' strength and spread the revolution.

The Red Guards Gain Power

For schools that were relatively quiet before August, the message at Tienanmen triggered activism. Students outside the capital also criticized teachers and education or wrote wall posters. For the vanguard institutes where school administrations toppled and revolutionary committees formed, the students had complete autonomy. The Red Guards continued with their criticism of the bureaucracy, but they became bored when their inventory of indictments was exhausted, and so they turned to more interesting issues.

The Removal of the Four Olds Movement provided this outlet, introduced the students to social issues outside the schools, and intensified the Cultural Revolution in society. On June 8, 1966, the government articulated the need to change ideology, culture, custom, and habit.[27] The student movement was still relatively weak, however, and the appeal brought little action. Then, on August 18, Lin Biao repeated the appeal at the first rally on Tienanmen: "We have to destroy old thoughts, old culture, old customs, old habits of the exploiting class, and all the superstructures that do not fit the infrastructure of the socialist economy. We have to destroy the worms that destroy our people and remove the millstone around our legs."[28] The students saw a new way to "make revolution" and responded enthusiastically.

The students had not been organized in June, but they were in August. The school administration was overthrown in many schools and universities, and this encouraged the belief among students that anything was possible. The "removal of the four olds," which had appeared so remote a possibility to the students in June, now appeared attainable. With the school administration removed and the revolutionary committees bowing to their every whim, the students had access to pens, ink, loudspeakers, and other materials for propaganda purposes. Their experience in criticizing the teachers and school administration also made the concept of removing the "four olds" more meaningful. This phase of the movement showed not only how one stage of the revolution prepared the participants for another, but also the delicate relationship between government encouragement and students' preparedness. The government planted an idea in the students' heads, and the students acted. If the students were not prepared for action, no amount of government urging could produce action, let alone a revolution.

Now that the Red Guards had acquired political consciousness and organizational strength, they were on the move the very next day: "From August 20, the Red Guards of the capital went into the streets. They posted revolutionary pamphlets and big wall posters, they had gatherings and speeches and ferociously attacked all old thoughts, cultures, habits, and customs."[29] The names of department stores, hospitals, and even product brand names were changed. For example, Wang Fujing Department Store became People's Department Store; Xiehe (Negotiated Peace) Hospital became Anti-American Imperialism Hospital; Tongren (United Clemency) Hospital became Worker-Peasant-Soldier Hospital; and Terrace of Phoenix Cotton brand became Worker-Peasant-Soldier cotton goods. Newspapers like *Da Gung Bao* became *Progressive Paper*, and *Wen Hui Bao* became *Shanghai Evening News*. Names of streets reflecting traditional culture were discarded. Perpetual Peace Street became East Is Red Street; East District People's Alley became Anti-Imperialist Road; and West District People's Alley became Anti-Revisionist Road. Wang Fujing, a main street in Beijing, was named Prevention of Revisionist Road, then Revolutionary Road, then People's Road. These rapid name changes showed not only the enthusiasm of the Red Guards but the lack of coordination among groups. The name-giving also served as a constant source of conflict among the groups, with each acting according to its whims and fancies. Sometimes skirmishes resulted.

Soon the Red Guards defined their mission in much broader terms:

> We should in a short period change the Hong Kong style of dress, cut the strange-looking hair, burn yellow books and pornographic pictures. Jeans can be cut into shorts and the remnants used for mending. The rocket [pointed] shoes should be blunted and turned into sandals, and the high heels into flat ones.[30]

Subsequently, their activities to root out bourgeois influences included ransacking school libraries; in some cases, half of the collections were burned in a week. The Red Guards also searched houses and dug up floors for evidence to incriminate "capitalist spies and bourgeois scum." In the beginning, the rebels focused on families in their neighborhoods that they considered to be bourgeois. As the movement escalated, they became more systematic, obtaining lists from the public security bureau.

Articles such as Western records or novels, family albums, heirlooms, and other memorabilia deemed bourgeois were confiscated. More organized Red Guard groups itemized the articles taken and gave receipts to the families, but others disposed of the articles according to their own fancy. Some were saved for displays to re-educate the population, others burned immediately, and still others the Red Guards pocketed. If they knew of youths fallen into "bourgeois ways," they would visit and persuade them to mend their ways.[31] These activities might have been motivated by the highest ideal in the communist culture—that is, to root out bourgeois influences—but they also imposed great strain on those under criticism. What followed was reported by numerous authors in the "wounded literature" of the late 1970s. The Red Guards were sometimes overzealous in carrying out their mission, which put unbearable pressure on those under scrutiny and led some to commit suicide.

Public places were not immune from Red Guard interference. Bookstores were asked not to carry "bourgeois" books, hairdressers not to perm hair, and tailors and shoe factories not to make Western-style dress. Shop windows displayed not goods but Mao's pictures, wall posters, and revolutionary slogans. Cultural artifacts that smacked of traditional and bourgeois influences were removed. It was in this frenzied atmosphere that cultural artifacts were desecrated or destroyed, that carvings and paintings in the Summer Palace in Beijing were painted over, and the Statue of Liberty overlooking Sun Yatsen Memorial Hall in Guangzhou was hacked to pieces.[32]

Not all Red Guard activities were destructive; others were more orderly or constructive. Most of my respondents proudly claimed that they had worked on assembly lines in the factories or helped in the harvest at one time or another during that period. According to a report in the New China News Agency, a group of 5,000 Red Guards in Sichuan carried not only their hoes but also Mao's pictures, quotations, and revolutionary slogans when they helped on the farms.[33] Farm work was inseparable from propaganda work.

The younger revolutionaries propagated Mao's thoughts in their own way. Primary school students set up little stands on street corners for passersby to rest while they read them Mao's works and offered them tea. They also posted news of the most recent directives and developments. Eighty-four Red Guards of Pengpei Number 2 Middle School wrote essays about the good acts and model persons in the area and posted them to provide examples for others to emulate. They helped younger children study Mao's works and taught them revolutionary songs, like "East Is Red" and "Navigation Needs the Great Helmsman." They also helped the residents in their housework by carrying water and

washing clothes.[34] These activities certainly created an atmosphere for
change and revolution in the larger society, which in turn fanned the Red
Guards' revolutionary enthusiasm and gave them tremendous confidence. This prepared them to take an even greater role in the Cultural
Revolution.

Mao's Revolutionary Ideology

Liu's policy of sending the workteams to contain mass involvement in
the Cultural Revolution in June and July was repudiated by the Communist Party's Central Committee, and he was demoted from the second-
in-command to the eighth position at the eleventh party plenum on
August 8.[35] But his continued appearances on Tienanmen Square could
be interpreted as a sign of considerable support in the central administration. In fact, Mao conceded that he had a difficult time convincing the
other leaders to accept his view. Liu also had considerable support
among the provincial and local bureaucracy, because administrators were
generally more willing to go along with his cautious and pragmatic approach. Mao now had the backing of the Red Guards, but they were
diffuse groups without a clear chain of command or tight discipline, and
their joint associations did not even have full control over the member
organizations. Mao could not depend on them as he once had on the
schools as an institutionalized instrument of political control; he had to
mobilize them through nonformal means, extorting ideological allegiance from each of the members.

Those who were politically astute, like the Beida and Qinghua rebel
students, realized as early as August that Liu was in political disfavor, but
to many others, only the school administration and mid-level cadres
were wrong and the Central Committee of the party was still a monolithic unity under the triumvirate of Mao, Liu, and Zhou. Liu's prestige
had not eroded in the eyes of the people, and so Mao had to wean the
students from their respect and support for Liu.

To win over the young was an easier task than convincing the other
central leaders of his views. Mao clearly enjoyed higher esteem among
the people than did Liu. Many Chinese considered him the founding father of the socialist republic, the author of China's communist philosophy, and the leader of the party. Adulations for Mao did not begin with
the Cultural Revolution; the people had always trusted him. As early in
the movement as June 9, the *People's Daily* reported how a group of students studied Mao's thesis on class struggle every morning for philosophical and strategic guidelines. It was also rumored that Kuai Dafu,

Qinghua University's student leader, read Mao's Hunan peasant report for inspiration. Recognition of the students' devotion may even have prompted the central government to launch the campaign to study Mao's thoughts.

In the following two years, the campaign to promote Mao's thoughts was intense. The populace was bombarded with Mao's works. The quantities of his *Selected Writings* (in four volumes), *Selected Works*, *Quotations*, and *Poems*, which were published during the Cultural Revolution, outstripped those of the previous seventeen years. In August 1966 alone, 120,000 copies of *Selected Writings* were distributed in Beijing, 340,000 in Shanghai, and 150,000 each in Nanzhou and Harbin—totaling over one million copies for those urban centers alone.[36] Yet there were not enough copies for a population of 700 million, and students who were literate and vanguards of the movement were given priority.

On October 10, Lin Biao called on the country to study Mao's "three constantly read articles": "The Foolish Old Man Who Moved the Mountain," "In Memory of Norman Bethune," and "Serve the People." He told them in a front-page article: "The thoughts of Mao Zedong unite the whole army and the people. Now the masses have created a new situation in the learning of Chairman Mao's work . . . we should raise it to a higher level of understanding and grasp his thoughts."[37] For six consecutive days, front-page stories exhorted people to study Mao's thoughts while other stories told of how different individuals and organizations successfully put Mao's thoughts into practice. As of late August, all major Chinese achievements—including the explosion of an atomic and a hydrogen bomb, the completion of irrigation projects, and the discovery of oil—were attributed to the power of his thoughts. Even the diary of 3111 Oil Team members who discovered oil was published to illustrate the contribution of Mao's thoughts to their success.[38]

Any message repeated long enough acquires credibility, and these continuous reports of Mao's greatness increased his image of ominpotence and omniscience. When I questioned a professor who had been a young tutor at Beida (the most prestigious university in the country) why he denounced Liu in 1966 despite his contributions to China's 1949 revolution and reconstruction, the professor justified it thus: "When Mao said one sentence, ten thousand sentences, he would always be right. Mao said that Liu was wrong; he therefore had to be wrong." The spontaneity with which he mouthed the slogan fifteen years later was astonishing. If he was sincere, and if an educated intellectual took these words at face value, one could imagine the blind faith of the average student. If he was not, it still showed that the mouthing of Mao's quotations must have been a normal practice during the Cultural Revolution.

The Red Guards' commitment to Mao might have been genuine, but they certainly also had much to gain from cultivating close connections with him. Mao's thoughts were the Red Guards' spiritual support— inspiring them, giving them confidence, and legitimizing their actions. The Red Guards knew that the organization's very emergence, proliferation, source of strength, and continued existence rested on Mao. Mao's support provided them tangible benefits; with his tacit consent or instructions, the bureau of public security, the factories, and other units stood by or complied easily with the Red Guard's requests in the Removal of the Four Olds Movement. Even the once-powerful cadres succumbed when the rebels invoked Mao's sayings.

Consequently, the Red Guards themselves also promoted this close association. They bestowed on Mao the honorific title of supreme leader, on Lin commander-in-chief, and on Zhou consultant of their nonexistent "national" Red Guard organization. On September 8, the Red Guard Headquarters distributed a documentary film on the first rally, called "Chairman Mao with His Million Soldiers of the Cultural Revolution," to be shown all over the country in theaters and to small groups.[39] The relationship between the Red Guards and the central government was symbiotic. The Red Guards were not just pawns in the center's struggle for power. The thoughts of Mao Zedong were used as much by the chairman himself and the other central government leaders as by the Red Guards. This ability to manipulate and exploit their connections with certain central leaders became even more evident when violence broke out.

Whatever the motivations behind the promotion of Mao's thoughts on both sides, his ideas at that juncture provided the unifying ideology of the Cultural Revolution and became the basis of communication and discussion among the Red Guards. Many of my respondents characterized this period as one of open discussions and, however short-lived, as invigorating. Many participants looked back to this period with nostalgia. One young Red Guard told me, "You won't understand our zeal at that time. We studied Mao's teachings, discussed his works, and tried to understand them. We debated late into the night, wrote big wall posters, and went on for days without sleeping." Another said, "It was like Hyde Park in England. We would stand at the entrance to the school and thrash out problems with passersby. People would stop and we would discuss and argue. It was a pleasant experience." For the first time, they were released from their teachers' authority to explore problems on their own— in this case, the interpretation and application of Mao's thoughts. The students were not only concerned with philosophical issues but they also tried to apply Mao's teachings to their actions. Like the scholar gentry trying to apply Confucian teachings in their daily life, Mao's sayings became a code of conduct for the students. They evaluated their behavior according to his teachings: for example, would it be disrespectful to trade Mao's badges? Was certain behavior appropriate to a true follower?

Mao's thoughts became the guiding light of the revolutionary movement, and the students aimed to create a new educational system, if not a new society, based on Mao's tenets. They had not worked out the details of their future programs nor how they would attain them. At the present stage, this did not matter. As Mao said, there would be no construction without destruction, and Mao's thoughts provided them the justification to dismantle the current system. Mao's thoughts legitimized the students' actions against the school authorities and gave the rebels confidence and strength. They provided the all-encompassing philosophy that shaped the students' every action, in theory if not in practice. Despite the different interpretations of Mao's thoughts, Red Guards from across the country could claim that they were one unified force and had joined together to form municipal or provincial organizations whose concerted strength was essential for the survival of revolutionary groups at that early stage.

The Great Link-up and Exchange of Revolutionary Experience

At the second rally on August 31, when Zhou Enlai had invited the Red Guards to Beijing group by group and at different times, the attraction of traveling was too great to resist and the students immediately converged on the capital. In their revolutionary jargon, this was the Great Link-up, when revolutionaries established contacts with one another. Although only a little over a million people attended the eight rallies, according to the official count, nine million had visited the capital by November.[40]

In August, students going to Beijing sought authorization from the schools, but that was a mere formality since the government had already sanctioned these travels and no local authority had the courage to veto this revolutionary activity. By the end of the month, when the Red Guard organizations formed, many simply left on their own initiative. For the first rally, some representatives from outside were flown in. After that, the Red Guards traveled by train. In the provinces, local authorities gave instructions to cadres to treat the student revolutionaries well and to provide them with transportation, food, lodging, medical and recreational facilities, and materials required for propaganda work.[41] A Red Guard identification would get the students free train rides and meals at a dime each. (Later, as the movement got out of control, many students traveled without showing their identification, stopped paying for their food, and even demanded loans from local government offices.) In the capital, similar facilities were available. Colleges and institutes, workers' cultural palaces, stadiums, and railway stations set up reception centers to accommodate the new arrivals. Traveling was expensive in China and far beyond the means of the average student. These government provisions made it possible for students to travel and spread the message of revolution. It is true that, in some cases, the students did finance their own travels. One respondent from southern China told me that his mother was so delighted he was going to see Chairman Mao that she borrowed money from relatives to pay for his trip. But for the majority, only the government provisions made traveling possible.

The first group of Red Guards took its mission seriously. Nanjing University students used a four-point strategy: "One, read [the big wall posters]; two, listen [to the different points of view]; three, record [the masses' good experience in learning Chairman Mao's thoughts]; and four, compare [their experience and observations with Chairman Mao's sixteen points and the situation on their own campuses]."[42] Accordingly, they went to the vanguard institutes of Qinghua and Beida. Qinghua had 50 reception stations on campus for these visitors, and Beida had twenty. The students were briefed on the history of the Cultural Revolution in these universities, and they received Red Guard publications. They copied the wall posters, attended the rallies and mass meetings, and discussed the situations in their own schools. On the train home, they reviewed their experience as a group, assessed the situation in their schools or universities, and planned a program of action. On their return, they promoted the revolution in their schools.

On October 22, an editorial in the *People's Daily* featured a story about fifteen students of Dalien Naval Transportation Institute who walked 600 miles to Beijing. The government openly endorsed this.[43] The Red Guards' train rides had strained the transportation system, and perhaps students traveling on foot would relieve the state's burden without discouraging the revolution; it would also spread the revolution to more remote regions. At the sixth rally on November 3, Lin Biao called for this "big exchange of revolutionary experience" on foot. Again the media played an important role in encouraging this development. In the following ten days, there were six reports of the bravery and stamina of students walking to Beijing, comparing them to the revolutionaries of the Long March in the 1930s. On November 15, the top government leaders, including Zhou, received 30 "long-march groups" at People's Hall; on November 21, a huge rally was held to honor them at Workers'

Stadium. At the same time, the newspapers were giving advice on how one should prepare for these journeys: what to bring and how to handle cold, blisters, and frost bite.[44]

The students' "exchange" brought the Cultural Revolution to the remotest parts of the country. If the students had continued to travel by train, they would have missed isolated communities en route. Instead, out-of-the-way places were visited by the Red Guards. Though traveling on foot, students carried not only their personal belongings but also propaganda materials, such as Mao badges and Mao's published works. One group of students carried 12,000 copies of Mao's works in a wheelbarrow. Whenever they reached a town or village, they beat their drums and cymbals, propagated Chairman Mao's thoughts, promoted the Cultural Revolution, and established contacts with the local groups.[45] It was winter and their presence, at least for the moment, was greeted by the peasants as a welcome break from the monotony of rural life.

The Red Guards even entered factories and schools to promote the revolution; there they received mixed receptions. When the students worked alongside the others, they were usually welcomed; but where they disrupted production, some workers resisted and sometimes attacked the students. The clashes between students and workers had become so widespread that, on September 7, Mao had issued a directive forbidding workers to interfere with the student movement, thus giving the students a free hand and official blessing to promote revolution wherever they went.[46] The students were unopposed, at least outwardly, in the schools. I was told that, in one primary school where the teachers were united behind the administration, whenever Red Guard groups visited them and demanded the escalation of the movement, the teachers would organize large criticism meetings for the visitors' benefit, and the school would quiet down again as soon as the Red Guards left. Other schools were not as lucky. A primary teacher in Shanghai complained bitterly,

> We had been holding classes even till November 1966. One day, a group of Red Guards from Beijing came in and demanded to know why we were not carrying out the Cultural Revolution. They called the students together and asked them to revolt. It was only then that the movement started in our school.

This incident indicates the power and prestige that the Red Guards had gained by November. The school administration did not dare to oppose these Red Guards coming from outside the schools, and it did as it was told. Through the Great Link-up, the Red Guards brought pressure on those lagging behind, and by December 1966, the Cultural Revolution had spread to almost every school in the country.[47]

Conclusion of Part I

Except for the brief setback in June when the workteams were dispatched into the schools, the Cultural Revolution gained momentum throughout the latter half of 1966 and escalated from an isolated incident within a university to a nationwide social movement involving over 100 million students. By December 1966, the student rebels had acquired all the elements necessary for a successful revolutionary movement. They had their own organizations through the formation of Red Guard units, controlled resources necessary for mobilization through sitting on the cultural revolution committees, and were unified under the revolutionary ideology of Mao's thoughts.

My informants, either because they were echoing the current official line or out of genuine conviction, blamed Mao and the Gang of Four for launching the Cultural Revolution. There is some truth in their assertion, since the government played an inordinately large role in promoting the revolution. Even if Mao did not initiate Nie Yuanzi's wall poster, the publicity given to it encouraged other students to follow her example. Reports of the educational proposals of Beijing high schools and People's University in the national press focused their attention on educational reforms. Coverage in the government-controlled media of students' successes in toppling university presidents exposed the administration's vulnerability and encouraged others to take similar action. The withdrawal of the workteams saved the student movement at a critical stage.

When the school administration was dismantled and the institutionalized machinery to mobilize the students gone, the repeated government urgings and directives reported in the national media sustained the excitement and put pressure on the students to continue the movement. The personal appearances of central leaders on university campuses lent respectability to revolutionary activities and generated enthusiasm. The same could be said of Mao's reviews of the Red Guards and of his wearing their arm band. The directives forbidding workers to interfere gave students immunity from retaliation and protected the movement. The provision of free transportation, food, and lodging enabled them to travel and spread the revolutionary word. With government material and nonmaterial support, the revolution took off and took shape.

This explanation fits the resource-mobilization theory, which holds that the infusion of economic and material resources makes revolution possible.[48] However, a more sophisticated version should also consider the social organization of Chinese society and particularly that of the schools. The revolutionary actions of individuals are situated within the web of social relations, which can ultimately facilitate or undermine a revolution. In China, the machinery of social control in the schools provided a convenient instrument for mobilization. The close school environment and the concentration of schools in cities and suburbs provided the infrastructure that generated an intensity in the movement, exerted strong pressures on the members to conform, and limited the alternatives open to the incumbents to do otherwise. The school administration not only provided the material resources but also organized criticism meetings, parades, and the writing of wall posters both during and after school hours, making it impossible for anyone to be uninvolved. These activities overcame students' initial inertia and nurtured their revolutionary élan. Once the school administrations were dismantled, the revolutionary momentum was sustained by the rallies, broadcasts, parades, and the mass media. In addition to disseminating news of the revolution, these activities shaped public opinion, kept the movement at a feverish pitch, and made nonparticipation in the movement socially unacceptable. The strong pressure of the tight control the Chinese social institutions had on the individual cannot be overlooked if we are to understand the speed with which the Cultural Revolution grew. These infrastructures in Chinese society—not the conspiracy of a few leaders in power—made the Cultural Revolution a reality.

A movement of that scale could not have occurred without a host of forces all acting in the same direction. Students' dissatisfaction with the educational system and their commitment to communist ideology were prerequisites for revolution. They were not solely responsible for the Cultural Revolution, of course, but, as Tom Bottomore has pointed out, no social movement could occur if the participants did not believe in its cause.[49] However strong the government control over its citizens, it could not organize a mass movement involving millions without the participants' commitment and volition. It would have been especially difficult in China to do so when the school administration disintegrated. The Cultural Revolution was a movement initiated by intellectuals and characterized by idealism. Students believed in communism and especially in its central tenet, equality. When they became sensitized to the injustices and other weaknesses in the educational system, they wanted to remedy them. Furthermore, they had internalized the value of obeying higher authority. When the schools organized them to revolt, they followed; when the central government turned against the school administration, they simply relied on the higher authority of Mao. Their communist ideology together with their unswerving trust in authorities made them susceptible to government instigations.

If the students were not prepared, no amount of government urging could have goaded them into action. The June appeal to "remove the four olds" fell on deaf ears; it was only in August, when the students had acquired political consciousness and perceived this goal as attainable, that they took up the challenge. When they were ready, they carried out the directives with little urging and even exceeded government expectations. They took the initiative and organized into revolutionary units, criticized education, and walked to the capital.

The Cultural Revolution is the result of complex interactions between the students' initiatives and government intervention in the closed climate of the Chinese educational institutions and society. The government introduced the idea and the students adopted it or even developed it further. If the students had a new idea and the government liked it, they disseminated it. Through these efforts, the revolutionary ideology of the students jelled, and the Cultural Revolution took shape with rallies, wall posters, and other paraphernalia. These developments, in turn, generated their own pressure and momentum. Many students participated in the movement because their peers joined, or attended the rallies because their friends went. They wrote wall posters and denounced bourgeois influences in society because that was the fad. When the administration resisted, the students formed opposition groups. The government supported the organization, and more students became Red Guards because everyone was a member. Not to do so would make a person conspicuous and a deviant. Under these circumstances, the movement spread.

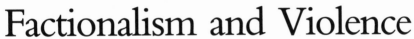

PART II

Factionalism and Violence

CHAPTER 3

The Outbreak of Violence

Clarence Crane Brinton has compared the different stages of revolution to a person falling sick, having a high fever, and recovering.[1] At the second stage of the Cultural Revolution, the movement degenerated into internecine fights that undermined the revolutionary cause. The students seemed to have abandoned their altruistic goals to revolutionize the educational system and instead became involved in politics in the larger society. Schools as an institution ceased to exist, and campuses were either deserted or battle grounds for group fracases. Instead of moving toward a more constructive phase of reforming the educational system, students continued to criticize the school cadres and fought their own comrades, the other Red Guards. The delirium of the second stage of the Cultural Revolution often appears senseless to outside observers. To fully understand the phenomenon, we must trace back to the structures of the schools, the cleavages among the students and faculty before the Cultural Revolution, and the complexities of the issues in the early stages of the movement. Each of these factors is seemingly innocuous on its own, but, interacting with the developments in the first few months of the Cultural Revolution, they created an explosive situation.

The Roots of Rivalry

The social organization of the schools played an important role in the group alignments and development of factional fights among the Red Guards. As noted in Chapter 1, schools in China were highly structured.

In the class committees, the good students had to help the poor ones; in the political organizations, members of the Young Pioneers and the Communist Youth League were responsible for recruiting more activists. Unlike peer groups in the West, where students with different interests rarely interact, those in China could not leave each other alone. This watchdog role of the class committees and the youth branches of the communist party, plus the constant pressure these members put on their fellow students, created friction. Weekly meetings were held and students had to criticize themselves or one another. The students did develop their own defense mechanisms to diffuse conflict by turning criticisms in these sessions into a ritual. They criticized each other in meaningless platitudes or warned their friends that they would be criticizing them.[2] Still, ill-feelings could not be completely avoided, and the overzealous often generated hostility.

In the West, students at the same school are typically from similar socioeconomic backgrounds; those in China are more diverse. Admission in the 1960s was based on a student's performance in the examination, and competition was keen. Because of parental help and other intangible advantages of family background, children of intellectuals did well in the examination[3] and so constituted a majority in the good schools. While some cadre children were good students, others were admitted because of their family ties. In many good schools, which were the vanguard schools in the Cultural Revolution, a predominant proportion of students came from these two backgrounds. In the best schools in the country (Guangya Middle School in Guangzhou, the middle school attached to Beida, and Number 101 Middle School in Beijing), 45 percent of students were children from cadre families and 43 percent were children of intellectuals.[4] There were often hostilities between these two groups. The cadre children distrusted the children of intellectuals because of their background, and the latter in turn despised the former, who were sometimes admitted "through the backdoor" (that is, because of their connections). As noted in Chapter 1, bourgeois intellectualism and bureaucratic corruption were precisely the issues raised during the Cultural Revolution, and this gave each group reason to attack the other.

The faculty was similarly divided between party members who valued political enthusiasm and intellectuals who treasured academic achievement. Theoretically, the party and school administration had different jurisdictions, but the distinction between transmitting knowledge and ideology was easily blurred. In practice, the party was usually supreme in Chinese society and the party members supervised teaching. Like the divisions among students, party members and intellectuals distrusted one another. Party members were particularly suspicious of intellectuals trained under the Guomindang or abroad. But there were not enough teachers, so those intellectuals had to be accommodated. Even some younger teachers, who were politically more radical, disliked the conservatism and snobbishness of their senior colleagues. In return, most intellectuals considered party members ignorant and doctrinaire. They disliked the policing role of party members who monitored their "ideological level," and the older intellectuals looked down on younger ones with less academic achievement. This mutual dislike between the party and the intellectuals and between the younger and older teachers became part of the basis of group loyalties in the Cultural Revolution. Party domination in the schools in 1966 helped to launch the Cultural Revolution, but once the movement started and party authority was questioned, dissatisfaction with party control surfaced and divided the faculty.

Not all the differences among the faculty members and students were based on principles; they also had personal grudges against one another. During the Hundred Flowers Movement in 1956, the government had encouraged intellectuals to speak out. Their hostile public statements— some attacking party rule—confirmed the party's fear. The rectification campaign in 1957 that accused these critics of being "rightist" further soured relations and confirmed the intellectuals' opinion that the party could not be trusted. Moreover, to the intellectuals, many policies of the Great Leap Forward in 1958 reflected the party's ignorance; quality steel could not be made in backyard furnaces, nor solid education acquired through laboring in the farms and factories. Then, in the early 1960s, the government had tried to root out abuses such as corruption and bureaucratism. Well-meaning as these campaigns might have been, they unavoidably involved exposing the culprits and generated suspicion and hostility among colleagues. Some of those accused waited for the next campaign to get back at their accusers.

The Cultural Revolution became another occasion to settle scores. The ease with which many party cadres singled out intellectuals for attack in June 1966 was symptomatic of the deep rifts within the school administrations. For example, Nie's big wall poster might have been her way of retaliating at Lu Ping, and in the Shanghai Foreign Language Institute, the first person to be criticized was a cadre who had made gains in the Socialist Education Movement.[5] My interviewees generally concurred with this view. They admitted that the long history of disagreements among faculty in some schools promoted factionalism during the Cultural Revolution—though, interestingly enough, all denied that it did in theirs. They pointed out that, when the movement was an occasion to settle personal scores, the situation was more explosive and the fights more acrimonious.

New Issues Reinforce Traditional Cleavages

During the Cultural Revolution, new and complex issues were raised. A critique of education was not a simple matter. It involved pointing to weaknesses in the system as well as suggesting remedies. Such a critique involved questions like: Were the previous seventeen years of education completely or only partly bourgeois? How important was the teaching of conventional knowledge compared with ideology, and theory compared with practicum? What constituted legitimate knowledge to be included in the curriculum? Who were qualified to teach? How was teaching to be carried out in the classroom? Should the examination be retained, or, if abolished, what were the options? It was only natural that all students and faculty members did not hold the same opinions.

Most faculty members saw room for improvement in the educational system, and yet they were cautious about the developments of the Cultural Revolution. Some were satisfied with the growing emphasis on academic achievements in the previous few years and suspicious of any change in policy direction. Others agreed with the direction of the movement in putting increasing importance on political orientation; however, they were skeptical of the way the movement was carried out. The students were more positive toward the movement. They, too, were critical of the educational system and especially of its bureaucratism and class bias. They were eager for change but were not sure what was to replace it. The differences among the faculty members were evident in the initial stages of the Cultural Revolution, but cleavages among the students were less apparent in their preoccupation to fight the administration.

Vanguards in a revolution are usually united in their animosity toward the establishment, though they rarely achieve consensus as to what is to replace the status quo. Indeed, they rarely present a blueprint of the future, especially since a revolution by definition aims at a radical transformation of the present to a future as yet unknown and unattained. In many cases, the specific objectives are modified and the reform programs tailored to meet the changing circumstances in the movement. The readiness to highlight an agreement in general principles can contribute to the rebels' initial success, but it can also contribute to their divisiveness later on when the specific goals and programs have to be worked out and differences emerge. In the Cultural Revolution, the students' differences surfaced and became a constant source of debate and violence once the school administration was overthrown.

Mao's writings did provide some rough guidelines for settling those differences. A collection of his sayings on education could be found in "Chairman Mao on Education," yet his statements were broad and general while short and pithy—and were therefore subject to different interpretations. For example, one of his statements was, "The years of education have to be shortened; education has to be revolutionized." It made no reference to how many years to be taken away, nor did it clarify whether revolutionizing education meant its complete overhaul and, if so, how this could be achieved. Even though the students would soon be fighting over other matters, these debates on education were for many students among the first issues to split their ranks, and they spent two years arguing and fighting over them.

Discussion about education could not remain at an academic level. It necessarily involved a review of the personnel, and such evaluations were difficult to resolve and often personal. People with different personalities preferred different teaching and administrative styles. A teacher or administrator could not please everyone; consequently, a staff member criticized by one group of students might be supported by another. With no resolution of basic educational issues, an acceptable teaching or administrative style became more controversial, and without an official position on these issues, no ideological constraint inhibited people from holding one opinion or the other. Numerous student groups sprang up to side with one view or another or to support one member against the next.

It was on such issues that traditional cleavages in the schools perpetrated and exacerbated the divisions among the students. The students were not unanimous in their judgment of the cadres. Generally, those students belonging to the youth branches of the Chinese Communist Party backed the party members, and the high achievers and children of the intellectual or bourgeois families were behind the academics. As the Cultural Revolution became a mass movement and the students grew stronger, the administrators courted student support to protect themselves; however, they often gained the support of one group but not of others, thus turning these groups against one another. Sometimes, to forestall their own turn to be criticized, the administrators would even mobilize students against their colleagues, who often also had their own support group. These manipulations poisoned student relationships, and ill feelings remained even after the school administration was dismantled.

The most obvious example of manipulation was the case of the workteams when they organized their own student groups, usually members of the youth branches of the communist party, to copy posters criticizing them and to take pictures of dissenters. These actions made their supporters traitors in the eyes of the other students. Another example was the disagreement over the so-called bloodline theory. This theory could be summarized by a couplet—"The son is a hero when the father is a revolutionary; the son is vile when the father is reactionary"— which advocated hereditary revolutionary spirit. The position was supported by high school students of cadre background because it put them in a superior position. They were also backed by cadres who stood to gain by this theory and provided material support. This backing emboldened the Red Guards to ostracize those from "bad" (bourgeois) backgrounds from their organizations, even to the extent of exiling them to farms and factories. When the students who were once persecuted returned in November 1966, after the government denounced the bloodline theory, they joined the revolutionary ranks, but some of these returned exiles hated their tormentors and sought revenge.[6] Thus, the misunderstandings were reinforced among the students of cadre and intellectual backgrounds.

Even if students agreed on their opinions of the cadres, they would often be split on the punishment to be meted out to the "guilty." Some students were more prone to use physical force than others. The latter objected to the inhuman treatment meted out to the accused, such as confining them in ox pens (rooms with windows boarded up), interrogating them for several hours, and occasionally taking them out for public humiliation with their heads bent about two feet above the ground and their hands raised high like the wings of an airplane. One respondent felt sick when she saw the campus cook leading a professor on all fours around campus on a rope.

Bitter feelings remained even after the evaluations came to a close. For example, after the workteams were discredited and left, some students demanded that the dossiers collected on them be destroyed, but others disagreed. Those "struggled" (punished) by the team members wanted to be rehabilitated, since the workteams had proven to be wrong. But not all agreed to this simple verdict; instead, they wanted each case to be reviewed individually. Neither could the students agree on how to deal with the workteams. Some were more benign and considered the matter closed; others wanted to punish the individual team members.[7] In the end, differences of opinion merged with the settling of personal scores. Fighting for one's convictions and personal revenge became inextricably linked and almost indistinguishable. New rifts were added to old ones, and old cleavages and new issues intermingled.

The Red Guards Proliferate and Splinter

The Red Guard organizations that united the students in the beginning also became a factor contributing to their constant disagreements and fights. In the first six months of the movement, students were united against their common enemy, the school administration; but with the enemy gone, their differences surfaced. Some disagreed about the evaluations of the educational system and the alternatives proposed; others differed on the evaluations of the cadres and the treatment of those found guilty, and members broke off to form their own organizations. The basis of a disagreement could also be personal. In Beida, Jingganshan broke away from New Beida Commune, not because of basic differences in outlook, but because its leader, Nie, "denied things said or done when they were to her disadvantage." Sometimes members in Red Guard groups were alienated from their leaders who aped the lifestyle of the cadres they toppled:

> They were incapable of doing important tasks and unwilling to take on minor ones. They indulged themselves with food and wine, had their own motor cycles, telephones, and borrowed others' padded jackets and kept them. They stayed up late and had evening snacks of eggs. Everywhere they went, they were accompanied by body guards and private secretaries and a large entourage.[8]

These perquisites might appear trivial to Westerners, but given the living standard in China, the scarcity of supplies arising from the chaos, and the lowly status of students, these were excesses if not corruption, especially in the eyes of critics. In their idealism, many students did not hesitate to start their own groups.

Whatever the origins of these divisions, the proliferation of Red Guard groups increased the parties involved and the occasions for disputes. Although a new organization might agree with its parent organization on the major issues of the revolution, the very fact that it broke away would create ill feelings, and the two would become rival groups. Furthermore, government had put resources formerly available to the school administration at the Red Guard's disposal. The limited supply, however, could not satisfy the needs of the growing number of Red Guard groups, and they fought over these scarce resources. For example, the same Beida respondent quoted above explained why Jingganshan attacked its parent organization:

She [Nie] denied them office space, so they had to invade and occupy a room. That was how different buildings came to be occupied by different groups. Nie was in control and denied others pen, paper, and materials required for propaganda. We were poor students, but the government had given us all these supplies. She would not share them. So students had to go and take them by force.

The presence of Red Guard organizations converted private differences into public issues. With the backing of the Red Guard's divergent opinions between individuals became public conflicts between groups. Each group protected and supported its members, and each believed that it was the guardian of the revolution and of Mao's thoughts and, consequently, that its views and actions were correct. Each group was dogmatic and clung to its positions, making negotiations or compromise difficult. Furthermore, such intransigence often turned peaceful discussions into shouting matches. Tempers flared, and shoving and fistfights followed.

The Red Guard organizations always sided with their members, and not necessarily because they agreed with them—they would also do so even when they knew the member was in the wrong. This approach was taken not only to gain the allegiance of the supporters by showing that the organization was always behind them, but also because the organization leaders felt that to admit the wrongdoings of members would undermine the group's prestige. A Red Guard explained: "If we struggled against them [bad elements in the organization], it would have been like struggling against ourselves. It reflected on us if we had such people in our ranks, so we protected them to the end."[9] The organization became so important that the definition of friend or foe rested on organizational alignment. Those who agreed with them were their friends, those who saw otherwise were their enemies, and any admission of the mistake of a member was considered a sign of weakness.

Minor personal differences could therefore lead to open conflagration. An example of how an innocuous issue could trigger fighting among the Red Guards was reported in one of their publications, the *Red Guard Rebellion*. On this occasion, a Red Guard from Beijing criticized another from Guangzhou for wearing pointed shoes unbecoming to a revolutionary. When the matter was couched in "revolutionary terms," it was not simply a matter of personal taste, but a serious issue that generated heated discussions; with members from two different groups involved, it was one group's position versus the other's. Since one group came from the north and the other from the south, other groups from the two regions were drawn in. Heated discussions followed. When shouting could not resolve the issue, they fought. In cases such as this, tens or hundreds of people could be drawn into the disagreement. As we shall see in Chapter 4, Red Guards allied with groups outside their schools and later outside their localities, thereby involving more and more groups and expanding the scope of the violence.

As the revolution continued, group rivalry became so important that group interest was paramount. Groups would join their allies in a fight even though they had nothing to do with the issues that triggered the dispute. Even in the vanguard institute Qinghua, the April 14 Group fought alongside the radical Earth Faction in Beijing, not the like-minded Sky Faction, because their rival, Jingganshan, was a member of the latter.[10] Principles were compromised for group politics. Group alliance was the only criterion for deciding who was revolutionary or counter-revolutionary. Narrow group interests—how to defend one's own group and defeat one's rival—became the only criteria for actions. Ken Ling, a Red Guard from Amoy, described these considerations during the period: "We were loyal only to our own organization...During the next two years, I was never to hear my colleagues describe how to defend Mao Zedong's thoughts or rule of the proletariat. All I heard was how to strengthen our own organization and weaken the opposing one."[11] The means had overshadowed the ends. The Red Guard organizations were supposedly instruments to protect Mao's thoughts and defend the revolution, but the security and expansion of the group became the overriding concerns and motives for action.

The New Dogmatism

In August 1966, more than a million copies of Mao's *Selected Works* were produced. By December 1967, the *People's Daily* reported that 80 million copies of the *Selected Works*, 35 million copies of his *Quotations*, and 57 million copies of his *Poems* had been distributed.[12] In 1967, the *People's Daily* carried full-page pictures of Mao and his close comrade-in-arms, Lin Biao, after each Red Guard rally and on the national day of celebration on October 1—an unusual practice for the national newspaper. Life-size pictures of Mao were distributed.[13] In May, a pictorial display of Mao, "The Red Sun in Our Heart," was held in Beijing, and two months later, a picture book with the same title was published.[14]

The heroes of the day were Mao's devoted followers, who listened to his every word. In September 1966, the government promoted the model Lei Feng; in October, Wei Fengyin; in March 1967, Liu Yinjun; in October, He Shenghui; in November, Cao Yangzhong; and in December, Li

Wenzhong. The next year, Meng He was the hero. These were not "great" men and women, but simple people who "listened to Mao." Wei and He were workers, the rest were members of the People's Liberation Army. However, they shared one characteristic: complete devotion to Mao, even to the extent of laying down their lives. Lei, He, and Cao gave up their lives to fulfill Mao's thoughts by preventing the derailment of a train, attempting to put out a fire, and saving children from being trampled by a horse, respectively. Their life histories were carefully documented in the papers and served as reading material in group meetings and as inspiration for all. Wei Fengyin, the hero of the 3111 Oil Team, was characterized as "growing up in nurturance of Chairman Mao's thoughts." She "listened to Chairman Mao's words and never forgot class struggle" and used "Chairman Mao's thoughts as guidelines and inspiration in technology." Liu Yinjun was honored with an exhibition in Beijing, and Meng He was commemorated during a rally of 130,000 people in Hefe on May 29, 1968.[15] The message was strict obedience to Mao's every word.

In addition, every unit across the country periodically picked their own model students of Mao's thoughts. These were heroes who put his thoughts into practice in their everyday life, but according to my respondents, some were dogmatists who took Mao's every word literally and believed that, with Mao behind them, every difficulty could be overcome even to the extent of defying physical laws. They were rewarded with the honor of seeing Mao. In promoting them as models of emulation, the government encouraged blind faith in Mao, and every medium was used to hammer home this point.

My interviewees interpreted this campaign of promoting Mao's thoughts as part of the Gang of Four's design to increase their power. By promoting the prestige of their mentor, they also augmented their own. Although this explanation is plausible, it is erroneous to concentrate on the government role without recognizing grass-roots spontaneity. As pointed out in Chapter 2, students' loyalty to Mao arose from genuine commitment as well as practical advantages to be gained by associating with him, and they too promoted Mao's image. Each unit produced its own Mao badge out of metal, porcelain, or bamboo. A foreign student in Beijing collected over 200 different badges fifteen years later, in 1982, and probably more varieties were available during the revolution itself. In April 1967, the Red Guard Headquarters, a conglomerate of Red Guard units, produced another documentary film, "Chairman Mao's Fifth and Sixth Review of the Army of the Great Proletarian Cultural Revolution"; each showing was followed by meetings and discussions.[16] In May, Qinghua University put up its life-size statue of Mao. Similar ones went up all over the country's campuses, including one on Jinggan-shan Mountain, the refuge of the Chinese Communist Party in the 1930s before its Long March.[17]

Besides the traditional rallies on Labor Day (May 1) and National Day (October 1), the Red Guards organized rallies to commemorate Mao's every involvement in the Cultural Revolution the year before: for example, on May 16, the rally celebrated the May 16 Directive; on July 26, Mao's swim in the Yangtze; on August 5, his wall poster "Bombard the Headquarters"; and on August 18, his first rally. There were also rallies and "meetings of resolution" to show support for the new directives as they came out and, indirectly, to show their faithfulness to Mao's revolutionary line.[18] These are only the incidents reported in the national newspaper, a small sample of the total number of rallies held across the country. With the breakdown of the educational and even the political systems at that time, it was unlikely that these activities were planned and coordinated by the center. They were more likely activities spontaneously organized by the Red Guards as their way to promote the revolution and forge group solidarity.

The country was saturated with Mao's image. The Maoist paraphernalia generated a revolutionary, but stifling, atmosphere that no one could escape. People were reminded everywhere that a revolution was going on. It is only against this backdrop that we can appreciate the pressure on the individual. When I questioned why the respondents acted the way they did during the Cultural Revolution, they invariably answered, "You were not there, you would not understand." The social climate of the time was such that it was impossible for anyone not to follow the tide, especially when not doing so would invite negative sanction. The accounts in the "wounded literature" of the early 1980s give us a sense of the ambience of the time.[19] One could not escape even in the private sanctuary of the family, since children brought the revolutionary spirit home and turned against parents. The atmosphere was much more stifling and pervasive than the tight control of the school administration had been.

In October 1966, Beijing was a sea of fluttering posters; Mao's quotations were posted on every wall, subway, bus, and train. Students from Sichuan University described their first few moments in Beijing this way:

> We got off the train to wait for the bus, [and] a boy of six or seven brought us hot water. He [had] memorized a few passages of Mao's quotation. We asked, "My little friend, why did you read us Chairman Mao's quotations?" He raised his head high and said, "Let the thought of Mao Zedong bear fruit in every heart."[20]

Before long, this scene was repeated elsewhere. The paraphernalia associated with Mao's cult proliferated—his slogans, his little red book, his pictures, his badges, and his statues were found all over the country. Groups of students stood on street corners reading Mao's works. Even the blind and the old could recite his passages; illiteracy was no excuse for ignorance of Mao's work. Every respect was shown to Chairman Mao. An old man carrying a bust of Mao in a basket hanging from his bamboo pole was criticized for irreverence. The word "invite" was the euphemism for buying Mao's memorabilia. Symbolism is important in maintaining a revolutionary movement, and there was no lack of it in the Cultural Revolution.

The stance first advocated by the Red Guards of "looking at both sides" (to be critical and objective) was abandoned; it was replaced by a blind faith in Mao that extended beyond the limits of reason. Any act justified by one of his quotations was tolerated; any action that violated his words was unforgivable. Maoism was elevated from a philosophy that could be discussed and questioned to a religion whose pronouncements were sacrosanct. The altruism of Meng He, the hero who used his satchel, his clothes, and his body to put out a forest fire, was laudable, but his actions went beyond common sense. They were certainly futile, if not foolish, but no one could question or protest even though this unwavering trust in Mao was thought to be unreasonable. Dogmatism and extremism replaced reason among the Red Guards. This attitude was reflected in the numerous examples given by the respondents. People who threw away scraps of paper bearing Mao's picture or name were criticized or jailed; students who scribbled over similar items were punished; and vendors who used paper to wrap their wares had to be doubly careful. A Red Guard leader recounted to me how he lost his "lieutenant":

> [The lieutenant] was planning strategy at a meeting. He wrote on a corner of *Yangcheng Wenbao* [a newspaper] and he didn't realize the characters "Mao Zedong" were among the words he scribbled over. I did not know how it happened, but our rival group got to know of this and accused him of "being against Chairman Mao," and he was jailed for a year. There was nothing I could do about it.

The reasons for his arrest were probably more complex, but this did reflect the atmosphere at the time: desecration of anything associated with Mao was an offense that no one could defend.

This situation can only be appreciated against the backdrop of Chinese cultural traditions. The government promotion of Mao's thoughts certainly played a tremendous role, but as noted above, the students were used to obeying a higher authority. This growing dogmatism was not a break from tradition. Rather, it was a cultural trait accentuated by new developments of the Cultural Revolution. The students were imitating the authorities they overthrew, and to bolster their position, they fell back on Mao. They too became authoritarian in their newly won importance.

Mao's thoughts became a weapon in Red Guard rivalries. Communication between individuals or groups entailed the exchange of invectives, each claiming to be the faithful follower of Mao and denouncing the other as wrong. Mao's writings covered a wide variety of topics, and there was a quotation for every occasion. "Revolution is not a crime, rebellion is justified" was most often cited. Students chanted it in their fight against the school administration. When they wanted to investigate the politicians, this quotation was useful: "If you cannot solve a problem, investigate the situation and its historical development. Once you understand the situation, you can take appropriate action." When they wanted to fight, a number of quotations were handy: "Whenever there is struggle, there is sacrifice, there is death"; "Revolution is not a dinner party"; or "Political power grows out of the barrel of a gun." But when they were losing a fight, they would shout: "Fight with reason, not force" or "Look at facts, and reason." When they lost a fight, they could even console themselves with this quotation from Mao: "Throughout history, all reactionary forces on the verge of extinction invariably conduct a last desperate struggle against the revolutionary force." In prison, "Be resolute, fear no sacrifice" was the rallying cry to boost morale. To justify infighting, this served well: "Factionalism in itself might not be a bad thing, since the proletarian factions had to fight bourgeois ones." Mao was liberally quoted so long as his saying fit the purpose; Mao's writings meant everything to everyone.

Quotations from other "faithful students of Chairman Mao" were also useful in justifying Red Guard rivalries. During the Cultural Revolution, Lin Biao analyzed the different types of criticism and struggle sessions:

> It was good when the good people struggled against the bad. It was also good when the bad people fought against the bad. It was not so good when the good fought against the good, but these differences could be easily resolved. It would be bad if the bad struggled against the good. But still the good would learn something good from it.[21]

The Red Guards derived the following conclusion from Lin's quotation: even Mao's closest comrade-in-arms declared that only benefits and no real harm could come out of fighting ("struggle"). Since the authority said it, fighting was therefore justifiable.

Another example of such Red Guard ingenuity had to do with Jiang Qing's famous statement on July 22, 1967: "Attack with words, defend with force." When a group was losing a fight, this slogan was often re-cited. However, when it was to the rebels' advantage to fight, they gave the quotation a strange twist. In May 1968, the *April 22 Bulletin* read: "In the spirit of Jiang Qing's instruction, "Attack with words, defend with force," we waged a defensive counterattack on the Allied Command, who waged a counter-revolutionary war against us."[22] The difference be-tween defensive and offensive attack was hard to decipher. The Red Guards had put Mao's writings, and anyone else's, to ingenious use.

My interviews were conducted in 1980. By that time, Lin and Jiang had already been charged as conspirators behind the Cultural Revolu-tion. My respondents singled out their statements—as opposed to Mao's more blatant ones, like "A revolution is not a dinner party"—as examples of the government's deliberate designs to encourage fighting and create chaos in the country. Yet given the history of the ingenious uses to which Red Guards put the leaders' statements and government directives, we must view such assessments with some skepticism. The Red Guards had reduced Mao's writings to rhetoric for every occasion. They used any quotation, even though it might be out of context, so long as it suited their purposes. Every action was couched in Maoist rhetoric. The Red Guards believed that rivals were simply enemies of the revolution dis-obeying Mao and that they alone were his faithful followers.

The suffocating atmosphere in which Mao's thoughts were supreme made fighting much more likely to occur. It strengthened the students' already strong commitment to Mao, reinforced their habitual obedience to authority, and generated dogmatism within the already intense revo-lutionary élan. Dogmatism per se did not cause factionalism or fighting among the Red Guards, but it certainly promoted them and reduced the possibility of any compromise among groups with different opinions. The interpretations of Mao's thoughts were a perpetual issue of debate and source of dissension. The Red Guards were already divided over their views on the revolution and its strategies; they were also protective of their own group's autonomy and interests. In the absence of any insti-tutional channel to settle disputes, each group clung to its opinions. There was no room for discussion, reason, or compromise. Communica-tion—the exchange and discussion of ideas—could not exist. Meetings of Red Guard groups were occasions for hurling rhetoric devoid of meaning, and cleavages only widened. Furthermore, any voice of moderation only invited criticism. Those who cautioned restraint could be criticized for being unfaithful to Mao's thoughts or, even worse, as counter-revolutionaries protecting the enemies. Words of caution or moderation were silenced. Teachers and students with second thoughts on these developments or the use of physical force remained quiet. Extremists could boast that they were faithful followers of Mao, and they rivaled each other in dogmatism and intolerance as expressions of revolutionary spirit or faithfulness to Mao's teachings. The situation was such that the dogmatism, extremism, and use of violence could only escalate, all in the name of the revolution.

Cultural Roots of the Growing Violence

Although the fighting was highlighted in the Western press, it was but one form of group rivalry. More often, groups competed in other ways to express their revolutionary zeal. To prove themselves faithful followers of Chairman Mao, the students organized rallies and meetings supporting central directives and celebrating the revolution. They were constantly waving little red flags and red books. They burned books, destroyed buildings, and damaged art works.

These activities across the country made China look irrational and chaotic to the rest of the world, but they were meant to express and raise revolutionary zeal and to keep the revolution alive. Nevertheless, to understand their particular form, we must trace their origin to Chinese cultural traditions. Many of these expressions of enthusiasm or hostility were deeply rooted in Chinese culture. The flurries of little red books, red flags, red wall posters, and red-ribboned trucks were not unusual. Red had always been the color of joy. Rallies and parades were also traditional expressions of joy and protest. In the 1920s and 1930s, urban intellectuals demonstrated in the streets to protest government policies and foreign encroachments. When happy tidings came, the peasants paraded the streets beating drums and cymbals to disseminate the good news. Since 90 percent of the peasants were illiterate and few radios were available, these parades were most effective in disseminating official information and promoting solidarity. Even after 1949, the national radio stations would give several hours' advance notice of the broadcast of major government policies, which were usually in the evening. The people would gather to listen to these announcements, and neighborhood committees organized residents to parade in the streets immediately after the broadcast to show their support. The parades and rallies of the Cultural

Revolution were part of this tradition, although the scale and frequency of the demonstrations increased and often became occasions for skirmishes among different groups. As we shall see in Chapter 4, Red Guard groups ambushed one another during these parades and sabotaged peaceful demonstrations, sometimes turning them into large-scale battles.

The Red Guards' incessant criticism meetings and parades of intellectuals to punish the "bourgeois enemies" can also be understood in the context of Chinese traditions. In the past, fugitives and criminals caught in China had been dragged through the streets. During the land reform movement of the 1940s and 1950s, the peasants humiliated landlords by shaving their hair, making them wear dunce caps, chains, and placards announcing their crimes, and forcing them to bow before mass gatherings. Mao made references to similar incidents in his report on the Hunan peasants, and William Hinton recounts such scenes in his work on the land-reform movement of the 1950s.[23] The students in the Cultural Revolution followed these peasant traditions: they denounced the "bourgeois intellectuals" before the whole school, paraded them through the streets, shaved their heads, and made them wear placards announcing their crimes. Even the term "ox pen" used for the prisons of these intellectuals on campus reflected this peasant origin. The students imitated their class allies, the peasants, in their treatment of their class enemies, the intellectuals. In some cases, the students were simply imitating the workteams, who had imposed harsh punishments on the accused, subjected them to long hours of interrogation, and humiliated them in front of the students. The repressive measures taken by the school administrations and workteams had backfired, and students retaliated by using similar measures. In other cases, excesses were committed when feelings ran high and the meetings got out of control. Whatever their origin, once these measures were adopted by some students, others followed, and because of the Red Guard network across the country, they spread quickly.

Although these expressions of revolutionary zeal were founded on traditional Chinese culture, the fact that students targeted the intellectuals and party members was, in some ways, a radical break from tradition. The teachers and school administrators were authorities to whom students usually deferred, and turning against them represented a triumph of the new culture in socialist China. The students justified their actions in the name of the revolution: "They saw themselves as vanguards of a new era entrusted with the task of cleansing away every vestige of the . . . humiliating past. If their work involved some violence, forcing people to submit to indignities, they felt this was unavoidable."[24]

The intellectuals were no longer the teachers that the students once respected; they were enemies of the revolution and, in the Chinese peasants' jargon, demons and monsters to be purged. The reduction of intellectuals and party members to such nonhuman categories made it easier to torture them. They were living embodiments of bourgeois traditions, and they had committed the heinous crime of disseminating these values. Therefore, they had to be punished. Fifteen years later, when I asked a student how she felt about her teacher's suicide at that time, she replied drily, "He deserved it; he tried to escape revolution through death." In like manner, the students justified defiling art works, burning library books, and destroying school equipment. All these artifacts encapsulated the bourgeois traditions to be destroyed. Campus buildings were burned, not as wanton acts of arson, but to eliminate the strongholds of bourgeois enemies; the use of physical force was only a means to protect the revolution. To the students, they were showing their revolutionary zeal and commitment to communism. These destructive acts were only the means to a noble end. Every act justified in the name of the revolution was acceptable. The training students received under the communist era had triumphed over the traditional respect for the intellectuals and Chinese culture.

When the school administration fell, group rivalry came to the fore. To each student group, their rival groups became enemies of the revolution. Just as seeing the school administration as devils and demons made it easy to inflict suffering on them, calling one's rivals enemies of the revolution produced the same effect, and competing groups attacked one another with vigor. The students had never had the same respect for their peers as they once had for their teachers, and so they did not have to overcome the inhibition of criticizing authority. Intellectuals generally shrank from violence, and the administrators and teachers without moral and material backing were generally passive. This was not the case when rival Red Guard groups accused each other of being counter-revolutionary. Fired up by their sense of revolutionary zeal and righteousness, they hit back with vigor. When resistance was strong, more powerful measures were used, and the violence escalated. One respondent gave me a graphic account of a bloody battle in which students on both sides were pierced by homemade spears, exposing their entrails, and yet they continued charging until they fell. Battles were fought and rivals were killed, not out of bloodlust, but as expressions of a group's dedication to the revolutionary cause (however it was defined) and as an unavoidable means to root out recalcitrant enemies considered counter-revolutionary. A university student articulated it best when questioned about the killings during the Cultural Revolution: "It's like asking the numbers killed in a war. When you look only at the soldiers killed on the battlefield, it of course sounds inhumane." The revolutionary cause, like a war, justified these actions. The value placed on human life was temporarily suspended on the battlefields.

As the movement continued, the use of physical force became a normal part of revolutionary life. This escalation of violence was gradual and imperceptible to those involved; it numbed the participants. If the rebels were initially repulsed by bloody scenes, they no longer were so as the violence became more frequent. Even a spectator like Neale Hunter became indifferent as the parades of the intellectuals increased: "It was a degrading sight at first, but so many people were exhibited in this way that the horror lost its edge for both the spectators and the victims."[25] As these scenes became more common, they no longer elicited indignation or sympathy. They became such a mundane part of everyday life that justification was unnecessary. A Red Guard described his exploits in the "exchange of revolutionary experience" with great gusto:

> The first day in Shanghai, we saw on a wall poster that a meeting was to be held in the workers' stadium. We went there. When the meeting ended, we were surrounded by members of a rival faction. We had to fight our way out. I even broke my arm in the scuffle and had to be sent to the hospital.

I interrupted to ask why he fought so enthusiastically when he was not even involved in the disputes, and why he supported one side and not the other. He only smiled.

However noble the original motivations, as the fighting continued it became a way of life, an accepted and effective way to settle differences. Differences of opinions, however highly motivated or platonic in the beginning, could not remain so for long. These differences were soon tainted by personalities and egos, blended with old vendettas and new grievances, and degenerated into factionalism. To seek revenge became an integral part of a group's motivation. Ken Ling, who had been attacked and beaten by the local Red Guards in Fuzhou, described this feeling clearly: "The more I beat them, the better I felt. The pent up anger of one month ago was finally dissipated."[26] As the vendettas continued, fighting and rivalry among groups proliferated and turned into battles of recriminations and counter-recriminations. The process could not be stopped, and factionalism became the students' major preoccupation.

The Violence Spreads

Like other developments in late 1966, the "exchange of revolutionary experience" promoted the revolution but also violence. Students who traveled to the capital then returned to their home provinces, and those from Beijing moved outside. Both groups helped to propagate the revolution as well as the tactics used by the "advanced" units. Through the efforts of these students, mass meetings, rallies, parades, big wall posters, the persecution of the intellectuals, the Mao paraphernalia, and fighting became national phenomena.

Since August 1966, disagreements had been acute in Beijing and rival groups had been fighting one another.[27] Many students did not fully appreciate the complexities of the issues involved—that is, the history of disagreements among the schools, the philosophical differences among groups, the dogmatic atmosphere of the time, and the lack of a recourse to settle disputes except through fighting. However, they picked up this form of settling disputes, interpreted it as an expression of revolutionary zeal, and recounted what they saw to their fellow students back home. Since they had been in the capital—thus, at the side of Chairman Mao— their opinions carried weight and their suggestions, including the use of physical force, were adopted. In many schools, the wanton use of physical punishment and fighting among the students occurred only after these students returned from their revolutionary tours. Many students and teachers remembered the early days of the Cultural Revolution in 1966 as a period of "blooming and contending," when everyone was involved in debates. A young teacher told me: "I would stand on a table, a chair or a box, and I debated with my colleagues and students. A crowd would gather and listen. Opposition groups might try to overwhelm me and tire me out, debating with me one after another." It was exciting, but when the students returned from Beijing and used physical force, he withdrew.

In the exchange of revolutionary experience, many Red Guards from Beijing also moved out to the provinces. Some of them saw this as an opportunity to build their strength and spread their ideas; others were simply driven out from their own campuses. Some used the names of parent organizations, perhaps to give themselves credibility, and they established liaison stations without prior consultation with the headquarters. In February 1967, for example, the *Capital Red Guard*, a bulletin published by Beijing Third Headquarters, made a statement dissociating itself from

Sharp Knife Combat Group, Third Headquarters Middle School and Technical School Section, and Third Headquarters Preparatory School Committee, and it declared that the group had stations only in Ganzhou, Wuhan, and Ningxia.

The local Red Guards were unaware of these complications. They only saw the outsiders as emissaries from Beijing—the fountain of revolutionary experience at the side of Chairman Mao—and hung onto their every word. But as different factions from the capital reached the provinces, each disseminating their own ideas, they sowed dissension among the local Red Guard groups. New issues were heaped onto local differences.

Having been involved in fights before, the Beijing Red Guards were not slow to do so in their new locations. Moreover, they were now away from the watchful eyes of family and friends whose expectations often conflicted with the needs of the revolution. In a strange environment, these outsiders felt little compunction to live up to their relatives' and friends' expectations to settle disputes peacefully. They acted with less restraint, often behaving in an audacious and cavalier manner (much to the admiration of the local Red Guards) and encouraging violence. Ken Ling expressed his feelings in this way: "In Foochow [Fuzhou], I had no restraint, no worry, at all. I had neither relatives nor friends nor even casual acquaintances. All this was so different in Amoy, where I had thousands of worries and constantly felt the conflict between my family and upbringing."[28] To the local Red Guards, the association of violence with those they held in high esteem made its adoption not only useful in their own expansion of power but also, to some, attractive.

This picture of audacity among outside Red Guards was corroborated by my respondents' accounts. They all recalled that the outside Red Guards arrived around November, the peak of the exchange movement, and that then the chaos started. A Yunnan University student recalled the coming of the Red Guards:

> This Red Guard came from Beijing. She was wearing a green military uniform with a thick black belt around her waist. Half of her head was bald, a sign that she was leftist. She was standing on the stage, with feet wide apart, and shouting slogans, including obscenities. Her speech excited the students. They all rose to their feet and shouted with her.

Another high school student remembered her first exposure to the Beijing Red Guards. Her group was searching the house of a former Guomindang member and interrogating him:

In the afternoon, a Red Guard from Beijing arrived. I did not know how she knew we were there. We were interrogating this old Guomindang. He was lying on the floor, face down. She took the thick leather belt from her waist and thrashed the old man. With every blow, skin and clothing came off where the buckles hit.

In Shanghai Experimental Primary School, the arrival of the Red Guards incited the students to violence. They broke windows and light bulbs, destroyed laboratory specimens, tables, and chairs, and even made a hole through the three floors to the roof so that the sky could be seen from the ground, just to show their revolutionary spirit. These incidents not only showed the influence of these nonlocal Red Guards, but they also epitomized the different "revolutionary" styles in the three educational levels. University students were the first to use physical force and instigated fights elsewhere, but in many cases the secondary school students did the actual fighting. On the whole, the secondary students were more willing to use physical force and were more violent than the university students, and the primary school students were relatively naive. But more important, these incidents showed that by December 1966 the use of violence had spread across the country.

CHAPTER 4 _____

The Year of Chaos

In the previous chapter, I have shown how the seeds of factionalism were embedded in the structure of Chinese society even before the Cultural Revolution but were brought out in the new developments of late 1966. Just as it was impossible to stay uninvolved in the Cultural Revolution in late 1966, student groups found it impossible not to be involved in Red Guard politics. In the following two years, more discord developed among the Red Guards, which embroiled them in more fighting. The student revolutionaries became so preoccupied with everyday politics and guarding group interests that they pushed educational reforms to the background.

The Radical Factions Dominate

As noted above, violence spread with the students traveling across the country in the exchange of revolutionary experience. However, to students and teachers who disagreed with the movement, the chance to travel meant an opportunity to leave school. In the beginning of the Cultural Revolution, everyone had to take part. For example, according to my respondents, a student of Beijing Aeronautics Institute was dismissed for staying out of the movement. Yet now there was a legitimate excuse to stay away. Regular classes had been discontinued, and no member of the revolutionary committee or the administration could prevent someone with no "political problem" from leaving school. Once the students spread across the country, it was hard to trace them, and even teachers took to the road. The chance to travel was a rare one in China, and many students, including the rebel leaders and young teachers, readily left campus. Some got involved in politics in the places they visited and never returned. Others stayed with relatives in quieter parts of the country, and many simply stayed home.

With the exodus of the Red Guards, many schools were emptied. My respondents could not give me any accurate estimates of the activists or the proportion of schools involved, but they said that the majority of the secondary and especially the primary schools were deserted. Even in universities that remained active throughout the movement, only about a third of the students stayed. This picture was corroborated by the May 20, 1967, issue of *Combat War Gazette:* "The majority of students did not come to school; the school looked quiet and desolate."

In most schools, only the teachers and administrators remained. Many of them had been criticized in the early part of the Cultural Revolution, so when the call to exchange revolutionary experience came, as "reactionaries" disallowed to participate in the revolution, they could not leave. In some ways, this came as a reprieve. One respondent, who had been criticized in the early months, breathed a sigh of relief with the departure of the Red Guards: "By the end of 1966, everyone was gone from the school. The Red Guards did leave a few behind to guard the compound. But we were left pretty much on our own and did whatever we liked." When pressed to elaborate on exactly how he spent his time, he would only say he just "walked and stood around, doing nothing." This amnesia of later developments in the Cultural Revolution characterized all the respondents. Most of them retained vivid images of the first few months of the movement, but their memory blurred soon after, perhaps because the movement lost its novelty. But, culling from these interviews, we can get a picture of these teachers spending most of their time studying Chairman Mao's works or doing manual jobs on campus, such as cleaning buildings and latrines. Occasionally, they attended criticism meetings. Those who were not targets of attack still returned to school every day but just sat around, read the papers or wall posters, or visited other vanguard schools in the movement. The pace was slow, though the tension remained.

Students who remained were also at a loss for what to do. They found little to sustain their interest. They too read wall posters, the most recent government directives, and visited other schools. Sometimes they were so bored that they played practical jokes on each other. A Red Guard complained:

There was really little that one could do. We could spend our days reading the posters over and over again. One day, while two girls and I were standing there reading the posters, we were hit by a water bomb and drenched. It was from one of our group. A boy guarding on the roof had nothing better to do.

Other students hanging around campus devised their own pastimes. It was a time to acquire new hobbies and expertise. A favorite hobby among high school students in Guangzhou was "three-line construction"—that is, knitting, sewing, and electronics—punned on the Chinese word "line" and "thread," or "wiring," used in these activities. By 1982, when I visited China, a faculty member of Shaanxi University had become an expert in oracle bones, a teacher had become a good calligrapher, and a student had mastered three languages since they took up these interests in 1967. To have a more objective overview of the Cultural Revolution, the frenzied activities that characterized the Cultural Revolution must be seen against this mundane and lethargic atmosphere on many campuses. Not all the students or schools took an active part in factionalism, but the participation of a handful was enough to throw the country into chaos.

Intense political maneuverings continued in a minority of schools. These schools were sometimes headquarters for conglomerate groups. In 1967, the umbrella organizations were not confined to student organizations but comprised groups from different sectors of society. For example, Liaoning University was the headquarters for Liaolian, a conglomerate of workers, government workers, and students with membership in the thousands. In such cases, the schools would be the center for strategy planning and the targets of constant raids. At other schools, like Beida and Qinghua, where opinions had polarized and the strength of the rival groups was equal, the campuses became battlegrounds. Rival groups occupied different buildings, boarded windows, hoarded supplies, dug trenches, and adopted other defense measures to be prepared for battle at anytime. The rest of this chapter will focus on the latter schools.

In schools where the core student groups were active, they controlled the campuses and exerted strong pressure on the others to conform. The school administration had been a tight chain of command bounded by specific rules and regulations. For those remaining on campus, this formal system of social control was replaced by a less structured and less predictable, though in certain ways equally effective, one. The central leaders communicated their directives through the newspapers, radios, and street posters, and sometimes directly to the Red Guards. Whichever channel used, the implementation of these directives was subject to the interpretation of the individual local leaders; as we have seen in their interpretation of Lin Biao's and Jiang Qing's directives, the Red Guards frequently added their personal touches or new twists of meanings. They also made arbitrary rulings, and the retaliations on transgressors of Red Guard "laws" and on opponents were swift. For example, in minor cases, jaywalkers stopped by the Red Guards had to memorize passages from Mao's works. In more serious cases, opponents of dominant Red Guard groups controlling the school revolutionary committees could be demoted or have their wages suspended or reduced.[1] At times, these Red Guards even created their own reign of terror by kidnapping, jailing, or torturing their opponents.

Many were cowed into silence or conformity and drifted along with the movement. A Red Guard justified her actions in this way:

> I was scared of the use of physical force and never took part in any of these fights. But I attended the meetings. I read the big wall posters at night. There were fewer people around. It was more convenient to read them. I slept during the day. You had to know what was going on, otherwise you would not be revolutionary.

The use of physical force turned many people away from the movement, but, in schools where the Red Guards were strong, the threat of it being used on them also kept many involved. Morale was low among these members. They would do the minimum to ward off retaliation—closely follow the developments, read the big wall posters, study Mao's thoughts, and attend meetings—but they avoided fights or any form of violence. By February 1967, this attitude had become so widespread that it invited criticism from the *People's Daily*. The government still wanted the revolution to continue, and these drifters were called "those viewing themselves as appendages of the revolutionary group and not members of the revolutionary ranks. Every time a meeting was held, they attended as spectators to make up the quorum."[2]

In schools actively involved in the Cultural Revolution, the movement was in the hands of those dedicated to it; "backward elements" merely tagged along. The vocal opponents had been purged, the moderate elements muted, and any voice of moderation or caution silenced. It was a vicious circle. Without any cautionary advice or restraint, participants could only encourage one another and become more radical. As fighting became more frequent in 1967, popular support further declined. The participants became more extreme, and even the "riffraff" of society was enlisted to fight.[3]

The Red Guards and Politics

In their isolation from fellow students, or perhaps in their concern to expand their group's influence, student leaders sought alliances with local leaders and extended their activities outside the schools. Some students even became heads of municipal and provincial revolutionary committees. Instead of carrying their revolution in education to its logical conclusion—that is, to seek remedies to the weaknesses they identified in the educational system and to translate their general educational philosophy into coherent proposals, now that they were in a position to do so—they expanded the scope of their revolutionary activities to national and local politics.

The campaign to remove the school administration and the "four olds" marked the beginning of Red Guard political involvement and apprenticeship for later participation in municipal and national politics. The students were encouraged by the local and central government; it was necessary for them "to get out of the small classroom of the schools to the big classroom of the society, to weather the storm, to face the world, to understand class struggle, and to let the new rain wash the political dust in our heads and remove the old class influence, to integrate with the masses and investigate society."[4] In December 1966, the students moved into politics.

Central Government Politics

A major issue in national politics was the criticism of government leaders. During the Cultural Revolution, most of the central and provincial leaders were purged and criticized at some point. Central leaders and veteran Chinese Communist Party members such as Liu Shaoqi, Deng Xiaoping, Bo Yibo, He Long, and Zhou Yang were dismissed. Out of the 26 ministers, vice-ministers, directors, and vice-directors of the ministries associated with education, nineteen lost their positions.[5]

The criticism of these high-level politicians was closely watched if not orchestrated by the Beijing government. The central government was certainly involved; it was split into factions, but the dominant group always acted in the name of the collective, which gave the impression of a unified coordination from above. In October 1967, the *South Guangdong Survey*, a Red Guard paper, read: "With the approval of Chairman Mao and the party Central Committee, those party persons in authority taking the capitalist road who have been criticized or repudiated by their name in the central government include. . . ." After the list of names, it continued: "Those party persons in authority taking the capitalist road who are to be criticized and repudiated publicly by name in the next stage of the central publication include. . . ." Finally, for the third category: "Those party persons in authority taking the capitalist road who are to be criticized and repudiated publicly by name in the next stage in local publications include. . . ."[6]

It appeared that the targets of criticism were carefully screened by the central government through directives sent to the Red Guards. Many Red Guard leaders admitted that, even though they did not have direct contact with central leaders, their actions were not completely brash— that is, they would not move against a political leader or a government department unless they had some indication of support from other groups or from above. They did not want to be isolated or held solely accountable.

Red Guards became astute in these political maneuvers. They were aware of divisions in the different levels of government and sensitive to nuances in official documents that could signal the fall of a particular leader. Red Guards from Beijing universities admitted they were aware that Liu Shaoqi was in trouble even in August, whereas the provincial Red Guards remained oblivious to this until early 1967. A veteran Red Guard explained that the criticism of political leaders developed in several stages:

> First there were indirect attacks, like "leaders in power taking the capitalist road." Through the details given and the political profiles of these leaders, we could recognize the targets. At the second stage, those criticized would be named in wall posters. At the third stage, the person would be identified by name in the national papers.

Everyone would jump in at that latter stage. But the politically astute would get involved at the second or even the first stage, and their political acuity gained them tremendous prestige. It also gave the impression that they might have friends in high places.

The criticism of Liu is the best example of this political maneuvering, since it is so well documented. At the end of the eleventh plenum of the Communist Party Central Committee, Liu was demoted. On August 23, 1966, the *People's Daily* urged "the overthrow of anyone who opposed Mao Zedong's thoughts, no matter how high his position, how great his prestige, or how long he worked for the revolution." On November 16, Liu was criticized by name in a wall poster in Beijing. On December 2, Qinghua and Beida put out a joint poster against Liu, though it still had a cautious tone: "We believe that Liu and Deng are the Number 1 and

Number 2 authorities in the party taking the capitalist road."[7] At that stage it was still a political gamble, because they could be wrong. A Red Guard explained how to act in such a murky situation. It was prudent "to pause a while to see the reaction of the central government and, if there was no sign of objection, to keep on going."[8] If the central government disagreed, it would let the students know. After some Red Guards attacked Zhou Enlai, for example, Jiang Qing and other central leaders came forward to denounce such actions, and the students held back. But in the meantime, before the central government made a stand, the different Red Guard groups would be debating among themselves and even fighting to defend their own positions.

To the students, government silence indicated tacit approval. Their suspicion was confirmed. On December 18, Kuai Dafu—the student leader at Qinghua University—met with Zhang Chunqiao in Beijing. On December 25, a mass rally was held, and the demonstrators chanted slogans against Liu and Deng. Mass meetings to criticize Liu in absentia were held. Finally, the Red Guards in the capital became so bold that they wanted to "struggle" Liu at a criticism meeting. On January 6, 1967, Qinghua University students tricked Liu and his wife, Wang Guangmei, out of their home, fabricating a message that his daughter had been in a car accident and his signature was needed for an emergency operation. Zhou Enlai intervened. Though Liu was criticized numerous times at criticism meetings all over the country during the Cultural Revolution, he only appeared at one mass meeting, in which Zhou chaired the session. His wife was not as fortunate. In front of a large gathering at Qinghua, Wang was forced to wear the gown she had worn on an Indonesian state tour adorned with a string of table-tennis balls for a necklace.[9] When the incident was publicized in the Qinghua bulletin, other Red Guard groups knew their limit: Liu could be criticized, but not in person. Thereafter, the indictment of Liu Shaoqi became a regular item on the Red Guards' criticism agenda.

Despite these attempts to contain the movement, government control over the Red Guards was never complete. Its control over the students deteriorated as the revolution progressed and local governments were overthrown. The dominant government faction might send its directives in the name of Mao and the Cultural Revolution central committee, but these were not necessarily obeyed. Despite the government's order prohibiting students from parading central leaders, Minister of Culture Xiao Wangdong was dragged through the streets on January 17, carrying a placard listing his "crimes"; the government could not stop it in time. The students became bold, ignoring and openly defying central directives. In August 1967, students camped outside Zhongnanhai, the central leaders' residence, demanding to criticize Liu in person despite government orders to disband. Toward the end, even the core groups of the central government leaders did not escape the Red Guard attack. Jiang Qing's residence was raided. Even Zhou Enlai was criticized as "China's Red Capitalist." He was surrounded for nineteen hours and released only to be taken to the hospital after a heart attack. Such incidents reflected the nadir to which the central government authority had fallen.

This interplay between government directives and local initiatives was a continuous theme throughout the movement. In the first months of the Cultural Revolution, central-government policies coincided with what the majority of students wanted, and the movement took off at a tremendous speed. As the revolution developed, both bodies had different ideas as to how to proceed. But the government had been so successful in promoting the revolution that the movement had acquired its own dynamics. Government leaders found it difficult to control or reverse the trend as the students became stronger and acted their own minds. This conflict was further complicated by the fact that the central government itself was divided. When a losing faction at the center could not have its way, it secretly encouraged student supporters to implement its wishes, galvanizing some students' defiance of central directives. Liu's fate, as well as that of other leaders, reflected the test of strength between the Red Guards and the central leaders. On one hand, the freedom of the Red Guards was circumscribed by the government, which exerted strong pressure on them to comply. On the other, the Red Guards took the initiative (at times with the prompting of some central leaders), and the central government could not completely control them. This tug-of-war remained a central feature of the period. Sometimes the students complied with, and at other times they defied, government directives. When the students fought among themselves, the government had a difficult time stopping them.

To back up their accusations of the central leaders, the Red Guards did research on these leaders and documented their crimes. Red Guards investigated politicians' pasts, even to the point of seizing official documents and raiding their residences. On December 4, 1966, Red Guards raided the residence of Peng Zhen, the former mayor of Beijing, and on January 8, 1967, that of He Long, the former chief of staff.[10] They visited the home provinces or places once visited by those being criticized, and they interviewed anyone who had previous contacts with them. The 124 Combat Group claimed to have traveled through ten provinces and cities and interviewed 400 persons on one such mission.[11]

This information was not only used in criticism meetings organized for their own members but was also widely circulated among their allies.

Sometimes it was compiled into documents and distributed. Again, the history of Liu Shaoqi was the best researched. In February 1967, Qinghua put out a pamphlet entitled *One Hundred Examples of Liu Shaoqi Resisting Chairman Mao,* which became the prototype for other Red Guard documents denouncing him. Liu was attacked for his policy of econo- mism (reliance on material incentives, such as private plots and free mar- kets to boost production), his "condoning exploitation" (holding that capitalist exploitation was necessary to produce class consciousness and workers' opposition), his educational policies, his undue reliance on technology and intellectuals, and his stalling of the Cultural Revolution. Even his behavior in the 1930s as an underground communist activist in the urban areas was condemned, and he was criticized for being the son of a landlord. In one case, his letter advising his sister to give up her land in the coming land-reform movement was taken as evidence of betraying a state secret. Some accounts of his actions and statements were incredi- ble, and even if they were authentic, the criticisms were unreasonable. In any case, such research on the leaders' backgrounds considerably demys- tified them and undermined the respect Red Guards once had for them. The circulation of the documents gave the accused little opportunity to defend themselves. It only whipped up negative emotions against these leaders and kept the revolution going.

The students might not agree with the central government, but nei- ther did they agree among themselves. Students held different opinions about the central leaders just as they had about the school administrators. They defended their positions and debated with those disagreeing with them. These discussions could often lead to skirmishes and fighting. The longer the government took to come up with a stand on the leader in dis- pute, the more protracted the debates and fighting. The government pro- nouncement on the leader usually increased the prestige of the group who took the "correct" side, and it spelled the disgrace of those who did not. These official verdicts on the leaders diffused the intensity of the de- bate but could not completely stop the fighting. The losing groups con- tinued to hold their stand and may even have been secretly encouraged by the losing faction at the central level. Criticism of central leaders split Red Guard ranks and fueled factionalism.

Again, we can take the example of Liu Shaoqi. After two months of debate among the students, the central government as a collective was ready to sacrifice Liu, and it denounced him in the *People's Daily* in Janu- ary 1967 as the "leader taking the capitalist road." His followers within the central government, if they still existed, were silent. At the local level, the majority of the Red Guards followed this position, but some students still expressed their support for him. On January 6, 1967, when it was already apparent that Liu was in disgrace, 400 members from United Action raided the anti-Liu Beijing municipal council and shouted "Long live Liu Shaoqi!" and "Down with the Central Cultural Committee!"[12] Even in such a clear-cut case, with the central government criticizing Liu, Red Guards still attacked government offices to express support for him. The split in student ranks must have been even greater when the government's position was less clear, or when central-government involvement was less direct.

Local Politics

To the Red Guards, except for those living in Beijing itself, the national leaders were distant figures; criticisms were couched in rhetoric, and the feelings toward these central leaders were less intense than in the capital. The evaluation of teachers and school administrators had touched the students' lives, but then only the school community had been involved. In local politics, however, the Red Guards' targets were closer to home: mayors, heads of local offices of education, members of the municipal committees, local party secretaries, and government and industrial administrators.

Since August 1966, the Cultural Revolution had spread to factories, enterprises, government departments, and other social organizations. What occurred in these units were similar to what had taken place in the schools: subordinates were exposing the leaders and criticizing the administration. By 1967, factionalism was as prevalent in these organizations as it was in the schools. Local politicians were, therefore, scrutinized not only by students but also by rebel groups from every walk of life. As more diverse groups became involved, opinions varied. Moreover, the political records of local administrators were more complicated than those of school personnel, and information to evaluate them was harder to obtain. Their files were classified as state secrets and accessible only through raiding government offices. Thus, judgments were often based on hearsay, verdicts based on personal opinions, and differences irreconcilable. In the criticism of national leaders, the rebels could still look to the central government for guidance. In the case of local leaders, the central government intervened only in an impasse or crisis situation. Their fate was left to the discretion of the local forces, which meant that a settlement would only be reached when one side was completely exhausted. Disagreements among student groups were prolonged and fights were numerous.

National leaders might number in the hundreds, but local leaders numbered in the millions. There were 26 levels of cadres in dozens of local offices, and each one of those cadres was a potential source of conflict. I do not have systematic information on these conflicts at the provincial level, but it is easy to imagine the chaos that resulted when the cadres came under attack one after another. Opinions differed and group alignments shifted; this in turn led to more disagreements and more skirmishes among the students.

There seemed to be no end to these disagreements, especially when they were compounded by repeated calls from the central government in 1967 and 1968 to include the fallen cadres in the revolutionary ranks but to exclude traitors and bourgeois capitalists. The definitions of "traitor" and "bourgeois capitalist" were naturally subject to different interpretations. Cases were opened and reopened, which led to more friction. The case of Liu Hsun, president of the Institute of Seventh Ministry of Machine Building, was telling in this context. Liu had been criticized as a reactionary who took the bourgeois line, for which he was "educated" by the masses. During the process, he befriended the September 16 Rebel Group, and they said he "carried out ideological work among the masses hoodwinked by the bourgeois reactionary line and exposed Zheng Zhun, party secretary of the Institute." To the September 16 Rebel Group, the case was closed. But 4812 Rebel Group continued to oppose Liu:

> They beat comrade Liu four times in January and February, and harassed him at home. On March 20, they changed Liu's public security file and branded him a spy of the Central Investigation and Statistical Bureau of the Guomindang. On April 15, they organized mass struggle against him day and night over [the] issue of wages.[13]

This case not only shows the breach between academic and party administrations as mentioned in Chapter 3, but, more important, it also shows the divided opinions of two rival groups, with one accepting and the other rejecting the repentant cadre, and how befriending one group through exposing another could absolve one from any crimes, at least in the eyes of one's allies. Many political leaders were quick to realize that they were at the mercy of the local forces. The central government would not or could not intervene on the local cadres' behalf. Red Guard support was necessary for their survival, and local leaders were quick to exploit divisions among the students.

When a city was divided over the highest level of leadership—such as in the cases of Chen Pixian, the mayor of Shanghai; Zhang Texue, the party secretary of Wuhan; and Duan Daming, the secretary of

Chongqing—it became a virtual battlefield. Wuhan, for example, experienced 320 clashes in the first half of 1967.[14] These were not minor clashes. On July 7, for example, the Million Heroes, in support of Zhang Texue, clashed with the Red Flag Combat Group when the latter held a rally to welcome mediators from Beijing; 2,000 members from the Red Flag Combat Group alone were involved. A skirmish could easily involve tens of thousands; when the army was involved and heavy artillery was used, the city became a war zone with the two sides occupying strongholds in different parts of the city and a no-man's-land in between.

Only in such severe situations would the central government intervene. The most dramatic case was again in Wuhan. It has been described in detail by Thomas Robinson,[15] but I shall recount it briefly here. In July 1967, Xie Fuzhi, a member of the Central Cultural Revolution Committee, and Wang Li, deputy director of the party's theoretical journal *Red Flag*, came to investigate the situation. When it appeared that the two emissaries favored the Red Flag Combat Group, Zhang arrested them, and when Zhou Enlai flew in to secure their release, the Million Heroes plotted to ambush Zhou as well, but this plan was discovered. The provincial capital came under siege by the air force, army, and navy. Zhang was then escorted to Beijing to be interrogated, and the Million Heroes disbanded. This incident showed the nadir to which central control had fallen: the provincial leaders were ready to defy central emissaries, and even top-level leaders and the military had to be mobilized to extort compliance.

The verdict from the central government resolved the balance of power in Wuhan. The quick demise of the Million Heroes and similar conglomerate groups in other cities—for example, the 60,000-member Scarlet Combat Group of Shanghai accompanying the fall of Chen Pixian—impressed on the Red Guards the vulnerability of their position. They knew they could not survive without these alliances: contacts with the "correct" local leaders lent them prestige; inside information from friendly local leaders helped them make judicious decisions, avoid mistakes, and act faster than their rivals; and tangible benefits like paper, ink, and weapons could be obtained from these government departments. Moreover, the experience and advice of the local cadres sitting on their group committee would be especially useful when students began to control local government administration. However, the Red Guards also knew that they had to be careful in making these alliances, because choosing the wrong friends would ruin their future. Politicking and cultivating alliances, in addition to investigating, criticizing, and supporting local and national leaders, became integral parts of their revolutionary activities.

The Seizure of Power

Red Guard activities soon extended beyond merely criticizing or evaluating one cadre or another. In 1967, they also took control of factories and government departments. The term "seizure of power" was used to describe such activities early in the year. The schools had been taken over in July and August 1966, but classes were suspended and running the schools lost its attraction. The students were not experienced and disciplined enough to reform the educational system. By November, the students were moving into the farms and factories to spread the revolution. Students from the Central Finance Institute Worker-Peasant Oriented Combat Group joined forces with workers of the Red Rebel Corps of Beijing Chienhua Steel Factory to take over production. Even middle school students were involved, like those in the Hongjiang Middle School in Shanghai, who were partners in running a local glass factory.[16] What made the January 1967 takeover different from what happened the previous summer was the level and scale of the coup. In January, the very top levels of the local, provincial, and national administrations were attacked, and the nation's administrative organs were paralyzed.

"Seizure of power" was first applied by Mao to what occurred in Shanghai. In December 1966, the forces of the two rival groups—the Scarlet Combat Group and the Workers' Headquarters—each numbered 60,000 and had split workers in almost every school, factory, store, and government department. The city came to a standstill. Factories stopped production, loading ceased at piers, the trains stopped running, and there was no water or electricity for four days. According to Zhang Chunqiao, the leader of the rebels, they only wanted to put vital services such as water, electricity, mail, shipping, and the railway back into operation.[17] If these were not Zhang's real goals, at least his rhetoric moved the students, which again reflected their idealistic and altruistic concerns despite their own internal squabbles. College students sold tickets, maintained order at the railway stations, and served as conductors and train attendants. Middle school students helped load and unload ships. On January 5, 1967, seven student groups in conjunction with four organizations from other sectors of society took over the newspaper *Wen Hui Bao* without consulting the leaders, and they sent a "letter to the whole municipality" appealing to the workers to go back to work. The next day, other Red Guards took over the Shanghai municipal party committee and the municipal people's council. On January 7, the Liaison Center of Public Organizations and the Suburbia Peasants' Association took over the district party committee and the East China Bureau of the Chinese Communist Party. Then they went to Beijing to seek central approval. On January 9, the central government gave its support.

The Shanghai incident again exemplified the uneasy relationship between government control and local initiative. The seizure of power was a local idea. Student and worker groups acted on their own, without prior consultation with their local leaders, let alone with the central ones. They also set up a Paris Commune type of organization in place of the municipal government, with 38 organizations favoring and 20 against it. However, the commune lasted only twelve days; in January, government influence in the provinces was still strong. The dominant group in the central government was against the new organization and considered a communal structure unrealistic. Zhang Chunqiao and Yao Wenyuan were summoned to Beijing and asked to abandon their plans.[18] With central support, minority opinion overruled the majority. The government suppressed news of the Paris-type commune and instead publicized the province of Heilongjiang's creation of a "triple-unity" revolutionary committee, composed of young revolutionaries, veteran cadres, and soldiers.[19]

However, the government did support the seizure of power in Shanghai, and it publicly encouraged similar developments elsewhere. This turned an isolated event into a mass phenomenon. On January 9, the government called for a "counteroffensive upon the bourgeois reactionary line," urging cadres in other areas to follow Shanghai's lead. Five days later, rebels took control of the Ministry of First Light Industry and the Ministry of Petroleum. In the following seven days, 21 ministries—including the ministries of forestry, coal, metallurgical industry, water conservation and electric power, higher education, culture, labor, post and telecommunication, finance, and railway—were taken over by the rebels. In the final count, three of the nine state commissions and 30 of the 40 ministries transferred power.[20] In their place, revolutionary committees (and not Paris-style communes) were formed.

The Red Guards were involved in all these activities, although they were no longer the sole participants. Among the rebel groups in the universities, each seemed to agree tacitly on spheres of control and each took over the ministry that once had jurisdiction over their institute. The Institute of Water and Electric Power engineered the coup in the Ministry of Water Conservation; the Red Flag Group of the Institute of Steel Industry took over the Ministry of Metallurgical Industry; Daqing Commune of Beijing Petroleum Institute took over the Ministry of Petroleum; the Jingganshan Group of Light Industry Institute took over the Ministry of Light Industry; and Rebel Corps of Sixteen Articles of Chemical Engineering Institute took over the Ministry of Chemical Industry. In the provinces, the leading local university controlled the pro-vincial administration. August 15 Group of Sichuan University took over the provincial revolutionary committee; Zhongda Red Flag, the provincial office in Guangdong; and August 31 Group of Liaoning Uni-versity headed Liaoning's provincial committee.[21] Occasionally, outside Red Guard groups were involved in local politics. Student groups from Beijing, Harbin, and Xian were involved in the initial seizure of power in Shanghai. On December 31, 1967, the Guangzhou Liaison Center of Wuhan Universities and Colleges, Beijing Aviation College Red Flag, and Harbin Military Engineering College were listed among the 24 or-ganizations taking over the newspaper *Yangcheng Wenbao*.[22]

Steel August 1, the publication of a rebel group bearing the same name, described its seizure of power on August 8, 1967, at a district office: "500 people of revolutionary organizations arrived at the office. They read aloud an editorial of *Red Flag* and then their proclamations in the takeover of power. Then they enumerated the crimes of the cadres and took over the seal."[23] The paper did not mention whether a report had been given to the central government. In most cases, rebels followed their coup with a report to the center that represented a request for cen-tral approval. In this case, the coup was a calm proclamation of crimes and a turning over of the official seal. In other cases, however, the local officials resisted, and fighting ensued. The rebels would then surround government buildings, storm the offices, and cart away documents. As in the "removal of the four olds," there was no coordination in these activi-ties. For example, on January 23, Dongshan Division of August 1 Com-bat Group wanted to take over the district office, but it arrived only to find that another group had accomplished the same thing earlier in the afternoon.[24] Government departments changed hands a number of times among different rebel groups and were put out of service. As the fre-quency of such takeovers and countertakeovers increased, the Red Guards could not decide which group executed the "authentic" transfer-ence of power from the bourgeoisie to the proletariat. The divisions among the Red Guards again proliferated.

What had taken place in the schools in late 1966 was repeated in the government departments in 1967. Like the school administrators, some government officials and factory managers tried to reduce pressure from their subordinates by encouraging the revolutionary workers to go away on the exchange of revolutionary experience. In some Shanghai factories, over half of the technicians were gone. In Shanghai Cotton Factory, some apprentices—whose average monthly income was about 30 yuan— were given 200 yuan for two months to stay on the road; in others, man-agers gave workers bonuses as large as 1,000 yuan to gain their support.[25]

Like the workteams transferring power to student supporters before they left, government leaders maneuvered their own "seizures of power." They recognized that, with the central government's approval and the rebels' enthusiasm, a takeover was unavoidable. It would be better to orchestrate one while they still had some influence. The rebel groups they chose, again like the student supporters of the workteams in the schools, were ready to comply, because it meant a warrant to share future power and an advantage over their rivals. Minister of Culture Xiao Wangdong and Minister of Foreign Affairs Chen Yi were accused by the rebels of engineering such transfers with the help of sympathetic Red Guard groups. The April 15 issue of *Red Rock Combat News* gave an account of how a transfer was accomplished in Chongqing:

> On January 17, Lu Tatung, Hsin Ichih, and Liao Suhua of the municipal party committee and Sung Bia of the Chongqing Bureau of Public Security met with leaders of the August 15 Group. They arranged another meeting on January 19. On January 24, they decided on a unified seizure of power all over the city. The next morning, it was accomplished without a hitch. The seizure of power and the rehabilitation of Hsin Ichih took less than eight minutes.

Many respondents confirmed that sham seizures of power did occur and that such manipulations further complicated divisions among the Red Guards. The interviewees added that even "real" takeovers meant only the transfer of the official seal. In fact, nothing changed. As in the schools, the revolutionaries did not have the experience or the administrative abilities to run the departments, and incumbents continued to perform their duties though they reported to a different person.

Theoretically, the measurement of a real seizure of power rested on the transfer of power from the bourgeoisie to the proletariat—whatever these terms might mean to the revolutionaries—and the evaluation of the political leaders was an integral part of the process. Like the evaluation of school administrators, the review of factory and government cadres divided the students who took part. The evaluation of cadres was complex, and it was a constant bone of contention among rebel groups. Sometimes 40 groups coming from diverse geographic regions and backgrounds were involved. Disagreements were unavoidable even among those who supported the initial coup. Those who felt left out in the distribution of power or dissatisfied with the new arrangements carried out their own counter-coups. Former allies became enemies.

With each shift in power, new targets of attacks were found, and former heroes became enemies of the revolution. The schools had experienced similar, though less complicated, developments. The intellectuals had been the first targets; then their prosecutors, the party members, were attacked; then the "revolutionary" students who supported the party were labeled conservatives and those who "opposed" the party and, later, the workteams, were considered heroes. In the schools this process had been relatively brief and ended when the school administration disintegrated and students turned their attention elsewhere. The stakes in the factories and government offices were higher, and, with rebel groups from other walks of life involved, there was no end to the seizures and counterseizures of power. Each change in political leadership blurred the distinctions between revolutionaries and counter-revolutionaries. Those who fell victim in the previous shift in power sought redress. The criticisms and charges in each case were worded in Marxist jargon, however, which made it difficult to establish "guilt" or "innocence." Victims were accused of being "antirevolutionary, anti-party, or anti-Mao" based on the flimsiest evidence and sometimes on fabricated charges.

Some victims argued that, since their accusers were now found to be "counter-revolutionary," then those whom they denounced would necessarily be "revolutionary." But not everyone agreed with this simplistic criterion. Furthermore, the review of these cases and the reversal of verdicts were not usually the priority of the new leaders, who were preoccupied with consolidating their positions. Their procrastination increased the dissatisfaction of the accused who were not cleared, especially when the central government seemed to be encouraging more magnanimous attitudes toward the cadres. Thus, new differences were added onto old ones. The scenes in the schools in 1966 were replayed, except that they did not come to a quick end. In February 1967, to curtail the scope of fighting, the government announced that only members of the same unit could seize power from their superiors,[26] but it was too late. The Red Guards were too much involved in these local politics to extricate themselves. Criticisms and countercriticisms, seizures and counterseizures of power continued.

Factionalism Grows

Increasing factionalism among the Red Guards must be seen against the background of Red Guard participation in national and local politics. Such involvement introduced issues that split their ranks and were constant sources of conflict among the student revolutionaries in 1967 and 1968. Cleavages widened and new scores were added to old vendettas until the misunderstandings and disagreements intertwined and could not be resolved. The demise of powerful political leaders impressed on the Red Guards their vulnerability and the importance of having political power, and they clung to their newly gained positions. The preservation of group interests was their only guarantee of safety. Since each Red Guard unit also considered itself the champion of Mao's thoughts, it felt that the revolution would only develop in the "correct" direction if that group held control. Therefore, increasing its power, forming alliances, and acquiring ammunition and other resources had to be given priority, if not for the group's own sake then at least for that of the revolution. Under such circumstances, whatever the ultimate intentions of these Red Guards, the pursuit of personal gains and revolutionary interests were intertwined. Fighting for group interests—that is, strengthening one's own group and defeating one's rivals—was a prerequisite for "revolutionary success" and became the only criterion for action. The means overshadowed the end. Factionalism dominated, and restructuring the educational system was pushed to the background.

The factionalism took different forms. For example, one battle was of words. To safeguard their power, the Red Guards published bulletins and distributed handbills to shape public opinion and gain support. In Beijing alone, 200 different bulletins could be bought in 1967.[27] In these, the Red Guards justified their every action while putting their enemies in the worst light. The August 1 Combat Group, for example, "in the spirit of making an investigation," published a chronicle of its own organization to show it had a long revolutionary history. It documented all the "glorious revolutionary acts" when it had obeyed the central government directives and especially the word of Mao. The Steel August 1 Group put out a special edition of its paper to deny accusations that the group's seizure of power was "illegal" because it had reportedly been "abducting and detaining responsible cadres." Instead, it showed that its actions were most democratic and had mass support.[28] Just as the repeated adulation of Mao made his omniscience "real," continuous propaganda on a group's virtues also enhanced its image.

Perhaps prompted by this rationale, Red Guards devoted a great deal of space in their publications to discrediting their enemies. A content analysis of *Zhongda Red Flag* in 1967 showed that it contained 89 articles attacking Guangdong Military Command, 15 articles against the provincial revolutionary committee, and 74 articles against its rival groups.[29] Similarly, *Zhongda Red Guard Papers* undermined the credibility of its rival, the Guangzhou Provincial Revolutionary Rebel Joint Committee, accusing it of fabricating names on its membership list. Sometimes these accusations were posted in the streets to gain wider readership. The Red

Flag Commune of Sanshui Middle Schools posted slogans like "Guangzhou Doctrine Red Guards fighting and looting in Sanshui will come to a bad end," implying of course that the latter looted and fought.[30]

Such Red Guard publications had wide readership. Work in farms and factories had stopped, and many peasants were in the city to deliver complaints on living and working conditions to the new government. They were eager for news of the revolution. Jean Esmein, who was in Beijing at that time, described the situation: "People went hunting for news and the crowd never ebbed in the city festooned with wall posters. Those who sold the little papers [Red Guard publications] did good business. Everybody wanted to know what was happening in Shanghai, Chungking [Chongqing], or Xian."[31] The official sources, such as the *People's Daily* or the People's Radio, carried central directives and developments approved by the central government, but the Red Guard papers mainly ran graphic accounts of new developments in the localities. The reliability of their reports might have been questionable, but their bent for sensationalism certainly made them more interesting reading.

The Red Guards fully appreciated the importance of symbolism in a mass movement and the need to rally members' support. They organized a rally for every occasion. In addition to the traditional celebrations of National Day, Labor Day, and parades to show support for new directives, rallies were held on anniversaries of major events of the Cultural Revolution—for example, the May 16 Directive and Nie's wall poster. On December 27, 1966, Red Guards across the country protested against Russian revisionism; on January 26 and February 6 and 12, 1967, against the Russian treatment of Chinese students; on May 15, 19, and 21, against the British handling of their comrades in Hongkong; and in July, against the Indonesian government treatment of the overseas Chinese. They also gathered to show support for friendly nations, such as on January 9 in support of Arab countries. There were also meetings to celebrate China's achievements, like the manufacture of insulin and the explosions of the nuclear and hydrogen bombs. Local demonstrations celebrated or commemorated a seizure of power and sometimes protested against the sham ones. As a result, large numbers of rallies were held. At Liaoning University alone, 141 public meetings of various sizes were held between April 1 and July 15, 1967, averaging more than one a day.[32]

In contrast to group fights, which turned many people away, parades were generally peaceful occasions that attracted a large attendance. By late 1967, contentious issues were no longer the theme of such mass gatherings. After the government prohibited dragging those being criticized through the streets, the rallies became joyous occasions or, at worst, indictments of enemies already removed. At Liaoning University, for example, 101 of its 141 meetings were against Liu Shaoqi and other central leaders and only 40 were against cadres in the Northeast Bureau, provincial, or municipal offices.[33] The verdict against those criticized was settled even before the meetings.

With work stoppages and schools closed, these rallies gave people a break from monotony. Attendance was large, sometimes numbering tens of thousands. The rank and file gathered in the streets and listened to the harangues of their leaders. A respondent described to me how these public meetings were organized: "At these meetings there were usually the main slogans put in front of the hall. At different corners of the room there were people to lead the shouting of slogans. The speakers would make their speeches punctuated by the shouting of slogans at the appropriate moments." After an hour or two, the meetings would end with a grand exit and parade in the streets amidst the sound of drums and cymbals.

Parades and rallies were also a form of intergroup rivalry. The leaders used these occasions to show off their strength and to gain visibility and public support. A Red Guard leader recalled how pathetic his small group looked in comparison to its stronger rival:

> We were a small group with only 50 members; our rival numbered 800. It was funny when we paraded in the street, beating drums and cymbals. We were so few and the noise we made so small; when the two groups crossed paths, the sound of their drums and cymbals deafened our ears and drowned whatever sound we made. Little children of eight or nine knew no better, they thought it was fun to follow a parade. So you can picture our little pathetic group with little kids carrying sticks and tattered flags trailing behind.

To improve the group's status, he invited his allies to join in just to show he had outside backing; Guangzhou Zhongda Red Flag sent a few trucks and tanks as reinforcements. According to the leader, after a number of these parades, public opinion did turn in his favor.

Parades could also be a way for a group to show that it was more committed to the revolution than another group. When new government directives were announced, the Red Guards competed with each other to organize the first rally to show support for the directives, and some would go so far as to sabotage their rival's rallies. When the government organized its own mass rallies and invited all groups to attend, rival groups "would not march along the same route and arrive at the same

time. Sometimes [they] even raced to see who would get to mass meetings first."[34] But not all parades ended with this touch of humor.

Occasionally, peaceful parades became bloody clashes, especially
when group rivalry was intense. Fighting could occur when two parading groups crossed paths and the exchange of invectives turned to the exchange of blows. Mayhem would follow. The parade of a rival group
offered an excellent opportunity to ambush the entire enemy group. It
was on such an occasion that the Million Heroes attacked the Red
Guards of Wuhan Central China Engineering College. When the 2,000
members of the latter group were marching down Liuchui Road to celebrate the arrival of Wang Li from Beijing on June 20, 1967, the Million
Heroes attacked them with spears and sticks, and they threw stones and
smoke bombs from windows above. The Engineering College Red
Guards were caught unawares. According to their own account, the
"brave" 111 Corps and 181 Corps engaged the Million Heroes in battle
to let the others escape, only to be ambushed again outside Number One
Middle School.[35]

Fighting was even more likely to occur when negotiation meetings
were held among rival groups. By 1967, the government was urging the
Red Guards to settle their differences. Negotiations were held, but frustration ran high when no solution was found, and the groups often
ended up fighting. For example, on February 17, 1967, a meeting between the August 15 Group and its rivals (Proletarian Revolutionary
Rebel Workers Army, September 21 Group of Chongqing City, August
31 Corps of Southwest Normal College, September 15 Fighting Group
of Zhedong College, and the Red Guard Headquarters of the Middle
Schools) was held to debate the legality of the former group's seizure of
power in Chongqing. According to its critics, the speakers of the August
15 Group threw down a piece of paper when they could not defend their
case. With this signal, their goons in the audience jumped onto the stage
and pinned their opponents to the ground.[36]

Fighting among Red Guard groups was just as likely to take place
when a local cadre faced charges at a public meeting. Groups differed on
their evaluations of local cadres—at times they supported or denounced a
cadre simply because their rivals did the opposite. When the participants
could not arrive on a verdict on the cadre through debate, they would
fight to settle differences, which only widened the gulf among the
different groups. Fighting could not even be entirely avoided when these
criticism meetings of cadres were restricted to members of the same
group. When the rival groups learned of such occasions, they sometimes
disrupted the meetings by breaking into the assembly hall and kidnapping the cadre under question. The search for the missing cadre would

start, accusations would be made, and raids and counter-raids of one an-
others' headquarters would continue.[37]

Every issue that arose in the course of the Cultural Revolution was a
source of dispute and every occasion an opportunity to fight, but with
the formation of these Red Guard groups and their alliances, the scale
and frequency of the fights increased tremendously. Most Red Guard
groups belonged to one conglomerate association or another. Disputes
between individual members belonging to two different groups could
easily draw those groups or even other allied groups into fights, and so
the fights became more frequent and the scale larger. A minor incident
could trigger a major battle. The following incident was a case in point.
Members of Guangzhou Corps in Guangzhou Technical School borrowed chairs from the Red Headquarters for a party. When the group
came to the Red Headquarters building, a member of Red Revolutionary
Successors of People's Number 1 Middle School staying there saw his rival, Pan, from the same high school in the approaching group and
shouted, "He is from Number 1 Middle School, get him!," whereupon
Pan was immediately beaten. Members of his group came to the rescue.
The Red Headquarters retaliated and surrounded the staff dining hall
where the party was being held. It attacked members of Criticize Tao
Zhu Joint Committee, Guangdong Drama Troop, and the Central South
Academy of Social Sciences, who were among the guests. Seventy people
were injured and 27 were kidnapped. The group also destroyed a record
player, utensils, tables, and chairs and took away valuables.[38] The serious-
ness of the damages can probably be discounted, since the report came
from the Guangzhou Corps, but it serves to show how group alliances
could turn a grievance between two persons into a fight involving at least
five groups outside that high school.

Red Guard groups had alliances both in and outside of their own localities. Conflict was therefore not confined to local groups, but could
spread beyond their area. When a group was attacked, reinforcements
would come from outside. In Qingshing of Guangdong province, outside help arrived from the provincial capital, Guangzhou, when some
Red Guards were detained by the public security bureau on June 13.
Fighting occurred between the local and outside groups on June 21, 22,
and 25.[39] Not only would the student Red Guards defend their allies, but
they would also do so even to the extent of defying the public security
bureau. When the group involved was large, like the Criticize Tao Zhu
Joint Committee of Guangzhou, reinforcements came from all across the
country—from Honan, Hunan, Guangxi, and as far away as Beijing.[40]
Such involvements prolonged and expanded the scale and frequency of
fighting.

Given such circumstances, one can surmise that fighting among the Red Guards, as well as in China as a whole, was ubiquitous. Perhaps in their concern for stability in an already chaotic situation, official sources in 1967 and 1968 never reported these clashes. They alluded to them only in the context of exhorting the Red Guards to make peace. However, Red Guard publications give a different picture. An analysis of such sources in the *Survey of China Mainland Press* shows that fighting frequently occurred. These accounts were not written to gloat over their success; more often, they were to show the inhumanity and deceit of their rivals. Whatever the motives for reporting these incidents, they showed that fighting was most intense in July and August 1967 when the radical factions in the central government were strong. In Guangzhou alone, fighting took place on ten days in July and seventeen days in August. This picture of pervasive turmoil was corroborated by Jean Daubier, who was in Beijing at the time:

> [G]roups armed with billy clubs and iron bars and wearing helmets fought each other at their place of work, and sometimes in the streets. . . I won't go so far as to say that these battles took place every-day and were so widespread as has been reported, but there is no doubt that the atmosphere was indeed tense.[41]

Esmein concurred, reporting 313 brawls between April 20 and May 10, 1967.[42] Despite the official silence, we can conclude that fighting was very much part of everyday life in China in 1967 and the first half of 1968.

The Red Guards Use Weapons

In the latter half of 1966, with government backing, the Red Guards had access to pens, ink, paper, paste, loudspeakers, vans, printing presses, and other materials required for propaganda war. When the war of words turned to physical fights, government involvement and intervention inadvertently allowed weapons to fall into the students' hands, turning skirmishes into more serious fights and escalating the violence.

Besides slandering one another in wall posters and pamphlets, rival groups broadcast the others' so-called crimes over loudspeakers. On one university campus, students of two rival groups occupying adjacent buildings turned on their loudspeakers, itemizing the other's crimes, and hurled rocks. But they would do so only after breakfast, stop for two hours at lunch, and resume again in the afternoon. At five o'clock sharp, both groups would recall their "troops" until the next day.[43] At first, innocent passersby were sometimes injured by the rocks, but people soon learned to avoid that stretch of road; nobody from the two groups themselves got hurt. On some campuses, fighting was even more like child's play. A Red Guard in a primary school told me that, even though they had no idea who the enemies were, her school was on alert all the time, with sentinels armed with knives guarding the buildings night and day.

On other campuses, real fighting occurred. Lethal homemade weapons were used. Metal and wood were sharpened to make knives, daggers, and spears. Soon students improved on their skills; gasoline or sulphur was mixed with insecticide to be used as incendiary bombs, and homemade tanks, hand grenades, and cannons were also used. Some schools outdid others in this expertise. Many respondents felt that fighting at Beida was not as ferocious as at Qinghua simply because the former was a liberal arts and sciences college, and the latter an institute of technology. Qinghua students were more skillful in making weapons and had workshops better equipped for manufacturing arms. Beida students continued to use bicycle tires as catapults to throw rocks at their enemies or sharpened pipes for spears, whereas Qinghua students made hand grenades, makeshift armored tanks, and heavy artillery. Similarly, the secondary and primary school students were less sophisticated and ingenious in making weapons compared with the university students. Yet what the secondary school students lacked in intellect was compensated by their physical strength. Many respondents indicated that high school students were particularly violent, especially when they teamed up with peasants and workers, who were less sophisticated and more dogmatic. As for the primary students, their major talents were employed in arson and vandalizing school property.

When the students turned to local politics, they looked to the factories and government departments for weapons. They were allies with these outside units and easily negotiated the supply. At other times, they raided government departments for trucks and cars, stole cranes and heavy hammers, and pillaged factories, stores, warehouses, and gas storage tanks to get materials for manufacturing homemade weapons. Red Guard bulletins carried graphic accounts of the use of the newly acquired weaponry. A typical report would run as follows: they were peacefully preparing for propaganda work in Mao's thoughts when they were encircled. The enemies set fire to the ground floor, using gasoline or sulphur mixed with insecticide, and pounded the roof with a crane used for demolition. They choked in dust and smoke. The fire department came, but the vicious enemies prevented them from putting out the fire. Brave members of their group tried to stall the enemies coming up the stairs and died heroically. Those who escaped by jumping from the upper floor windows only fell into enemy hands. Girls were molested, boys robbed, and others still missing. It is likely that these incidents did occur, though the "vile" culprits and the "innocent" victims were not so clearly distinguishable.[44]

The fights became more violent when weapons fell into the hands of the student revolutionaries. In early 1967, the central government supported the rebels throughout the seizures of power: on January 13, Xia Fuzhi made it illegal for the public security bureau to confine or attack members of the revolutionary organization, and on January 20, the Central Military Commission ordered the army not to intervene in local politics. The central government's endorsement of the triple-unity combination of revolutionaries, cadres, and soldiers in the organization of the revolutionary committees changed all this (although the military did become an integral part of this revolutionary rank). Finally, a January 28 directive advised the People's Liberation Army to support the leftists.[45] Like the workteams before them, the soldiers found it difficult to decide who was on the left without specific guidelines from above. Sometimes the soldiers and militia cooperated with local officials to restore order because they represented the party. At other times, the soldiers supported the revolutionary groups or even took power themselves until the rebels were strong enough to assume control.[46] Whichever side the military took, it pleased one group and offended another and became a partisan member in an already complicated situation.

The army itself was split into three broad groups, and these too were looking for support.[47] The conservatives under He Long supported Liu Shaoqi; the moderates under Yang Shangkun and Fu Chongbi, head of the Beijing garrison, had more in common with Zhou Enlai; and Lin Biao and his army supporters favored Jiang Qing. The provincial military commanders were generally split along similar lines, and like the local civilian governments, the local garrisons supported the Red Guards that sided with them.

Throughout late 1966, the military kept out of the movement in the larger society. The military had been undergoing its own Cultural Revolution, but that was mild compared with what was going on in other sectors. It was only in 1967, when the local government disintegrated, that the central government called in the military; even then, it was careful to restrict the military's role. Perhaps this reluctance stemmed from the fear of the more conservative elements in government that, by involving an already-divided military, the country might be further destabilized and plunged into civil war. Despite this collective decision, the extreme radical faction at the center under Wang Li and Qi Benyu (deputy director and editor of *Red Flag,* respectively) spread word on its own that there were "capitalists in the army," and it encouraged Kuai Dafu, leader of Qinghua's Jingganshan, to gather information on the army movement and establish twenty military information stations across the country.[48] There is little information on the motivation of the radical faction. It is likely that the army was, on the whole, more supportive of the conservative elements in the central government, and to undermine the unity of the army would have weakened the influence of these moderates.

The government gave blanket protection to all revolutionary groups in the beginning, but later it made a distinction between rightist and leftist groups. It asked civilians to stay out of army politics, and yet some government representatives encouraged civilians to spy on soldiers' movements. These contradictions reflected the internal splits within the central government, which could not agree on how to handle the Cultural Revolution. The changing policies over time represented the fluctuating fortunes of these different factions in the central government, and 1967 was perhaps the most volatile year, with the conservative and radical factions alternating control of the central government in rapid succession. Conflicting contemporaneous policies were indicative of a delicate situation with no one faction having full control. Such inconsistent policies, all announced in the name of the central government, added confusion among rebel ranks. Many Red Guard groups had realized that the central government was divided, but they were too embroiled in their own factional struggles to give it too much thought. It was more important for each rival group to hang onto the central directives advantageous to them, and to claim to be the central leaders' faithful followers. The central government might not have encouraged or condoned violence per se, but through its inconsistencies and ineptitude, it certainly did so.

The most important effect of the army's involvement in Red Guard politics was to make heavy military weapons available to the rebels. When the rebels had seized power, some local governments had resisted with guns and weaponry. Just as the repressive measures of the workteams had invited strong resistance, these harsh measures of the local governments had radicalized the rebels. They attacked the army installations and raided arsenals and barracks for supplies and armaments such as rifles, carbines, and machine guns.[49]

These raids became so numerous that, as early as February 1967, a military commission directive posted in the streets forbade attacks on the army. At the same time, soldiers were forbidden to use their weapons, perhaps to avoid provoking further violence. On April 6, a six-point directive again stipulated that the People's Liberation Army was to use persuasion, not force.[50] However, this precaution backfired because it made the army ineffective, and to many Red Guards this meant official sanction of their tactics. In any case, the raids for weapons were not random—especially since the army would have been too strong a match for the rebels—and, indeed, on some occasions they were pre-arranged. A faction in the local army units might support one group against another and be willing to stage a raid to reinforce the rebel group with supplies. A Red Guard who was on such a mission in Kunming described to me how the raid went: "We arrived at the arsenal in two trucks. The soldiers read us passages of Mao Zedong and [tried to] persuade us to abandon our mission. When this failed, they fired in the air and then got out of the way." To him, it was a joke and only reflected the tacit support of the People's Liberation Army. He admitted that the students would not have carried out the raid without assurances of support from the local government and army unit. The Red Guards could not have gotten away with it had stricter measures been employed.

If one Red Guard unit had guns and tanks, its rival also needed them for protection. For logistic reasons, both had to raid the neighborhood arsenals, and so the raids increased. The arsenal raids went unabated in the first half of 1967, and the fights became more frequent and bloodier. The casualties were high. According to the September 5, 1967, issue of *Survey of Mountains and Rivers,* Dizong and Doctrine Red Guards conducted 30 raids between August 17 and 22 against ten schools and universities supporting the Workers' Alliance; 151 were killed and 552 wounded. When one group reinforced another, it was not just supplying money and manpower, but also weapons. Wu Qunbun, the leader of Guangzhou's Criticize Tao Zhu Joint Committee, admitted at his self-criticism meeting that:

> In June, we organized men to bring weapons secretly from Wuhan, Hunan, and Guangxi. We asked Wuhan Steel Works and Third Headquarters for support. The Hunan Xinjiang Wind and Thunder and Guangxi April 22 Group sent guns. They also contributed food and money. With the money, we went to Beijing for help. Wuhan and Hunan also sent a contingent each.[51]

Such chaos probably prompted the government to change its policies in August 1967, when it ordered the people to return the weapons. On September 5, the government condemned these raids as counter-revolutionary acts.[52] It was announced that those involved would be arrested and prosecuted, and, if the rebels resisted, the soldiers could fight in self defense.

It was too late. Many weapons had been circulated among the Red

Guards, and to turn in these weapons would put a group at the mercy of its rivals. Moreover, the local government or army to whom the weapons should be returned were as partisan as the groups themselves and were likely to use the occasion against them. A Red Guard leader blamed the demise of his group precisely on making this wrong move: "Once I handed in the weapons, they [members of the rival group] surrounded our building. We defended ourselves as best as we could. Finally I had to abandon my men. I stole out of the building and swam across the river." Such examples put the students on their guard. To protect themselves, they had to have more weapons to gain the advantage over the enemy.

The students were not necessarily proud of such exploits. None of the Red Guard bulletins boasted of bravery on those occasions; instead, they condemned their enemies for their ferocity. However, these condemnations did not prevent either side from acting aggressively. If they did not fight, they would be destroyed. They were caught in a situation from which they could not extract themselves. This period, like the mobilization for revolution, generated its own momentum, making it virtually impossible for the participants *not* to take part. Once the trend started, it was difficult to call it to a halt. Consequently, despite the government's appeal, many rebel groups continued to raid army barracks. The Criticize Tao Zhu Joint Committee raided People's Liberation Army units 40 times between September 1967 and September 1968, and it seized over "500 pistols and guns, tens of thousands of bullets, tens of trucks, and large quantities of military supplies."[53] The rebels in Guangxi even looted government military supplies heading for Vietnam that were passing through their province. They used heavy and light machine guns, antiaircraft guns, and antitank guns, probably spoils from past raids on army barracks.[54] This defiance of directives showed the decline of central control. I have only concentrated on the chaos resulting from student involvement. One can imagine the scale and scope of the confusion when it is recognized that other sectors of society were equally involved and their potential for violence rivaled if not surpassed that of the young. By late 1967, these factional fights threatened to take on—if they had not already done so—the proportions of large-scale warfare or even civil war.

Conclusion of Part II

A revolution is telescoped social change with one event precipitating another and often a number of events happening at the same time. It is a time of intense political struggle when the balance of power changes at every juncture. It is a process that does not end with the overthrow of the privileged group; that point is only the beginning of a protracted power struggle among the different revolutionary groups until a victor (group or individual) emerges to fill the void.

One point stands out in the confusion of the Chinese Cultural Revolution: the Red Guards were preoccupied with increasing their power at the expense of revolutionizing the educational system. This pursuit of power took the form of factionalism, or action prompted by group interests. The Red Guards spent their time building community support through propaganda and putting forth points of view in wall posters, pamphlets, and broadcasts. They organized public meetings and parades to rally their members. They formed alliances with groups in other sectors of society and became involved in local politics to extend their power base. They fought to destroy those they considered enemies.

It is impossible to give a straightforward inventory of the causes of factionalism among the Red Guards, because many causes were rooted in the structures of the schools prior to the Cultural Revolution and only emerged as factors when reacting with the initial developments of the movement. Other factors contributing to factionalism arose only in the period of mobilization, and still others emerged in the events of 1967.

Differences of opinion, the existence of committed and institutionalized groups, and a volatile political situation were prerequisites for factionalism, and these were all present in the Cultural Revolution. Divisions among the Red Guards can be traced to the dichotomy between the party and the school administration, and between the children of cadres and those of intellectual families among the student ranks. Their differences had been brought to the fore occasionally during ideological campaigns prior to the Cultural Revolution. These broad groups within the faculty and the student ranks had different views on education. By focusing attention on educational issues and the evaluation of school personnel, the revolution accentuated these differences and revived old grudges, which precluded many schools even from moving on to the discussion of educational construction. The rifts became more complex when the school administrators and workteams manipulated students to protect themselves, turning one student group against another. As the revolution developed and students became embroiled in national and local politics, cadres manipulated students for their own interests, and the story was repeated. The local officials, too, capitalized on the student rifts and turned one group against another. New issues were added to old ones, and personal vendettas were fused with group concerns. The students were divided first on the evaluation of education and the administration, then on their opinions of the meaning of the Cultural Revolution and the strategies to be taken, and later on the evaluations of the central and local political leaders and the legitimacy of each seizure of power. The issues became more numerous and complex, and the numbers of factions increased. Differences over principles became entangled with personal feuds, and settlements were difficult.

The formation of Red Guard units, which at one time had united the students, institutionalized these cleavages and made compromise impossible. Groups were identified with a particular position, which made moderation difficult, since any shift of positions was taken as a sign of weakness and thus, in Chinese traditional culture, as a loss of face. Furthermore, the aggregation of students into Red Guard groups turned personal differences into group antagonisms. Groups protected members' interests, and any slight to a member would be an insult to the group. As the Red Guards made alliances with one another and with revolutionary groups in the government and factories, both in and outside of their localities, the scale of conflict grew. Other allied groups intervened when they would have otherwise remained neutral.

As Barrington Moore points out, a revolutionary situation is one in which there are no institutionalized channels to settle disputes; otherwise, revolution would not have taken place.[55] However, even the successful launching of a revolution might not resolve this issue. The initial success of the Cultural Revolution only brought the differences among the revolutionary ranks to the fore and increased the occasions of conflict among the former allies. The dominant group was overthrown and the structures of control dismantled, but a channel to resolve disputes could not be instituted immediately. In the absence of rule or regulation for arbitration, debates occurred and oratory was used to convert the unconvinced. To elaborate on Moore's theory, one can add that the revolutionary groups' recent experiences in the movement only increased their commitment to and confidence in the correctness of their position and the efficacy and necessity of using physical force. When their former allies—now opponents—failed to be convinced and clung to their own views, tempers would get high and physical force would be used to assert one's opinions. This explains why factional struggles in a revolutionary situation often take the form of physical violence. Once fighting starts, it generates its own dynamics. No group can compromise and pull out, because to do so would mean the end of that group.

In China, with the school administration dismantled, the local government offices moribund, and factions in the central and local government under attack, there was no recourse to settle group differences through established channels. The only guidelines for settling disputes were the thoughts of Mao, which meant everything to everyone. In the growing intensity of revolutionary élan and dogmatism exacerbated by the government promotion of Mao's thought, the students were in no mood to listen to the opposite point of view or to compromise. Each considered him or herself the authentic interpreter of Mao's thoughts. When peaceful negotiations failed, students resorted to the use of force.

The students saw the authorities toppling around them and recognized the utility of holding onto political power. They had to protect their group interests and establish a power base—that is, a large following, powerful allies, and control of resources. The constant parades, publication of bulletins, distribution of handbills, and purging and punishing of their enemies were all for that purpose. Rivals had to be eliminated, not only to preserve the purity of the revolution but also for their own security. Carrying out the revolution and protecting group interests became inextricably intertwined.

Protecting group interests became the only and immediate consideration. The means had become the end itself, and the preservation of group interests overshadowed revolutionizing education. Expanding their power base, making alliances, increasing group solidarity, and amassing weapons were the students' everyday activities. Exacting revenge, planning strategies, and carrying out offensives and counteroffensives were the major preoccupations. Fistfights gave way to the use of homemade weapons, and with the soldiers' involvement, students laid hands on machine guns and other artillery. Once this process started, fighting escalated and the amount of damage grew. If any group held back or exercised restraint, they would be destroyed. The Red Guards were trapped by their own rivalries; factionalism had acquired its own dynamics, and it dominated the movement. Revolutionizing education was pushed to the background.

PART III

A Call to Order

CHAPTER 5 ———————————————

Tug-of-War

It took only three months in 1966 to mobilize the students and the nation to take part in the Cultural Revolution, but it took at least two years for the country to return to order. The years 1967 and 1968 witnessed a tug-of-war between two trends. On one hand, the revolution was gaining momentum. The students were becoming strong, even to the extent of ignoring government directives and defying the public security bureau and the army. On the other hand, the government—that is, the moderate faction in the government—tried different means to restrain and finally to stop the students. Even as early as January 1967, the government tried to contain the violence. Although there was no specific date separating the period of violence from the return to order, it can be said that factional fights were much more widespread in the early half of 1967 than in the latter half. In late 1967 and 1968, such fights decreased and were replaced by the growing efforts to introduce changes in the schools.

The Cultural Revolution is divided here into phases, such as the growth of factionalism and the return to order, only for the sake of clarity of presentation. The developments recounted in the first part of this chapter occurred concurrently with the growth of violence described above. Here our focus is on the call to order.

Chaos Across the Country

The Cultural Revolution had serious repercussions in China, economically as well as politically. Red Guards crisscrossing the country strained the transportation system. Trains were packed with passengers huddled on luggage racks, and they displaced the transport of essential commodities; this, together with work stoppages, created shortages of food and other items in some areas. In January 1967, the docks in Shanghai came to a standstill when workers went on strike. In August, the navigation on Pearl River was held up by just 50-60 rebels.[1] There were probably many such incidents that came to public attention, but these examples show that even sporadic attacks by a few revolutionaries could create bottlenecks that held up the whole transportation system.

Many factories stopped production. In some Shanghai factories, three quarters of the technical staff, a quarter of the workers, and half of the management left their posts.[2] Supplies were low, machines were in disrepair, and hands were few, so factory production dropped. From 1965 to 1968, industrial production fell from 206 billion to 178 billion yuan.[3] Farming was less affected by fluctuations in personnel, since a guaranteed food supply was deemed essential by the government. In the busy sowing and harvesting seasons of March, June, and September, the government appealed to the city residents for extra help. On February 20, 1967, those who had left the countryside for the cities were asked to return. On March 13, the lead in a *People's Daily* article read, "Do not carry on the seizure of power during spring harvest." The revolution was interrupted for agricultural production; thus, grain output remained stable at 200 million metric tons between 1966 and 1969.[4]

The Cultural Revolution also had international repercussions. Relations with Britain, France, Indonesia, India, Burma, Italy, the Soviet Union, and the Eastern European bloc nations were strained. Chinese zealots overseas carried out their own little cultural revolutions, antagonizing host governments in Moscow, Djakarta, Hong Kong, and East European capitals. Ambassadors were recalled, leaving only the chargés d'affaires. In Beijing, Red Guards fired on Cambodian visitors. On August 9, a Mongolian diplomat was accosted in the street. On August 17, the Soviet consulate was attacked and a diplomatic vehicle burned. On August 22, the British Embassy was stormed and the Reuters correspondent, Anthony Grey, held hostage.[5] Such incidents created international crises that no government could ignore.

Disunity Among Central Leaders

The government was far from united. There were not only differences of opinion between Mao and Liu, but as the events unfolded, rifts also appeared among those supporting the Cultural Revolution. Like the students who became divided over revolutionary strategies, this latter group in the central government disagreed on the course of the revolution. Among Mao's supporters, the radicals did not see eye to eye with Zhou Enlai and the bureaucrats. The radicals were Chen Boda and the famous Gang of Four; with the exception of Wang Hungwen, the young worker from Shanghai, they were from the cultural circle. Jiang Qing was interested in contemporary drama and art; Chen was Mao's cultural secretary and speech writer; Zhang Chunqiao was director of propaganda in Shanghai; and Yao Wenyuan was correspondent for Shanghai's *Wen Hui Bao*. There was also an even more radical splinter group represented by Qi Benyu, the editor of *Red Flag*, who favored the direct involvement of the army.

The radical faction was influential in the cultural circles, yet even there it was not as strong as Yang Xianzhen, head of the party school, nor as influential as "Three-Family Village," who had come under attack at the beginning of the Cultural Revolution. Hence, the radicals justified their every act in Mao's name. They did not have a cogent political ideology, but, like Mao, they believed that ideology could transform society. Because they had little experience in governance or revolution, or because they saw something to gain from the turmoil, they wanted to maintain the revolution at a fevered pitch.

In contrast, Zhou Enlai was the seasoned administrator who went along with Mao because he recognized that the bureaucracy needed a shakeup. Like Liu, Zhou's support was in the bureaucracy; but unlike Liu, he did not engage in philosophical debates with Mao. He was the "man in grey," the administrator and pragmatist who kept the government running.[6] He worked for moderation during the Cultural Revolution; he protected top-level cadres like Chen Yi, the foreign minister, and often opposed the Gang of Four and its even more radical splinter faction, which opted for extremism and wanted to maintain the revolution at any price.

Even before Liu's fall in 1967, the central government could not agree on whether to continue the revolution, push it further, or stop it. As the accounts released in the 1980s showed, the atmosphere at the central level throughout the movement was tense. Meetings were frequent and long, and each was a test of strength among the different factions with each side accusing the other of conspiracy, subverting the revolution, and working for their own interests. Because the moderates and conservatives were the minority, their attempts to restrain the movement in February 1967 was derogatorily dubbed "the reversal of currents," and their concerted attempts to question the radicals were called "exploits"— that is, attempts to undermine the movement.[7] Even though the central

government was split, directives were still sent in the name of the collective, usually the Central Cultural Revolution Committee, Communist
Party Central Committee, and the State Council.

However, each directive was really the outcome of a compromise
among the different factions and was sometimes phrased in such vague
terms as to make it ineffective. One example was the appeal on September 5, 1966, to students to use words and not force. There were no teeth
in the government order, however, since the populace and the law en-
forcing agency had been asked not to intervene in the student movement.[8] Sometimes, because of fluctuations of power among the different
factions, conflicting directives were issued. In September 1966, the students were asked not to fight, but in August 1967, rebels were reminded
that power only came with military might. In January 1967, the government called for acceptance of and compromise with cadres; in June, the
revolutionaries were told to "hound the enemies to the end."[9] These conflicting messages, compounded by the breakdown of mechanisms of social control, increased confusion that further undermined the
government's influence. Sometimes the Red Guards openly defied central
directives;[10] at other times they used whichever directives suited them
and ignored the rest, then accused their rivals who did likewise of dis-
obeying central government orders. In the following pages, I shall examine in greater detail how the different central directives to restore order
were received.

The Call for Restraint

In early 1967, the government wanted the student revolutionaries to
carry out the movement in a more orderly fashion, though not to put a
complete stop to it. These efforts centered around two official slogans:
"economize and make revolution," and "achieve great unity."

On January 16, the government asked the rebels to "economize and
make revolution"—that is, they were not to destroy public property or
confiscate government trucks, and they should use national resources
with restraint, limit the use of ink and paper, and make fewer wall
posters. Furthermore, they were to lower the volume of their loudspeakers and respect curfews to give the neighboring residents some
peace and quiet. Finally, with regard to their exchange of revolutionary
experience, they were to walk and not to take the train.[11] On February 23,
the exchange was outlawed, but this directive had to be repeated on July
21, October 24, and November 26. On March 16, 1967, the appeal to refrain from destroying books and written documents or from stealing

trucks also had to be repeated, which showed the futility of the earlier directives.[12] When many schools reopened, "economize and make revolution" took on a new meaning. Students were forbidden to vandalize public property; furthermore, they were to repair facilities damaged in the previous months, such as chairs, tables, and other school amenities. This appeal, like others during this period, was repeated throughout 1967 on February 9, 15, and 22, May 15, June 15, and 16, July 14, and August 26; it was even repeated as late as 1968. Government orders were simply ignored.

The student fights grew more frequent as the rebels became involved in the seizures of power in January 1967; yet the government-controlled *People's Daily* appealed for moderation and unity. This official appeal did not call a halt to taking power from the authorities; rather, it only called on rebel groups to unite before doing so.[13] Perhaps the government hoped this prior understanding among the rebel groups would avoid the seizures and counterseizures of power that were plaguing the nation. Although these two messages ("seize power" and "achieve great unity") were not mutually exclusive, the former tended to promote revolution and the latter restraint, which reflected the differences of opinion and the uneasy power balance at the center.

When the situation became chaotic, the State Council and the Central Military Commission on January 26, 1967, forbade the seizure of power.[14] When these coups were banned, the original meaning of "great unity"—that is, rebel forces uniting prior to a takeover—was no longer relevant. On February 22, the *People's Daily* explained that the touchstone of unity was now the triple-unity revolutionary committee, which was to comprise cadres, members of the army, and representatives of mass organizations. The cadres had administrative experience and the soldiers provided the stabilizing force. The government's way of trying to resolve the competition among the different revolutionary groups was to tailor the meaning of a directive to suit the occasion. For example, on May 26, Zhou Enlai gave the term "great unity" a slight twist to fit the situation at the Academy of Sciences.[15] There, triple unity referred to cooperation between the young, the middle aged, and the elderly. But this new interpretation only added to the confusion. The appeal was repeated on March 26, May 20, and July 3, again demonstrating that the rebels never did unite.

The calls for restraint were punctured in June 1967 by aggressive messages in the official media. On June 2, the *People's Daily* carried an article titled: "Save your courage to hound the enemies to the end." On the surface, this seemed to be another appeal to the rebels to stop infighting, but the cadres were considered enemies of the revolution, and so this message effectively counteracted any calls for leniency toward them. Instead, the rehabilitation of cadres in February and March was ridiculed as a "reversal of the current."

The new government appeals coincided with the rise of the radical faction in the central government. In June, Qi Benyu and Wang Li were riding high. On July 20, Xie Fuzhi and Wang received a hero's welcome in Beijing on their return from Wuhan. On July 22, Jiang Qing made the famous call to "attack with words, defend with force," which encouraged many Red Guards to launch "defensive attacks."[16] In August, *Red Flag* published the article arguing for the need to "ferret out class enemies in the army."[17] Instead of restraining the revolution, the government was promoting it. This reversal of the official stand widened the scope and increased the intensity of the movement.

There could be two explanations for the radical central leaders' actions. First, like the Red Guards, the radical factions came to power through the revolution and thus had a vested interest in its continuance, at least until they had consolidated their power. My informants all pointed to the popular interpretation that the Gang of Four promoted turmoil to allow its supporters to take control when the local administrations were deposed and the rebels engrossed with infighting. This view credited the radicals with a well-planned strategy. But as many Red Guards also pointed out to me, so much was happening that the radicals were only reacting to immediate pressures. Not even Mao had full control of the revolution.[18] A more plausible explanation for the radicals' action was that the Gang of Four, like Mao, saw some degree of violence and fighting unavoidable in a revolution. They did not promote violence per se, but did so by inaction and by pronouncements that lent respectability to the use of physical force. The indiscriminate use of violence was an unintended consequence beyond the foursome's complete control, but that was a price they were willing to pay for promoting revolution. Once the fighting started, the four were quick to take advantage of the situation. In this volatile atmosphere, the leaders' own security, like that of the students, depended on clinging to power. This consideration for one's survival permeated all the parties involved, from the lowly radical and moderate Red Guards to the different factions at the local as well as the central level.

The increased fighting and chaos that accompanied the ascendancy of the radical faction alienated its support in the central government, and in late 1967, the moderates were again dominant. The government resumed its appeal for restraint. Radicals such as Wang Li and Guang Feng were dismissed, and Jiang Qing denied that she encouraged the use of force. The call for great unity was resumed. The political triumph of the radical faction might have been short-lived, but the repercussions of its exhortations to revolt were prolonged. It would take another year before the central government restored order to the country and in the schools.

Red Guard Reaction to the Call for Restraint

On one hand, the government's call to order was undermined by its own inconsistencies. On the other, the Red Guards were strong enough to defy the government. To the many Red Guard factions, every move was seen in political terms. Obedience to central government requests for order meant giving up what they had gained and even jeopardizing their safety. To unite and stop fighting were political actions that would upset the balance of power by giving a voice to weaker Red Guard groups and readmitting deposed cadres into their ranks. Even the decision to "economize and make revolution" would affect the strength of their organization. Damaging public property, such as burning a building, was sometimes necessary to destroy the enemy's base. Confiscating public records was a way to collect evidence to indict rivals. The exchange of revolutionary experience offered opportunities to expand their sphere of influence, and for the losing factions it was a chance to make graceful exits. Indeed, even the use of loudspeakers and the distribution of handbills had ramifications on the balance of power for the different groups. Such resources were all part of a group's support system. To surrender them would give its foes an advantage and ultimately affects its own security. No group could risk making the first move, which resulted in an impasse.

There were practical problems to resolve even if the Red Guards had been willing to negotiate a peaceful settlement. To unite meant incorporating cadres into their ranks, and the cadre question posed a major obstacle. On February 23 and 25, 1967, the government called for leniency to include the "liberated" cadres into the new organizations.[19] The government gave advice on how this was to be done. It put up wall posters to caution people: "We must know how to judge cadres. We must not confine our judgment to a short period or to a single incident in a cadre's life but should consider his life and work as a whole." This quotation was set to music and sung over the radio.[20] But this did not offer much help. Cadres asked for review of their cases; some declared themselves victims of the "bourgeois revisionist line," and others argued that they were "revolutionary on the whole" and their crimes only occasional misdemeanors. The students were as divided as ever. Instead of promoting restraint, the call for leniency reopened cases that were a constant source of conflict.

As before, the cadres manipulated the students for their support and capitalized on dissension among them. They supported one group against another. At Tongji University, some students accused the cadres of using legal technicalities to destroy the revolutionary committees, and they labeled the cadres "the class enemies [who] controlled a group of rightist and anarchists and used them to carry out these activities on the front."[21] Rightists and leftists were not easily discernible at that stage of the movement. Such manipulations or suspicion of manipulation complicated the issues and further divided the students.

Representation on the revolutionary committee was another source of conflict. As noted in Part I, revolutionary committees were formed in some schools; in many others, these organizations were not formed but the administrators and support staff kept the schools running. With the government's appeal for unity, students realized that it would be politically wise to have revolutionary committees in their own schools. The function of these committees, however, was different from that in late 1966, when a committee's primary role was to mobilize the students and promote and facilitate the active phase of the Cultural Revolution. Its role in 1967 was to restore normalcy in the school—that is, resumption of classes. To organize such a committee was difficult enough in late 1966, but it was much more so in 1967 since the number of groups had proliferated and the rifts had grown deeper. Rival groups had difficulty settling their differences and coming to a working agreement even on simple matters like the name of the organization. Issues such as the representation of different student groups and the division of responsibility on the revolutionary committees were even harder to settle, because the manner in which these issues were resolved had important political implications. Each group fought hard to have greater representation on these bodies.

The Red Guards were afraid of disbanding, which was a precondition the government had put on forming the revolutionary committees. The following passage from a Red Guard bulletin, *Little Soldiers Wish Chairman Mao Long Life*, expressed this fear: "In uniting, one should not forget the March storm [reversal of current]; in uniting, one should not forget the disintegration of Mao Zedong's Thought Combat Group; in uniting, one should not forget the August 20 martyrs." The "March storm" referred to the disintegration of Mao Zedong's Thought Combat Group, and the August 20 martyrs' incident was a battle in which the

Red Guards' allies lost out to rivals. The Red Guards were suspicious because they had experienced betrayals in the past.

With the breakdown of local government, there was no official organ to monitor the interpretation and implementation of central directives. Red Guards exhibited the same ingenuity they had in using Mao's words: they interpreted central directives to their own advantage, even when it meant distorting their meaning. The July 12, 1967, issue of *Middle School War Gazette*, published by a high school Red Guard group, gave "great unity" a unique interpretation: revolutionary organizations were the nuclei of great unity and had to be strengthened, not disbanded; those disbanded were to be rebuilt and supported. The paper further emphasized, "We should absolutely, faithfully carry out what Chairman Mao emphasized: to build and expand leftist ranks, the foundation of the proletarian ranks of the Great Proletarian Cultural Revolution and the red line." Thus, great unity simply meant building up organizational influence, making continuous fighting more probable. This definition of unity was certainly far from any version of the central government's directive on the issue.

Some students simply gave the directives lip service, since that would be good for public relations, group prestige, and solidarity. Red Guard groups prepared wall posters and handbills and organized mass meetings, rallies, and parades to show their support. Rival groups even competed to be the first to organize such rallies and sabotaged the others' gatherings if they could not be the first to do so. Even nationally prominent student leaders such as Nie Yuanzi, Kuai Dafu, Tan Houlan, and Han Aijing found it politically advantageous to write articles for the *People's Daily* to support great unity.[22] The public statements by these national leaders indicated that it was still important for Red Guards to show their support for central government policies, but such statements made as late as June 1967 only revealed that little progress had been achieved in restoring unity or peace on campus.

When pressure from the central government was strong, especially in late 1967 and early 1968 when the moderate faction in the central government gradually reasserted its control, Red Guards had to make more tangible gestures of support for great unity. Rival factions met, but not before each group had caucused to plan its strategy. A Red Guard leader gave this advice at one such caucus:

> Now under the strong pressure to unite, we cannot resist. Even if we do not want to do so, we should verbally express our support and write lots of slogans. If the other groups are unwilling, they will be guilty of

stalling great unity. If they are willing, we should stand firm on the question of representation and the flag. We should have an equal number sitting on the committee. On the flag of the new group, we should have the word "big" in it. If not, our followers will say we betray them. ["Big" was probably part of the name of this Red Guard organization.][23]

These attitudes were not conducive to unity; even if the students came to an agreement, settlements built on such mutual suspicions were shaky and the unity short-lived. In the case mentioned above, the peace made in the morning was broken in the afternoon.

Some Red Guard groups used the meetings to ambush their rivals. For example, the Rebel Corps invited Red Flag, another Red Guard organization, to a negotiation session in Jiangmen Municipal Number 3 Middle School on December 13, 1967. Given the political climate of the time, this was a request Red Flag could not refuse, even though it might suspect foul play. The group explained in its bulletin, "We recognized that it might be a trap, but in the spirit of letting bygones be bygones we returned at the risk of our own lives."[24] When the Red Flag members entered the school, they were surrounded by the Rebel Corps and its allies from Red Flag Commune and Jiangmen August 1 Fighting Team of the Technical Institute. Stones were thrown at them and many were hurt. Such conspiracies diminished the chances of peaceful settlement.

The Red Guards also used the call for great unity to augment their strength in another way. Instead of forming alliances in their schools, they joined with external units to extend their scope of influence. Red Guard groups from different schools and localities already had contacts with one another because of the exchange of revolutionary experience, and now they formally joined "in the spirit of achieving unity." One disillusioned Red Guard wrote: "We had become adept at turning the Communist Party Central policies to personal use; mutual exploitation had become the real basis of the relationship between the central authorities and us."[25] On January 14, 1967, institutes of higher learning in Shanghai "achieved great unity" and formed a revolutionary committee. On February 22, the Second and Third Headquarters in Beijing accepted the jurisdiction of a representative committee; the first Red Guard Congress was formed on the same date. On March 4, high schools in Xian and the universities in Tienjin followed suit, and on March 6, the high schools in Beijing held their own congress.[26]

The forming of revolutionary committees or alliances waxed and waned with the changing pressures from the central government. It slowed down in mid-1967 when the radical central leaders were in power and the pressure on the Red Guards to settle their differences was off. In January 1968, when the radicals were discredited, the central government renewed pressure on the Red Guards, and the forming of Red Guard congresses again sped up. On January 3, Guangzhou universities joined together, and on January 20, Shaanxi province universities had their own representative organization.[27]

However, these revolutionary committees could not control their member organizations, which divided as soon as they were formed. In Beijing, despite the formation of the Red Guard Congress, the Red Guards split between the Sky Faction (headed by the Aeronautics Institute) and the Earth Faction (headed by the Geology Institute). In Guangzhou, fighting continued between Red Flag and the Doctrine Red Guards. So far as the Red Guards were concerned, the government's call for restraint was just another issue to be dealt with in the politics of their everyday affairs, and they tried to make the best of the situation. Some complied only to what was unavoidable, others did so because it worked to their advantage. Thus, the government's call for unity backfired in the volatile atmosphere. The amalgamated groups succeeded only in involving other groups in fighting that might have otherwise been avoided.

Return to the Schools

Not all of the government's efforts were futile. In some schools, different factions came to a peaceful settlement. In February 1967, students in Beijing Number 80 Middle School made peace. On April 13, Shanghai Number 6 High School did so; the next day, so did Shanghai Financial Institute. On June 15, students of Beijing Shijingshan Middle School and, on June 19, those in Beijing Aeronautics Institute were united. In July, students from East China Normal University and, in August, those from Beijing Normal University buried the hatchet.[28]

By July 1967, seven universities in Shandong and four in Heilongjiang had negotiated truces, and in Beijing, rival groups in 130 middle schools, less than half of the total in the city, had made peace. The number increased to 200 by October.[29] In Shanghai, sixteen universities and 273 middle schools, about half of the school population, succeeded in negotiating a truce in September.[30] By March 1968, eight more universities were added to the list.[31] These were the only data available and, if complete, they represented only a small fraction of China's schools and universities. Few details of the settlements were given. The alacrity with which government-controlled media publicized these events showed that they must have been rare occurrences and were used as models to exert pressure on others. Even if a school was cited, that did not mean peace was restored. For example, a revolutionary committee was formed in Qinghua in September 1967 and widely reported in the newspaper,[32] but disagreements broke out soon thereafter and fighting continued until July 1968. Peace settlements in these schools were fragile ones.

If the Red Guards made peace in a school, the next step would have been to reopen the school and have classes. Revolution was to be redirected to its original cause—the reform of education—and was to proceed to a more constructive phase in a more peaceful atmosphere. While the government was calling for unity, it also issued directives to "resume classes and make revolution." The first came in February 1967, after some primary and middle schools had reopened. Like the call for restraint, the directive had to be repeated and the frequency of these reminders fluctuated with the power balance among the different factions in the central government.

The success of this directive was limited mainly to primary schools, where the Cultural Revolution was weakest. The disruption in primary schools had been minimal compared with the high schools and universities. The students had been young when the movement began, and most of them had returned home and let the teachers carry out their own revolution. Cases were rare when students criticized teachers or students spoke against students, but when these did occur, the students usually came from the higher grades; often, it was teachers against teachers. The fighting and disunity were not as intense as among students in high schools and universities, and hence settlements were more easily achieved. Besides, parents were eager to keep their children off the streets and have them back in school. These young students had to obey. Most respondents who taught in primary or junior high schools reported that classes were disrupted only for a few months. In one primary school I visited in a Guangzhou suburb, the principal even claimed that classes had never been disrupted. In February 1967, most of the primary schools in Shanghai reopened, and by September the majority of primary schools were holding classes.

Nevertheless, no revolution in education was carried out in these primary schools. The students were too young to take on the task, and the teachers were too insecure to attempt to change the system. To play it safe, the teachers used mainly government documents or Mao's works as teaching materials. Teachers taught passages from Mao's works and told stories about Mao and about the heroes who followed in his footsteps. Classrooms across China reverberated with Mao's words: students read, recited, and sang them.[33]

Classes were held, but the classroom atmosphere was never the same as before the Cultural Revolution. Young children were not as respectful to their teachers; they might not have criticized their teachers, but they knew that teachers had been—and still were—targets of criticism in schools. Some had even seen their teachers interrogated and humiliated. The teachers' status had dropped in the childrens' eyes. A teacher told me that she maintained her image by wearing "a red arm band with the word 'revolutionary' on it." I asked if she belonged to a particular faction and she said no. She explained that "anyone could buy a red arm band in the stores and write whatever they wanted on it. I wore it every-time I stepped into the classroom, that was the only way to keep the students' respect and make them listen to you." The revolutionary atmosphere at the time was so constraining that teachers had to use such measures to maintain discipline. This again showed the naiveté among some of these students—they believed that a red arm band connoted a revolutionary. Other teachers added that the atmosphere was tense and they had to be careful of what they said, lest a young child inadvertently report it to parents or other adults and get them into trouble.

In many high schools, the students did not make peace and no classes were held. Informants commented that Shanghai was the base of the Gang of Four and the first city to return to normal life. Yet even in Shanghai, only 107 of the 273 high schools that made peace resumed regular class schedules.[34] The number of schools that reopened in other cities was probably lower. The calls to the students to halt their exchange of revolutionary experience and return to school, which were repeated eleven months after the initial calls, showed that many students were still traveling across the country. Others simply refused to return. Neither the government nor the teachers could enforce attendance. In early 1968, the *People's Daily* continued to report that many campuses were empty.

No regular classes were held even among schools that reopened. The schedule of a boarding school at the time looked like this: the first class (9–10 A.M.) studied Mao's thoughts and central directives; the second (10:30–11:30 A.M.) was composed of criticism meetings and the study of wall posters; the third (3–5 P.M.) studied industrial and agricultural skills or military training; and the last class (8–10 P.M.) again focused on the Cultural Revolution.[35] Schedules in other schools were probably organized along similar lines, and regular classes were seldom held. The focus was on Mao's thoughts and the developments of the Cultural Revolution.

Regular classes could not be held because many students did not have the patience to sit through them, nor the teachers the authority to enforce discipline. Teachers were reluctant to use regular textbooks that had been criticized earlier in the movement, and Mao's works were the only safe ones. Since the students regarded Mao as their greatest leader, studying his works was something they could not refuse; to disobey would expose them to criticisms of not being revolutionary or simply of disobeying Mao. Such activities did not promote revolution in education, but they did occupy the students enough to prevent further violence.

It was even more difficult to control university students. In July 1967, only two out of eight universities in Mongolia, three of eleven universities in Xian, four of nineteen universities in Heilongjiang, and five of thirteen institutes of higher learning in Tienjin reopened.[36] Information on the other universities is not available, but based on the figures above, I would estimate that at most one-third of the universities reopened. Perhaps more telling of the failure of that government directive was the omission of it in all except one of my respondents' accounts. When I reminded them of this central directive, they inevitably replied that they knew of it but, nonetheless, classes were not held because the conditions to resume classes were not there. Government influence had dwindled so much that the people simply ignored or seemed oblivious of its orders.

A lecturer from the University of Inner Mongolia described how classes went in 1967:

> The were no chairs or tables. Many of them were broken in the chaos created by the students. We made the best of what we could. The first day of class, ten to twenty students appeared. But their minds were not really there. By the end of the week, only one remained. And so the class was discontinued.

Even though the newspapers reported that a university had reopened, it might be of short duration because of continuous fighting. Sometimes teaching simply stopped because of low attendance. More often, universities cancelled classes until 1969 and did not admit new students until 1970 and 1971.

The same respondent, commenting philosophically on the lack of student responsiveness, said, "The conditions were not ripe." Many other respondents echoed her view that the preconditions for conducting classes were absent. The schools were in disarray: chairs and tables broken, equipment in the laboratories destroyed or looted, books burned, and sometimes even buildings charred and in ruins. More important, holding class required the cooperation of both teachers and students. In 1967, many teachers and administrators were disillusioned and reluctant to take responsibility, let alone initiative. They had suffered under the students who were still in power. It would be embarrassing to face a classroom of students who were once their critics. To take the initiative in giving lessons might even invite criticism of promoting thoughts of personal advancement and propagating bourgeois educational thoughts. True, they could teach Mao's writings, but unlike the curriculum at the primary level, Mao's writings were no substitute for a university curriculum. Moreover, the nonactivist students were enjoying their cloistered life, pursuing their own hobbies. They were reluctant to return to the strict schedules, if not discipline, of the schools after their taste of freedom. Others were still on the road and in no rush to return. The activists were preoccupied with the day-to-day matter of revolution: reading central directives and other government and Red Guard publications, attending meetings and rallies, preparing wall posters, distributing handbills, selling Red Guard papers, and occasionally fighting. They were too preoccupied with factionalism to attend classes.

Mass Media Urge Restraint

The government could not expect students to return to school on their own, let alone to reform the educational system. Like the mobilization for revolution, the government had to create the appropriate conditions if classes were to be held. It had to change the course of the Cultural Revolution by mobilizing the students to settle their differences, return to school, and attend classes. This proved to be a much more difficult task than initiating the movement. The channels of control used in mid-1966 had been dismantled, and the government had to depend on noninstitutionalized and informal means. It increasingly resorted to the media to disseminate its policies.

Messages in the official media in this period were diametrically opposed to those promulgated at the beginning of the Cultural Revolution. In mid-1966, students had been exhorted to rebel against authority and carry on the revolution to the end. In late 1967, the government promoted a very different set of values, calling for restraint, moderation, and unity. The newspapers published numerous articles that discussed self-restraint, discipline, and self-criticism and that denounced anarchism, "mountainism" (factionalism), and infighting. Red Guards were no longer addressed as "revolutionary little generals" but as "revolutionary students and teachers," reminding them of their primary role in the schools. Instead of exposing the bourgeois line and others' mistakes, the students were told to examine their own ideologies and deeds. A popular slogan embodying this idea was "Struggle against oneself and criticize revisionism."

Revisionism no longer meant deviant, bourgeois policies imple-

mented by the cadres, but personal ideological shackles. Without removing these bondages, the students were told, they could not carry out the
revolution. Discipline, not audacity or courage, was the quality of a revolutionary; it was only through discipline that revolution could succeed.
Even class struggle took on a personal note. The official press no longer
emphasized the proletarian struggle against the bourgeoisie, or the removal of class enemies, but fighting against oneself and one's weaknesses. The students were to treat their enemies, including overthrown
cadres, with leniency and restraint.[37]

Instead of students being encouraged to form Red Guard units, these
organizations were denounced.[38] The rebels were criticized for forming
their own little groups, with each trying to overshadow the others. The
media dubbed it "mountainism." Those who refused to negotiate peace
were derided as anarchists who only wanted freedom and not discipline.
They only wanted to do what they liked and made no effort to compromise. They were selfish, not revolutionary; they thought only of themselves and not the interests of the party, the people, or the country. In
early 1967, the use of physical force had been denounced as "simplistic
militarism." Toward the end of the year, even the idea that different
groups or circles could peacefully coexist was derogatively labeled as a
"theory of many centers" that undermined great unity.[39]

In the first half of 1967, the messages of peace were interspersed with
calls for violent action, or the messages themselves had a militant over-
tone. But the government appeals for peace became more sustained and
consistent in the latter half of the year. Articles denouncing factionalism
and promoting discipline increased, and these became the dominant
themes in late 1967 and 1968. At the outset of the Cultural Revolution,
the government's silence on these issues could be taken as support for
factional fighting, but now the message was unequivocal: the government denounced fighting. If the government was too weak to actively
intervene and effectively stop fighting, these messages at least undermined the prestige of those engaged in squabbles. The rebels could no
longer claim they had the government's blessing.

The Central Leaders Intervene

As in the mobilization for revolution, the government resorted to Mao's
personal appeal. Despite the many distortions of his pronouncements, his
prestige was still high among the students. Toward the end of 1967, the
government again promoted the study of Mao's works, hoping this
would discipline the students and prepare them for classes. But now the

messages were different. The government no longer highlighted the works that condoned and glorified revolution; instead, it emphasized his appeals for peace. For example, Mao's observation on March 29—"I am not in favor of people everywhere overthrowing too rapidly the organization of the government and the party"—was publicized.[40] His earlier articles on similar themes were reprinted. On June 9, the *People's Daily* carried his essay, "On Correct Handling of Contradictions Among the People," written in 1962. The accompanying commentary gave a brief history on its composition, summarized the article, and pointed out that the major contradiction was between Liu Shaoqi and the people, not among the Red Guards.

The government especially popularized three articles: "To Serve the People," "In Memory of Norman Bethune," and "The Foolish Old Man Who Moved the Mountain." As their titles imply, the first article praised altruism and sacrifice as basic values in communist society; the second eulogized a Canadian doctor who helped the communists during the war against the Japanese and died while taking care of the communist guerrillas; and the third referred to an allegory of an old man who wanted to turn a mountain into flat land. These writings extolled altruism, sacrifice, patience, and perseverance, and students were exhorted to follow every word of Mao's instructions.[41]

The study of Mao's works began to be more systematically organized in mid-1967. His works, as we saw earlier, constituted the curriculum in schools that reopened. When the army later moved into the schools to help, it organized similar study classes of Mao's thoughts for the students. When the central government mediated among the different Red Guard units, it also organized such classes. Ken Ling described how the central government organized one such study session on Mao's thoughts at which leaders of rival factions spent several days together and shared the same bedroom, dining room, and study hall.[42] These sessions provided an opportunity for student leaders to conciliate and for central leaders to review the "evidence" brought before them. At the end of the study sessions, the students met with the central leaders and presented their cases. Some Red Guard documents suggest that they met with central leaders as soon as they arrived in Beijing. In any case, the central leaders would pass judgment after listening to both sides. The students, "armed with Chairman Mao's thoughts," were to accept the verdict and return to promote unity within their own schools.

Since the central government was organizing these sessions, Red Guards also felt the pressure to do so. In September 1967, the Beijing Aeronautics Institute held a conference entitled "The Study and Practice of Mao Zedong's Thoughts." Three hundred representatives from various schools attended to show their faithfulness to Mao and their revolutionary spirit.[43] On May 9, 1968, the universities in Beijing, Tienjin, and Shanghai called similar meetings.[44]

As in the earlier period, when Mao had associated himself with the Red Guards to promote revolution, he now was associating himself with the call for peace. He, too, met with the student revolutionaries and arbitrated their disputes. In July 1968, he summoned five nationally famous student leaders—"the five heavenly kings," including Nie of Beida and Kuai of Qinghua—to communicate his disappointment in their failure to stop fighting. When the workers went into the universities to enforce order, he sent the workteam at Qinghua University a gift of mangoes to show his appreciation.[45] When the message was this clear that Mao himself was behind the policy, anyone who opposed it could no longer invoke his name for support. Those groups that still fought lost prestige and support.

With the political and educational institutions dismantled, communication between the central leaders and the grass roots was broken. Policies did not reach the lower echelons as fast as before, and, in any case, the government had no way to enforce them. The media was one way to communicate with the citizens; another, more effective but less efficient way was through personal involvement. The central leaders had met with students since 1966 to communicate their views and to expand support at the grass-roots level. In 1967, when the majority in the central government decided to restore peace, central leaders made personal appeals to the students and mediated in local disputes. In June, Xie Fuzhi and Wang Li were emissaries from Beijing to settle disputes in Kunming (Yunnan province) and Wuhan (Hubei province). Chen Boda mediated in his native province, Fujien, and Jiang Qing in her native province, Shandong, and its neighbor, Liaoning.

Because of his prestige, Zhou Enlai was in greatest demand: "He was everywhere: in the ministries, in the factories, in the schools, in [Beijing] and in the provinces, talking to the workers and Red Guards, tirelessly explaining the sense and substance of Mao's directives and how to apply them."[46] He mediated among the delegates from Guangzhou on August 14 and 16, October 19, and November 9 and 14, 1967. He was in Guangzhou twice to bring some peace to that city.[47] On September 28, 1967, he met with delegates from Heilongjiang and Liaoning; on December 9, he mediated among factions from Honan; on December 13, he settled disputes in Beijing; and on July 25, 1968, he did the same for the delegates from Guangxi.[48]

An arbitrator rarely satisfied all parties; moreover, given the complexities of the disputes among the Red Guards, it was difficult to make an objective assessment. In early 1967, the central leaders often backed one group and condemned another. Such pronouncements sometimes signaled the demise of one group and the triumph of another. At other times, the "fallen" group defied government verdict and continued fighting. Toward the end of the year, the central government leaders abstained from passing judgment. Instead, they asked for compromise from both parties and appealed to the delegates to stop fighting.

Yet the violence continued. Central leaders could not be present whenever fighting broke out, and they intervened only when conflicts became serious and widespread. Nor were truces permanent, because factionalism was too entrenched and misunderstandings too deep for persuasion alone to solve the problems. Sometimes fighting broke out as soon as the student leaders returned home or when the central government emissaries left. The second visit of Zhou Enlai to Guangzhou in March 1967 was a sign of the failure of the first truce. Also in March, Zhou mediated between the 2–7 Commune and the Leftists of Zhengzhou in Henan, but fighting broke out again in May and Zhou had to order the Military District Command to intervene.[49] It was apparent that verbal appeals, personal interventions, and social pressures alone could not restore peace. More tangible measures had to be used if the students were to stop fighting.

The Army Moves into the Schools

As early as December 31, 1966, the Chinese Communist Party Central Committee and the State Council had issued a directive to the students and teachers that the People's Liberation Army would send small contingents to conduct "short-term military and political training" in the schools in the following six months.[50] The local party committees and the revolutionary committees were to coordinate these activities by organizing students into squads, platoons, and companies to undergo military training for fifteen to twenty days. Soldiers would conduct classes in "the study and application of Mao Zedong's thoughts." In addition to the "three well-read articles," works by Marx, Engels, Lenin, Lin Biao, and Chen Boda were included.

This represented the first active attempt to gather students and restore discipline in schools. The People's Liberation Army was not to exercise military control but to calm the students and prepare them for classes in the fall. This directive was soon followed by another, appealing the students to return to school to finish what they had set out to do—that is, to revolutionize the educational system. As usual, students expressed support because it was politically astute to do so. On February 3, 1967, a rally of 10,000 people was held in Shanghai, and "meetings of resolution" were organized all across the country.[51]

Little was accomplished. The teachers would not or could not take the initiative, and, despite the students' participation in the rally, they were not interested in actually attending classes. It was still early in the revolution, and students were preoccupied with the seizures of power that had begun in January. The resulting turmoil probably caught the central and local governments by surprise and overshadowed the implementation of the December directive. In the following three months, there was little evidence of soldiers entering the schools. The minority that did, as we saw in Chapter 4, became involved in local struggles, which only made order more difficult to enforce.

The soldiers were sent to the schools more systematically after the March 7 Directive, once the seizures of power had died down. In this directive, Mao instructed that:

> The army should enter universities, high schools, and the senior grades of primary schools in different groups to carry out military training. The soldiers should reopen the schools, reorganize them, and establish the triple-unity leadership organizations to carry out struggle, criticism, and changes...They should convince the students that it was only through liberating themselves that they could liberate the proletariat. Teachers and cadres who made mistakes should be included in the military training.[52]

This directive had been prompted by the report, "Yenan Middle School in Tienjin Used Class as the Basis of Unity, Succeeded in Achieving Unity, Reorganized the School, and Strengthened and Re-educated the Cadres." Yenan Middle School members had spent more than twenty days discussing the issue. Instead of using proportional representation of the different Red Guard groups, they established unity on a class-by-class basis, avoiding direct confrontation between the competing groups. On reading the report, Mao wrote a letter to Lin Biao, Zhou Enlai, and members of the Central Cultural Revolution Committee approving these measures. The content of the letter became the basis for the March 7 Directive.[53] Thus, even at that stage, local initiatives could shape central government policies constructively.

There were some isolated reports of the army's successes. The Shanghai Institute of Light Industries achieved unity through the intervention of the People's Liberation Army.[54] On the anniversary of the March 7 Directive in 1968, the army in Beijing had given military training to the students in 385 high schools, 834 primary schools, and some universities, though this constituted less than 0.01 percent of the national school population.[55] Most high schools and primary schools in the capital probably received military training, but such activities were not systematically implemented across the country. Many respondents in the provinces said that the soldiers came to their schools only in mid-1968, and some were completely ignorant of the soldiers' presence in the schools in 1967. In the March 7 Directive, Mao did state that the People's Liberation Army was to conduct military training first in a small area, learn from the experience, and then gradually widen its scope. The stationing of soldiers in the schools remained on a trial basis and limited to a few areas for a long time.

The soldiers' mission of carrying out study sessions was by far the easiest task. No student had the audacity to refuse to study Mao's works. A student described how these activities were organized in his school:

> In the first class, comrades from the People's Liberation Army talked about the wisdom and greatness of Chairman Mao and led us to compare our ideology with Mao Zedong's thoughts. The next lesson was the recall of the bitter past. A woman comrade recounted her suffering under the capitalist reactionary road. Her story was very touching. On the third day, the soldier comrade talked about individualism and revisionism and about Chairman Mao's latest directive: "If the two organizations are revolutionary, they should unite according to the principle of revolutionary unity." He said, "Chairman Mao asked us to talk less about others' mistakes and more of our own."[56]

Study materials included Mao's "three well-read articles" as well as "Combat Liberalism," "On Correcting Mistaken Ideas in the Party," and the works of Marx, Engels, Lenin, Lin Biao, and Chen Boda. The emphases were on discipline and tolerance as the means of convincing rebels to make peace with their rivals.

The students had undergone military training in school before the Cultural Revolution, including hand-to-hand combat, tracking skills, and target practice. In 1967, however, combat training was not given, since that would only sharpen the students' fighting skills. Students were divided into platoons, squads, and battalions, but these were nomenclatural changes that did not affect the organization of the schools, and the class remained the basic unit. They received one to two hours daily training in assembling and marching, no doubt to work off their energy. Discipline was the core of their military training. They were constantly reminded of the code of conduct of the soldiers:

Three rules: obey orders
                    take nothing from the people
                    hand over all captured goods

Eight points: speak politely
                    pay fair price for purchase
                    return what you borrow
                    give compensation for damages
                    do not beat or insult people
                    do not trample property
                    do not importune women
                    do not mistreat prisoners[57]

To establish unity was a much more difficult task. Students in May 1967 were still traveling on the exchange of revolutionary experience, and others were preoccupied with seizing and counterseizing power. The soldiers tried every means to get the students to make peace. Resistance was lower when individuals or groups were isolated in different classrooms and thus deprived of their larger group support. Nevertheless, group membership influenced relationships among classmates to the point that some students would not even sit down with—let alone talk to—their enemies. Meal times were staggered so as to avoid running into rival groups, and some students stayed in their own rooms during study sessions. In small group discussions, they sought out their own group members; in large ones, groups sat in their own corners.

Reconciliation meetings organized by the soldiers were not new to the students, because weekly class or group meetings had also been held before the Cultural Revolution. The students drew on these experiences. They had learned to talk in generalities and to reveal their own minor faults while exposing their enemies' "big" mistakes. Some students recounted the history of fighting in their school in great detail, only to show that their rivals had provoked them. Some even made notes during their enemies' self-criticism, in case the information might be useful later on. Such behavior was hardly conducive to reconciliation.

As always, the Red Guards found ways to circumvent the government's intentions and even to manipulate the soldiers. The Red Guards had increased their strength in 1967 by soliciting the support of rebel groups from industries, agriculture, service sectors, and government departments. To them, the soldiers were just another potential ally to be won over, and each group of students used every method possible to convince the soldiers that it was the "left" worthy of support and that its rivals were the "rightists" to be suppressed. Each group was on its best behavior, acted in a disciplined manner in the soldiers' presence, invited the soldiers to criticism meetings of its own members, and even volunteered to work in the factories. At the same time, it smeared the reputation of its rivals, spreading rumors of their wrongdoings.[58] It was impossible for outsiders, like the soldiers, to separate facts from fabrications and to judge who was right and who wrong. The issues were so complicated that no judge could possibly establish who was on the left, who started the fight, or who was more responsible. Any decision favoring one group would antagonize another, and to accommodate all the groups would turn them all against the soldiers. The soldiers thus became embroiled in local politics.

This difficult position of the soldiers could be seen in the many statements in Red Guard bulletins indicting their judgment and action. For example, the Three Red Corps and the Red Flag Commune of Guangzhou Number 29 Middle School expressed their displeasure and "disappointment": "We adopted the attitude of trusting and relying on the People's Liberation Army. We expressed our hope that the military training group would learn from Meng He and his clear-cut class standpoint and handle questions correctly."[59] Instead, the soldiers "fired on the Red Guards [probably the Three Red Corps or their allies], killing some of them." There were many other Red Guard publications and wall posters that accused the military of not "highlighting proletarian politics, not following Chairman Mao's latest directive."[60] In essence, the Red Guards were angry that the soldiers did not side with their group and therefore betrayed "proletarian principles."

The People's Liberation Army in China was well integrated in civilian life during peacetime. The soldiers worked in factories and on state farms, and they provided social and medical services in the outlying areas. School textbooks always conveyed the image of the helpful, friendly, and trustworthy People's Liberation Army cadet. The students never had the awe and fear of the military as citizens in other countries might feel about the armed forces. Yet now these soldiers had defied Mao's directive to support the left and had "colluded with rightists," and the Red Guards felt they deserved to be punished. They executed their own justice on the soldiers as they had on the school administrators, factory managers, and government officials.

The party and the government, which had once seemed invincible, had given way before the rebels; the soldiers, to the Red Guards, were equally vulnerable. The central government explicitly forbade soldiers to fire on civilians, and soldiers guarding arsenals had given up arms without firing a shot. The students knew this and attacked the soldiers. On May 14, 1967, Red Guards attacked 58 soldiers and members of August

24 Revolutionary Rebel Group of Kaifeng Normal School, and two days later they ambushed another 190 soldiers: "[Red Guards] dragged the People's Liberation Army fighters from the trucks, beat them, and tore off their army insignia and collar badges. Those [soldiers] captured were forced to labor during the day and struggled [criticized, possibly punished] at night."[61] Five days later, they wounded and kidnapped another contingent of 200 soldiers.[62] Some soldiers' plight could be clearly seen in this teacher's account: "I was awakened in the middle of the night by sounds on the lower floor. I had boarded up windows and doors for protection. I went downstairs and found two soldiers huddled in a corner. They had just escaped harassment by the students."

It was because of the growing number of clashes between the soldiers and the rebels that, in April and May 1967, the government called on the people to support the army.[63] But this was of no avail; skirmishes between the two groups continued, and the call was repeated as late as January 1968.[64] The soldiers were isolated, with usually only one or two sent to each school. Moreover, because they had explicit instructions not to defend themselves with arms, they were defenseless against belligerent students. Without power or the students' confidence and respect, the army could not be an effective arbitrator among the factions. The government's hopes of using the soldiers' presence to halt student fighting were dashed.

The government exhausted every measure short of martial law to halt the fighting. The school administration was dismantled, so the government could not use this institutionalized system of command. In its absence, the government relied on the mass media and the personal prestige of Mao and other central leaders. These measures were similar to those used in promoting the Cultural Revolution, except that the message had changed: the mass media called for restraint and demobilization, not mobilization; and the central leaders met with students not to learn from the "revolutionary generals," but to arbitrate in their disputes. Soldiers were sent not to support the leftists, but to discipline them. The government hoped that these steps would create an atmosphere of reconciliation and generate the pressure for peace.

Like the government's call for action in 1966, its call for peace in 1967 was meant to generate mass response and a social movement counter to that of the students' movement. This time it failed. The government's control was weak; both the central and local governments were rife with dissent, and the vacillation in policies that accompanied the changing fortunes of the different factions undermined further their effectiveness. The teachers and administrators who supported the directive were disheartened and powerless. Students not active in the movement were apathetic. More important, those who were active were strong and in no mood to return to class; they had become astute politicians who turned the government pronouncements into weapons for their own power struggles. Thus, the government's attempt to mobilize a countermovement made little headway.

CHAPTER 6 _____

The Proletariat Takes Power

The Chinese government's lack of control in the country and the students' unwillingness to lay down their arms were the main impediments to peace. In this chapter, I will show how the government reversed the situation, not by converting the students, but by appealing to a different sector in society: the workers and peasants. The government mobilized them to check the students, introduced a program of educational reforms, and brought the Cultural Revolution in the schools to a close.

Over 90 percent of the adult population in China at that time were workers and peasants. They, too, had grievances against their superiors in the workplace, and they participated in the Cultural Revolution. Although the students had certainly created chaos, their movement did not have any immediate disastrous impact on society. In contrast, work stoppages by peasants and the industrial workers created a shortage of food and other essential consumer items. As early as January 1967, managers who had encouraged workers to join the exchange of revolutionary experience were criticized for disrupting the economy. "Revolutionaries" in the communes who distributed the grain and tools owned by the collective were also attacked.[1] The government as well as the workers were quick to recognize the linkage between the revolution and the lack of supplies. Farm work was never entirely neglected, and, in early 1967, many factories reopened when workers returned to their stations. In the latter half of 1967 and early 1968, the national media reported that a number of the workers' associations and factories had achieved unity. Farm and factory facilities, such as trucks and loudspeakers, which had once been loaned to their student revolutionary allies, were reassigned for production purposes. Cutting off these supplies weakened the students, and their insistence to get access to such resources only antagonized their former friends in the industrial units. Even if students did not harass the factories, their constant infighting inconvenienced the populace and restricted movement. By the end of 1967, the majority of the population was tired and alienated by the students' fracases.

Popular support for the government's efforts to put a stop to the student movement could be seen in the communal assistance to schools that reopened. Parents who returned to work were anxious to have their children back in school. The Chinese had traditionally valued education and harbored a high respect for intellectuals. Despite all the criticism launched against the schools, parents still liked to see the teachers disciplining their young. They cooperated in bringing their children back to classes.[2] In addition, workers and peasants volunteered to lecture in school. They told stories of their past, comparing their sufferings before 1949 with the blessings received from the communist party since then. The students lacked the discipline to sit through five or six hours of regular class, after being out of school for so long, and the workers and peasants entertained them with their stories. Sometimes they took the young to help in the fields or do simple tasks on the shop floor.[3] In the latter half of 1967, many primary and secondary schools opened with community help. This became so popular that, in May 1968, even universities followed their example. For instance, Tongji University in Shanghai joined an architectural firm to form the May 7 Commune to start a work-study program, and the Shanghai Engineering Factory had its own technical institute to train workers as engineers.[4]

These developments, like those that had sparked the Cultural Revolution, originated locally, but the government appreciated the benefits and gave them wide coverage. The increased media coverage in early 1968 showed that the government endorsed and deliberately promoted these efforts toward peace. In December 1968, the *People's Daily* ran a series of articles that debated the pros and cons of having factories and farms in charge of schools. The government hoped that these reports and discussions on educational reforms, like those in June 1966, would focus attention on these issues, generate enthusiasm, and encourage other communities to follow suit.[5]

In the early half of 1967, central government policies vacillated between compromise and radicalism with the changes in the balance of power among the different factions. On May 22, the central government came out with the first explicit statement in the *People's Daily* asking the revolutionaries to stop the violence; such requests were superseded by the brief triumph of the radicals in August calling the revolutionaries to ferret out enemies in the army. In September, the moderates again dominated and made sustained efforts to contain the movement and end the fighting. Students were asked to stop the exchange of revolutionary experience, to unite, and to support the army. Although the directives were not completely successful, they did undermine the strength of the student revolutionaries and put them on the defensive. The students' continuous fighting brought economic havoc to the country, and their attacks on foreign diplomats put the country in an embarrassing position. These problems increased the support for the moderates and strengthened their resolve to restrain the students; the more active phase of the Cultural Revolution thus came to a stop. Government agencies also reconciled their differences and established revolutionary committees. By June 1968, revolutionary committees had been formed in 26 of the 29 provinces, municipalities, and autonomous regions across the country, thus establishing a formal channel of official communication and a chain of command in those places.[6] The radical central leaders' policies of advocating the use of physical force were discredited by the growing turmoil; however, as the trial of the radical faction in 1980 showed, they also achieved their goal of eliminating the conservative supporters of Liu. Between July and December 1968, 103 members of the party central committee, 52 members of the national people's congress, and 76 members of the political committee were indicted as traitors, spies, and antirevolutionaries.[7] The radicals were ready to reach a settlement with the moderates. With these developments, the government achieved some degree of unity, reasserted control over the provinces, and, backed by popular support, could directly confront the students who continued to make trouble.

The government turned to the workers and peasants for support. These groups had been exploited by the capitalists and the landlords before 1949, but since then their lives had improved. They were grateful to the party and to Mao; furthermore, their efforts in helping schools to reopen showed the government that they could be relied on to bring the movement to a peaceful end. The government also had tactical reasons for choosing the workers and peasants: they were the proletariat and, by definition, the revolutionary class whose attitudes and behavior were most "correct." The students had carried out the Cultural Revolution in the name of the proletariat, and its involvement was therefore something the students could not oppose. The government had exhausted all of its own peaceful means, including limited use of the military, and they had proven ineffective. There were over 500 million people in China who could be considered part of the proletariat, compared with only three million People's Liberation Army members.[8] Despite the internal rifts among the peasants and workers resulting from the factionalism of 1966–1967, the dominant groups were still numerous enough to overwhelm the students. Their presence in the schools would not call forth the same sense of oppression or prompt the same international outcry that a massive military presence would. Perhaps based on all these considerations, workers and peasants were sent into the schools.

Proletariat Propaganda Teams

The dispatch of proletariat propaganda teams into the schools was probably the government's last resort, and it was a successful one. On July 27, 1968, about 30,000 workers from 62 factories in Beijing moved into Qinghua and surrounded the buildings occupied by Kuai Dafu and the hard core of about 300 radicals who persisted in fighting. A detailed description of what occurred is given by William Hinton; he reports that the workers exhibited great restraint during that three-day siege, overwhelming the radical students through sheer numbers until the student stronghold in Qinghua collapsed.[9] This success led to others. Within a month the workers entered 136 universities: 59 in Beijing, 38 in Nanjing, 23 in Shanghai, and 16 in Tienjin. In October, workers also entered high schools and primary schools,[10] although their role there was not to overcome recalcitrant rebels like those in Qinghua, but simply to take over the administration.

The workers acted with restraint in Qinghua, but it was unlikely that they could do so throughout the country. Physical force was sometimes used to overpower the students. Some respondents in Guangzhou told me that the atmosphere was tense:

> I was away from campus the night before. When I returned in the morning, I could not enter. The campus was cordoned off. No entry or exit was permitted. I saw workers beating some of the students even as they were dragged away into the trucks. These were to be sent to the public security bureau to be interrogated.

Many respondents who belonged to the losing factions were bitter about this move of the central government. The workers had been as much involved in the factional fights as the students; now the workers were supporting their protégé groups and sending the "troublemakers"—leaders of the opposing factions—to the public security bureau. It was at that point the students felt betrayed by the central government. In 1982, a former Red Guard leader cynically described the situation: "First the government turned against the intellectuals, then the party members, and then the students. We were all being used."

Throughout 1967, the students—alone or in cooperation with other revolutionary groups—had assumed leadership both in the schools and in the government. Some students had become members of the revolutionary committees in the farms, factories, and even city and provincial governments, yet now they had to relinquish control to the workers. They resented the workers' new importance in the leadership.

It should be noted that the students did sympathize with the proletariat. The educational system before 1966 had violated the rights of the proletarians by keeping them out of school, and hence the "bourgeois intellectuals" responsible for this deserved censure. The students wanted to redress the abuses and champion proletarian rights, even though they were unsure how to change the system. However, they did not think that the intellectuals' control of schools should necessarily be supplanted by the proletariat.

Although students considered themselves to be intellectuals allied with the working class, most students harbored paternalistic attitudes toward the workers and peasants and saw them as ignorant, uneducated, and unqualified to take up the responsibility of reforming education. Students sympathized with the workers and peasants and felt that their rights and privileges had to be protected, but they nevertheless wanted working-class intellectuals to control education on behalf of the proletariat, not the proletariat itself. Workers and peasants were to take a supportive and subordinate role. Respondents who were activists during this period suggested that experience confirmed their belief. They were doing all the real work, whereas the workers only followed their suggestions: "The workers did not know anything about education. I prepared the lesson or the reading materials, and the workers looked at them. They would always make the same suggestion, 'Highlight Mao Zedong's thoughts.' It was really pro forma. They did not know what else to say." The students and young intellectuals in the universities were especially resentful of workers who had once been their fellow high school students but did not make it into the university because of poor grades, and yet who now held administrative positions in those same institutions. The students and teachers found them to be "proud, obnoxious, and inconsiderate" and looked on them with disdain.

The central government recognized this tension between the workers and the intellectuals. On the day the workers moved into Qinghua, the *People's Daily* carried a lead article with the heading, "Stop the Bourgeois Intellectuals' Domination of the Schools." This was perhaps an attempt to forestall the intellectuals' opposition to workers' intervention in the schools. On August 26, Yao Wenyuan published an article in the *People's Daily* titled, "The Working Class Takes Leadership in Everything," which was reprinted in *Red Flag* and also as a pamphlet. The article traced the development of the Cultural Revolution and concluded that, "Under these circumstances, we cannot accomplish the struggle, criticism, and change and the other responsibilities on the educational front through the students alone; we have to have the workers and the People's Liberation Army leadership." On August 27, Mao sent a directive stating that, "The worker propaganda teams will remain in schools to take part in the struggle, criticism, and change, and to lead the schools forever. In the rural areas, we need the peasants, the most trusted ally of the workers, to look after the schools."[11] The new directives even implied that the students themselves were bourgeois and must therefore hand control over to the workers. As usual, the central government used the mass media to clarify its position.

Mao further backed the workers on August 5, 1968, when he sent the Qinghua University proletariat propaganda team mangoes given to him by Pakistani dignitaries. Like the pinning of the red arm band on Mao on August 18, 1966, this personal gesture of regard and concern created a stir and secured the workers' dominance in the schools. The mangoes were not eaten but preserved. That same night, replicas were made by the workers in Qinghua and distributed to other propaganda teams as symbols of support from the highest quarters. The prestige of the proletariat was never so high.[12]

Beginning in August 1968, the national and local newspapers carried numerous articles praising not the zeal of the revolutionary young generals, but the progressiveness and intelligence of the workers. The *People's Daily* gave examples of workers besting engineers in solving difficult industrial problems. Intellectuals, with all their theories, could not handle the simplest problems on the shop floor. In one case, a professor and steel expert could not distinguish high-quality steel from that of average quality, but an ordinary worker did it from the sound of the bars hitting each other.[13]

The government's strong stand and the messages in the mass media seemed to have an impact on the schools. By October 1968, newspapers reported that the students were quite supportive of the workers.[14] This outburst of support might have been genuine, but with the government and the community against them, the student activists had little choice. Supporting the workers was a better political move than resisting because it might assure them a place in the newly constituted revolutionary

committees. To those Chinese tired of the confusion of the previous two
years, the workers were a better alternative than the Red Guard leaders.
At least the workers had restored peace on campus. Even in 1981, after
the government rejected the educational policies of the Cultural Revolution, intellectuals in China still spoke favorably of the workers' contribution in 1968. A teacher whom the workers had sent to labor in the
countryside admitted, "The workers did achieve something for the
schools. Without them, the students would have continued fighting.
They would not have listened to anyone else." The workers' efforts
reflected popular sentiments that many had not dared to articulate when
the Red Guards were controlling the campuses.

Teachers and students still operated according to the norms of the
Cultural Revolution; they expressed their support by organizing rallies
and parades, writing poems, drafting posters, and making public
speeches. When the workers entered universities in Shanghai, students of
rival factions in the Foreign Language Institute, Normal University,
Number 1 Medical School, and Fudan University joined to welcome
workers with drums and cymbals and invited them to attend their criticism meetings denouncing the capitalists and the reactionary intellectual
authorities who looked down on workers and peasants. Students confided their problems to the workers and asked for advice.[15] Even at
Qinghua and Beida, students and teachers once again resumed a peaceful
criticism of education:

> The golden sun gilded Qinghua campus. The music "East Is Red"
> wafted in the air. People in rows and in groups were in the shade, on the
> playground attentively studying Chairman Mao's works. The little
> bright red books of Chairman Mao's quotations were lights on a dark
> road guiding the people.[16]

These reports might have reflected the workers' success in restoring
order, but given the tension in the previous two years, it was more likely
that these descriptions of the relaxed campus atmosphere served an ex-
hortative purpose. Just as reports of the toppling of the university administration in late 1966 fanned student revolutionary activism, the
media in 1968 encouraged pacificism and increased the sense of isolation
of those who wanted to resist. Instead of mobilizing for revolution, the
pressure was for demobilization. The revolutionary elements were those
who stopped fighting; the counter-revolutionaries were those who continued to do so. Students who did not conform were ostracized or sanctioned by their own peers.

Restoring Order in the Schools

The workers' success in reopening the schools when other measures had failed raised their prestige and strengthened their position on campus. However, their problems were not over. The workers had to find ways to bring students back to school. Many students had stayed home throughout the movement. For example, only 300 of the usual 10,000 students were on campus when the workers entered Qinghua on July 28.[17] Some did return voluntarily when friends told them that schools had reopened, because it was boring to stay home. Others came back when they received official letters announcing the resumption of classes. Still others hurried back when they heard that the government was giving out job assignments to graduates—the only channel to employment in China. As one respondent told me, "I returned to school only because I heard that they [the schools] were assigning us jobs." But not everyone was in a graduating class, and so workers and teachers sometimes had to visit students at home to recruit them.

Another problem was to get the teachers' cooperation. The teachers felt betrayed by the government, which had instigated the students to rebel against them, and they felt uneasy about facing students who had criticized and sometimes tortured them. Sam Ginsburg described his feelings after the Socialist Education Movement of 1964, a much milder and smaller-scale criticism campaign compared with the Cultural Revolution:

> I just could not imagine myself entering the classroom and facing the students whose minds I had been accused of having been poisoning. Nor did I have any desire to sit down together with other members of our teaching staff; relations had been thoroughly spoiled by the "postering," though we took care not to show it.[18]

These sentiments would have been equally if not more intense and prevalent during the Cultural Revolution. Many teachers probably complied with the workers' requests to resume their teaching responsibilities, though without much enthusiasm.

A more serious problem involved pacifying the contending groups. Large-scale battles were over, but old grudges remained and sporadic fighting still occurred. Nevertheless, the workers had an easier task than the soldiers did. In 1968, the momentum for peace was stronger than that for turmoil. The students were deprived of their resources as well as popular support, and the government had come out strongly against fighting. Furthermore, the workers, unlike the soldiers, did not have to make judgments about "left" and "right." They only had to prevent fighting. They isolated student leaders who made trouble or simply handed them to the public security bureau. They organized criticism meetings and study sessions of Mao's writings and the central directives. If there was too much antagonism in the class, the students would initially meet in separate groups, and then in enlarged sessions when they were in a more conciliatory mood.

The workers were more numerous than the soldiers had been in the schools. Initially they numbered in the hundreds, and only when sporadic fighting stopped did the majority withdraw. Even then, ten to thirty workers—much larger than the initial soldier contingent—remained. This was a sufficient number to oversee each important committee or department on campus and even to approach the students individually.

The measures taken by the workers were strong reminders of the revolutionary strategies of the students at the opening of the Cultural Revolution. Resources used to promote the revolution were now used to diffuse it. Workers "used broadcasts, big wall posters, discussion groups, and individual approaches. They also formed over a hundred teams and penetrated the classrooms, the shop floors, and the dormitories. They carefully and patiently carried out their educational work."[19] The Communist Youth League was no longer available to oversee the other students. Instead, workers used their student supporters. They grouped the Red Guards in twos or threes with one supportive or model student to encourage them to study and apply Mao's thoughts.

The workers also talked individually to the Red Guards, especially the leaders, and urged them to examine their mistakes and reconcile with their enemies. They told the students about their "bitter past" (their sufferings under landlords and capitalists before 1949) to make the young appreciate their blessings and the pettiness of their fights. Workers also showed a personal concern for the students.[20] In one incident, Liu Jingxia, a worker and member of the local revolutionary committee, won over Wang Bauer, a high school student, through perseverance. The first time Liu approached Wang about being friends, he said, "Why should you be so magnanimous?" With that, he shut the door and left. She approached him several times and each time he "shook her off and would not even turn his head." But "Liu Jingsha patiently and carefully did her educational work with Wang Bauer. She tried whenever and wherever she ran into him."[21] Finally, her persistence paid off; Wang agreed to cooperate in the activities organized by the school. This was not an isolated case. According to many newspaper accounts, students were touched by the workers' concern and example, and they "repented." They became ashamed of their selfishness in pursuing their own power and private or narrow group interests.

My respondents' impressions confirmed this picture, especially when team members were older workers. Many intellectuals recognized that the workers were simple and often dogmatic, but they admitted that many, especially the older ones, were understanding and sympathetic. A typical comment from my respondents was, "They might seem pugnacious in criticism meetings. Perhaps they felt they had to do this in public. But after the meetings, the workers comforted me and were very sympathetic. They would ask if everything was all right and told me not to be afraid." Even though workers and peasants were secure in the new social order, they had to live up to their roles as overseers of the schools and act tough. They shouted and admonished the students and teachers vehemently in public, but were gentle and solicitous in private. Their behavior offers a glimpse of the tremendous social pressures that participants of the Cultural Revolution were under. Once the norm was defined, even victors like the workers and peasants felt pressured to conform to their perceptions of the role assigned them. We can imagine what greater pressure fell on those who were less lucky.

Dealing with Recalcitrants

As early as June 23, 1968, the government took harsh measures against the recalcitrants. A directive commissioned the new school authority to "clean the class ranks." Student revolutionaries were held responsible for the continued violence: "One reason why order was not restored is the small number of persons who pretend to make revolution. In reality they are opposing the revolution and making trouble."[22] Those who would not stop fighting were accused of being counter-revolutionaries engaged in double-dealing and sabotage, and they had to be investigated and punished. The State Council and the Central Cultural Revolution Committee, however, vetoed the use of physical force and prohibited torture or coercion during interrogation. They cautioned against hasty investigations and passing verdicts with insufficient evidence.

With this mandate, the workers and peasants investigated the student activists. Actual physical force was seldom used to extract confessions, but psychological pressure was great. The workers held endless criticism meetings, some of which lasted through the night. Even when classes were resumed, meetings were held in the evening. A young teacher described her plight:

> My child was only three at that time, and there was no one to look after her in the evening. Everyone had to go to meetings. So I tied her to the bed. She told me she was scared. But what could I do? So I just said, "Mother has to go out." And I would not be back until after ten o'clock.

At the sessions, the workers acted as if they had prior knowledge of wrongdoings and asked participants to confess and make restitution. Another respondent from the same university described how such a session went: "We would be at the meeting. There might be eight or ten persons there. The worker would look round and say: 'There were some of you here at Zhongnanhai on such and such a date [referring to the radical Red Guards' attempt to get central leaders to face mass criticism]. Those who were there better own up.' " In more serious cases, the Red Guard leaders were isolated and put under workers' custody for months, sometimes years. A leader who was under arrest by the workers for nine months described his days:

> I was not allowed to return home, and I spent my days living in a small room under constant supervision. My guards even followed me to the washroom, lest I should commit suicide. I was not physically tortured, I was given food, and usually allowed to sleep. They kept asking me what I did, whom I had contacts with, and to write my self-criticism again and again.

Just as they had resented the party's domination in school administration, the intellectuals disliked this policing role of the workers. They compared introducing workers in the schools to "putting sand into clay." The workers were spies who watched their every move and waited for a chance to incriminate them. My sources explained that, during the Red Guard period, the students had extorted confessions through torture, but these did not go into one's file. In contrast, the workers' accusations and verdicts were official and went on one's record permanently. Those found guilty of rape or murder were sent to prison, and others with less serious offenses, as one respondent cynically put it, like "taking the wrong side during the revolution," were re-educated in the countryside.

Not all the rebels were defined as counter-revolutionaries. A more effective way to rid the campus of this generation of student revolutionaries was to give them new job assignments so they could assume their

adult role of earning a living. As of mid-1968, the government had organized a media campaign to prepare the students to accept work in the
countryside. On July 9, the front-page headline of the *People's Daily* read,
"Go Where Your Country Needs You Most. Grow up in the Big
Storm." The *People's Daily* published numerous articles written by youths
working in the rural areas on how they were welcomed by the peasants,
adjusted to the new life, and contributed to their country. Some potential
graduates were prepared with a two-week retreat and study sessions
where they discussed works on altruism and central directives that exhorted them to go wherever their services were needed. At the end of the
session, they were asked to indicate their choices. With such strong social
pressure, many put down, "Where the country needs me most." Some
were genuinely committed to serving the country; others did it out of
social pressure. At the end of 1968, the classes of 1966, 1967, and 1968 in
the high schools and universities were given job assignments, and about
two million students left for the countryside.[23] For the university students, job assignment carried the possibility of a later transfer from the
rural areas; but for the high school graduates, it meant permanent settlement on the farms.

Many teachers and administrators also left campus. The spirit of
"economize and make revolution" now took on an entirely different
meaning from that of 1967 or even early 1968. Given the changed circumstances, economizing meant that the students and teachers were to
repair the school facilities and equipment and that excess personnel were
to be eliminated. Some staff members received new appointments in factories and on farms, where they would remain for the next ten years.
Others were sent to the May 7 Cadre School, where they underwent re-
education; still others attended the divisional schools set up during this
period. Qinghua and Beida both had divisions near Poyang Lake in
Jiangxi. Middle schools had branch schools of their own, and these were
usually located in the wilderness, where the cadres cleared land, built
their own shelters, and planted their own crops. Few academic activities
went on in these divisional schools; teachers and administrators worked
during the day and held meetings in the evening. Some remained for two
or three years until their services were again needed in the cities, and others stayed until 1976, when the Gang of Four fell and policies changed.
The majority of the original leaders and participants in the Cultural Revolution saw the end of the movement only in exile. In a superficial sense,
bureaucratism had been eliminated from the schools by removing these
"bourgeois" intellectuals from campus. Now the ranks in the schools
were pure: only workers and peasants—and their faithful supporters—
remained.

Schools Reopen

The official policy emphasized decentralization and grass-roots initiatives, and educational reforms were left to the workers, peasants, and soldiers who sat on the revolutionary committees. Although workers and peasants had entered the schools in July 1968, some soldiers had also remained. In urban areas, the workers were usually the most powerful; in rural areas, the peasants were. Only in rare cases did the soldiers hold power. Membership on the revolutionary committees changed periodically, since workers and peasants from the same factories or communes took turns in the schools. In many schools, representatives from the People's Liberation Army were absent altogether, though at Qinghua University a member of the army, Qi Zhuan, dominated until 1976. The reason for these different committee formations is unknown, but it is likely that the government wanted to keep a closer watch on key universities such as Qinghua. The use of soldiers also meant a greater degree of continuity on the governing body.

As early as February 1967, many primary schools in Shanghai reopened. Primary schools were the first to do so, because parents supported it and the children were young and more manageable. Some secondary schools opened in September 1967, and most were operating by September 1968. When the student revolutionaries graduated and were assigned to new posts, and when the recalcitrant young teachers and old guards were sent to the factories, farms, and May 7 Cadre or divisional schools, the campuses were rid of the opposition. Only the faithful remained, and the new and younger students were more cooperative.

Nevertheless, conditions prior to 1966 were never restored. It was difficult for students to settle in to the routine of learning, since they had stayed away from school for more than a year, and except for the very young, they had taken part in the Cultural Revolution in one way or another to criticize their teachers. Intellectuals no longer commanded the same respect as before; in the 1970s, they became the "stinking ninth category," the lowest in the social stratification scale of China. Students recognized this and teachers had a difficult time maintaining discipline. Respondents who were teachers had many stories of difficult students. One teacher told me:

> I set my students' class assignments and told them they could only leave after finishing them. I sat close to the door to make sure they would not run away. Instead, one student jumped right out from the second floor

window. He was disciplined later on, [since] the worker in charge of the school was behind me. We found out that he had an appointment to fight another student in the park.

If discipline problems were serious in the schools that reopened, teachers singled out for criticism as bourgeois intellectuals or as revolutionary leaders now denounced as counter-revolutionaries had an even harder time. A party secretary recounted this story:

> I was visiting the school and sitting at the back of class. An old teacher was teaching. It was close to lunch hour. A student took a bamboo pole and tapped the teacher's head and said, "You old devil, quickly finish your class." The only response from the teacher was, "Don't disturb me."

Another young teacher who had headed a Red Guard faction was called "bad leader" by the students to his face. This was the extent to which teachers had fallen from the high status they once enjoyed before the Cultural Revolution. Even though the revolution was over, the prejudice against bourgeois intellectuals that had prompted the movement remained. The teachers' concerns before the resumption of classes seemed to be well founded.

During the Cultural Revolution, the curriculum was declared bourgeois and a new one had to be developed. In the meantime, effective teaching depended on individual ingenuity. Only those who were politically naive or obdurate used the old textbooks and were thus criticized as "bourgeois intellectuals" poisoning the young minds. The majority had learned that teaching Mao's works was the best insurance, and they became the focal point not only of political classes but also of language classes and, later, of mathematics, science, and the arts. The government did not legislate the study of Mao's thoughts into the curriculum; the atmosphere was such that many teachers did it spontaneously.

Another Revolution in Education

Reforms in education had started in late October 1967, when some schools reopened. With peace restored to the schools, efforts to reform the system became more sustained and systematic. Groups of trusted teachers and cadres went to factories and the countryside to consult the workers and peasants on the kind of graduates they needed. This method of soliciting community input and the ideas collected were very much in line with the philosophy that had prompted the Cultural Revolution in the first place. There were, of course, differences of opinion expressed on the new program. For example, some advocated eliminating physics and chemistry from the curriculum, while others argued that such information could be useful to industries and agriculture as well as national defense. Others debated whether foreign languages should be offered in the rural areas.[24] However, the population was affected by the more radical ideas put forth in the previous two years, and with the clearing of class ranks among the teachers to root out spies, many people with more conservative views remained silent. The peasants and workers voiced their practical concerns, and their opinions—which were more in tune with the dominant political ideology of the time—prevailed. Their suggestions were incorporated in the new program. When one school adopted the program, others followed. As in the early stages of the Cultural Revolution, teachers visited other schools and emulated one another's examples. Shanghai set up its Educational Reform Communication Station, and universities in Shandong held meetings to discuss and disseminate new ideas on educational reform.[25]

In the new educational program,[26] primary education was shortened from six to five years and sometimes to four; secondary schools were shortened to four or even three years. Courses considered irrelevant were removed to accommodate this new schedule, and new courses with a practical bent were introduced to prepare the graduates to meet the needs of society. History, geography, and literature were eliminated because of their lack of direct practical value. Industrial skills replaced chemistry and physics, and agricultural techniques were taught in place of biology. New texts were drafted based on the workers' and peasants' suggestions, and when the manuscripts were completed, workers and peasants were again consulted on their relevance and suitability. A considerable amount of time, sometimes as much as a quarter of the school term, was allocated to working on farms or in factories. The final examination was reduced in importance, and a system of recommendation based on the applicant's love of the proletariat was introduced. By 1968 and early 1969, with the encouragement of the central government, most schools had developed their own variant of this new educational program.

The proletariat propaganda teams proceeded with greater caution in the universities. Revolutionary committees were formed much later; for example, a committee at Beida was formed only on September 27, 1969, and one at Qinghua on September 21, 1970. Some universities accepted new students only in 1970 or 1971. The drafting of the new university curriculum followed essentially the same procedures as in high schools: through grass-roots democracy, with school personnel conferring with the community. The new curriculum and teaching techniques were introduced on an experimental basis to small groups of students recruited directly from the workplace. The committees started with short training courses of one to three months before offering regular university programs, and many began with one- or two-year programs and then expanded them to two or three years. Like the curriculum in the primary and secondary schools, the number of required courses were cut and the course content was streamlined. Anything theoretical—that is, without direct relevance to the economy—was taken out. Academic excellence was downplayed and admission was based on recommendations, which in turn were based on a person's behavior, not academic achievement. Educational structures and practices that had once put the workers and peasants at a disadvantage were eliminated.

In 1966, the Red Guards knew what they disliked about the educational system, though they did not have any cogent educational program to replace it. However, they certainly did not expect the extent to which their criticisms were carried. They had not anticipated the significant influence of workers and peasants in formulating and especially in implementing the changes. The students might have called for a closer integration of theory with practice and of the curriculum with the economy, but they certainly did not want all theoretical knowledge eliminated, nor did they want physics and chemistry replaced by industrial skills and biology by agricultural techniques. They valued working on farms and in factories, but not as such a large part of the curriculum. Although they denounced the bourgeois influence in education, their writings did not suggest that workers and peasants ought to dominate education.

Although the Gang of Four was blamed for diluting education in the 1970s, those leaders should not be held completely responsible—at least, not with the information currently available. It is true that Mao's thoughts provided the framework for educational reforms and that the government manipulated the media to create the social climate for change and disseminated information on models it approved, but it did not dictate the specific goals or the way they were to be achieved. The government adopted a policy of decentralization, whereby each school made its own decisions and formulated its own programs. Only potentially vocal opponents were exiled; the workers and peasants controlled the schools, and those who were trusted were sent to consult community opinion. Within the community, the people were so tired of turmoil that any alternative was acceptable; moreover, they could suggest educational changes that had direct and immediate benefit. To many intellectuals, it was the beginning of a new age. The pragmatic educational programs that emerged were the result of these joint consultations between the intellectuals and the proletariat, at a time when Mao's thoughts were held as the supreme truth.

It is easy to say, in retrospect, that the reforms did not work and to conclude that the intellectuals were coerced into making these proposals. At that time, however, many intellectuals did believe in the utility of consulting the proletariat. It was also difficult to foresee the abuses that would arise. Many of my respondents admitted that they were enthusiastic because it seemed that the anarchists and troublemakers had been removed and they could return to what they set out to do in mid-1966. Many had abstained from the fighting and now returned to the revolutionary fold. They plunged into the reforms with great zest. A university lecturer described his efforts at the time: "I traveled all across the country and visited the textile factories. I think, more than 60 of them. It was hard work. I spent more energy and time on my work than I am doing now." With the information gathered, he helped develop the new curriculum.

Teachers found this new curriculum challenging and needed more preparation than for the traditional one. Another teacher explained:

> For example, if you are teaching mechanics, you only need to know the theory. But if you are teaching about the weaving machine you have to know not only the theory of mechanics, but also the construction of the machine. You have to know something about the property of steel, something about the property of cotton, and a number of other things. You have to integrate your knowledge.

The results of their teaching were immediately felt, and they were appreciated by the workers and peasants. In this particular example, the graduates took up their responsibilities in the workplace with greater ease than those of the early 1960s, and the weaving machine was immediately used in production. Mid-1968 to 1970 was a period of optimism, when new programs were instituted and modifications were made.

At the twelfth plenum of the eighth Chinese Communist Party Central Committee meeting in October 1968, Liu Shaoqi was expelled from the party. This almost certainly signified the decimation of his support at the central level. By 1969, when Lin Biao declared that one phase of the Cultural Revolution had come to an end, a revolution had perhaps not occurred in the larger society, but in the schools, a revolution in education had certainly taken place. The direction of education for the next decade was set. New structures were created in the schools. Party control was replaced by workers who were once excluded even from attending schools. Young intellectuals and teachers took an active role as advisers and executives of these new holders of power, although the students remained the subordinate group and many of the original revolutionary leaders did not oversee the introduction of the new educational programs. Power had changed hands, and a program that benefited the new leaders was in place.

Conclusion of Part III

The end of the Cultural Revolution was not as abrupt nor as dramatic as its beginning. Developments in this third phase at least initially overlapped with the second one. In 1967, the growing violence and factionalism among the students had been interspersed with the government's attempts to restrain them. It was only in late 1967 that the attempts to restore peace gradually eroded popular support for the movement and dampened the momentum for factionalism. Although the government's initial call for peace did not achieve its goal, each renewed call did undermine a little of the prestige and power of the students. They could no longer claim legitimacy for their actions. Their continued fighting split student ranks and alienated the community; student revolutionaries were reduced to isolated pockets of resistance with little possibility of outside help. Reinforcements from farms and factories stopped. Soldiers arrested those who tried to get military supplies from barracks and arsenals. Red Guard liaison stations were closed. In their desperation, these students became more extreme, condemning any dissident as the enemy, which further turned public opinion against them and increased the people's desire for peace.

These developments can be seen as the demise of the student movement, but they also mobilized the workers and peasants in the peace movement. Like the first demonstrations of student unrest in 1966, the participation of workers and peasants in restoring order in the schools probably came from local initiative. The government, as in 1966, liked the idea, took it up, and publicized it. In turn, the government's call for peace struck a chord in the populace and further shaped and fanned this sentiment until the community took action to restore classes in schools. The media and the central leaders praised the workers' and peasants' political purity and intelligence, as they had once praised the students, and urged them to intervene in schools. The government also gave the movement material support, putting not only the resources in the schools but also those of the local government, factories, farms, and the Public Security Bureau at their disposal. In short, the favorable conditions that once helped launch the student movement now worked for the proletariat movement.

A revolution is not a single movement but a number of movements, acting sometimes in concert and sometimes with diverse and even opposing purposes, whose genesis can be traced to an original social cause. The proletariat movement to restore peace in the schools was a case in point. The students' prolonged infighting galvanized the workers' and peasants' resolution for peace, and they joined forces with the government. In the end, the students—like the school administration before them—were isolated, caught in the pincers of government demands and pressures from the community. They were no match for the workers and peasants, who were backed by public opinion as well as by resources in the factories, schools, and public security bureau. Deprived of their moral superiority and supplies, the student organizations disintegrated and their movement collapsed. The proletariat movement triumphed.

The new educational program emanated from a consultative process between the community and the schools. However, because of the workers' and peasants' numerical majority and, more important, because of their rising status in society and power in the schools, their suggestions carried the greatest weight. Their views did not coincide exactly with what the students had in mind, however vaguely, at the beginning of the movement. The reforms introduced, like the students' critique of the educational system, were guided by the hegemonic ideology of Mao's thoughts, yet the resulting changes were different from what the students had envisioned. Workers and peasants came to dominate in the schools, and education became more pragmatic and vocationally oriented. In this process, the changes brought about transcended what the students had anticipated and supported in their ideological fervor.

PART IV

Conclusion

CHAPTER 7

The Revolutionary Process

Observations from one case study are not a sufficient basis for making generalizations. Nevertheless, given the rarity of revolutions or social movements on such a scale as the Cultural Revolution, one would be remiss not even to attempt to do so. In this chapter, I shall hazard some observations on these events in China and relate them, where appropriate, to existing theories on revolutions. Readers should bear in mind the limitations of these observations: they are based on just one aspect (what occurred in the schools) of just one revolution (whose designation as such is still debatable).

A revolution is a complex process. It is not a single social movement but a series of inter-related movements involving different institutions and sectors of society in different regions and localities. What happens in one sector of society has ramifications in others, and events there further define developments elsewhere. The Cultural Revolution in China's schools was affected by developments in the government, in factories and on farms, in the cultural circle, and in the army. The foregoing chapters document the interactions between the schools and these institutions. In sum, the student movement, while relatively autonomous, took off with the encouragement and support of the central government, industries, and agriculture. Factionalism among the Red Guards was fed by the divisions in those sectors of society, and the student movement collapsed when their support was withdrawn. The unrest in the schools was not an isolated situation, but was closely related to what occurred in other institutions. It was a revolution within a revolution.

A revolution is often broadly defined as an attempt of a subordinate group to wrestle power from those above. This assumes just two primary groups: one on the offensive, the other on the defensive. In China's schools, however, the movement involved at least three levels of power: the administrators, the faculty members, and the students; moreover, there were divisions in each echelon. Although the antagonism between the "dominating" and "dominated" groups was most pronounced, especially at the initial stage, the factions also maneuvered against their rivals in the same echelon and against groups in other strata. What happened within China's schools was an example of different factions in the different hierarchies—administrators, teachers, support staff, and students—immersed in group politics. It is easy to envision the complexities and number of groups involved when the circle widened to include other sectors of society. The Cultural Revolution and, I believe, revolutions in general, are a complex interplay of different groups from different levels in different institutions fighting to achieve their goals, forming and strengthening alliances, and attacking and weakening their enemies.

So many groups were involved in China's revolution that even allies did not see eye to eye. Given the fluidity of the revolutionary situation and the many issues that arose, groups changed their positions and alignments in the course of the movement. Some student revolutionaries saw increasing their power base as most urgent, while for others, introducing a program of educational reforms had prior claim. The workers and peasants supported the students in the beginning but preferred stability toward the end. Each group strived to achieve its own ends; each mustered its resources and mobilized its own social movement, which was not necessarily supportive of existing ones. A revolution can thus be seen not just as a number of social movements working toward similar goals in different social sectors, but also as movements and countermovements vying for dominance. This set of circumstances was evident throughout the Cultural Revolution in China's schools. In the initial phase, it was a struggle between mobilization and containment of the student movement; in the second phase, it was a power struggle among the different groups; and toward the end, it became a tug-of-war between preoccupation with continued revolution—whatever its definition—and mobilization for peace.

Although revolutions share similarities with one another, each is also unique. A revolution as a social movement is situated within its own cultural-historical context and can be appreciated only against that background. Thus, the Maoist faction's instigation of students to rebel can be understood only by referring to Mao's communist philosophy and repeated attempts to reform the government. The initial success in so doing must be seen against the background of the organization and geographic distribution of the schools. The reaction of the Chinese students can be explained only within the Confucian tradition and their exposure to communism. Their expression of allegiance to Mao can be traced to practices of their revolutionary predecessors, and the concerns of the peasants and workers for peace toward the end must be seen against the background of their material deprivations prior to the communist takeover and the subsequent relatively low level of economic development and standard of living in the country.

Given such complexities in the internal structure of a revolutionary movement, as well as the size and regional differences of China, it is not surprising that the Cultural Revolution even in the schools was not a homogeneous movement. The Cultural Revolution in each school had its own character and time table while it shared the goals and stages of the movement at large. The movement in the universities started earlier and came to a close much later than in the secondary and primary schools. Although the patterns were usually more alike in schools from the same level of education, city, county, or province than those that differed in these respects, events in each school were different depending on the internal organization, history, personalities involved, and particular issues and power balance in the locality. Nevertheless, the movement in each school interacted with that in others; changes in one school impinged on another, which in turn sparked chain reactions elsewhere.

A revolution offers a valuable opportunity to study human beings in situations rarely available in normal circumstances; however, it is so complex and so fluid that it is impossible to provide an authentic and objective description of what occurred, let alone to capture its developments in a single theory. Social scientists are interested in explanations and in identifying patterns of relationships that can be generalized to other situations, and yet it is difficult to accomplish this when events change so rapidly and apparently haphazardly. That is perhaps one reason why comprehensive theories of revolutions are not available.

Most theories focus on the causes of revolutionary outbreaks. James Davis posits social psychological origins with the rising but unfulfilled expectations of the masses.[1] Studies of smaller-scale contemporary social movements have used network theories to explore how friendship patterns and media exposure could facilitate recruitment into protest groups.[2] Theda Skocpol offers a structural explanation for the outbreak of the French, Russian, and Chinese revolutions: they began because the ruling group was weak.[3] Mayer Zald, John McCarthy, and William Gamson hold that the rebels' economic and political resources are more important prerequisites for revolutions to occur.[4]

These theories offer partial explanations, in the sense that they could be applicable only to certain occurrences in the Cultural Revolution in China's schools. Davis's famous J curve, which showed that social unrest broke out in times of prosperity when expectations were raised but not satisfied,[5] does not explain the student vanguard's participation in the movement. The vanguard was certainly not prompted by economic concerns or even by the frustration of blocked upward mobility. Only one out of a hundred high school graduates attended a university, and the future of those university students on graduation was assured; thus, any change in the status quo only jeopardized their prospects. Instead, they were motivated by altruistic and idealistic concerns.

Nevertheless, the idea of discontent as the root of a revolution is not entirely irrelevant, even though the particular motivation attributed to the participants may be inaccurate. Students are never completely happy with school, and Chinese students—with their commitment to communism—were cognizant of the incongruities between the ideal culture represented in the curriculum and the reality within the schools. As Jacques Ellul points out, recipients have to be prepared for the propaganda so that the messages can take effect.[6] The appeals in the officially controlled media in China jelled the discontent and gave students confidence to act to make the communist ideals a reality.

Skocpol's explanation of a weak regime conducive to revolutionary outbreak is logical and generally applicable to other revolutions, but is not applicable here.[7] The Cultural Revolution in China's schools took off because of the central government's tight control of the school administration, whereby it coerced some administrators into organizing the students. In turn, the school administration's strong influence on the students spurred them into action. This official intervention has led some sinologists to label the Cultural Revolution as manipulation from above rather than as a mass movement.[8] This pervasiveness of social control in Chinese society and, subsequently, the scale of popular involvement in the movement also render the network theory—which attributes recruitment into social movements to friendship patterns—inappropriate here.[9] Without the resources and encouragement from those higher up, many students would not have taken part initially and turned against the authorities. The campus protests would probably have remained isolated occurrences and not have developed to the scale and intensity that they did. Ironically, the school administration used its strength to mobilize for its own demise.

This latter situation points to the relevance of McCarthy and Zald's and Gamson's social mobilization theory here.[10] Mao's appeals transformed the students' diffuse discontent into action, and the political and material resources made available to them allowed the movement to ignite. The developments of the Cultural Revolution were shaped by the possibilities and constraints that the social structure put on the movement. Both material and nonmaterial support allowed the movement to spread, just as their withdrawal contributed to its collapse. For example, resources such as propaganda tools and weapons allowed the students a far wider range of expression than had ever been possible. Moreover, the accessibility or withdrawal of these resources shaped the students' assessment of the situation and prompted them to take or withhold action. Many students defied the school administration only when they were certain of central government support. They observed and weighed the circumstances before criticizing the central leaders. The same careful rumination preceded attacks on the armory. Material resources therefore not only facilitate or constrain a social movement depending on how these are being used, but they also have a psychological impact on the actors shaping the decisions they take.

The material resources—or, at a more general level—the social forces that shape a social movement are many and varied. However, they do not influence a revolution in the same way in its different stages. To take the example of the Cultural Revolution, their influences waxed and waned in the course of the movement so that even the school and party administrations, which figured so prominently in the opening stages, ceased to be significant in late 1966. More important, the nature of social influences changed and shaped the revolution in diverse and even opposing ways in the different stages, promoting the revolution at one point and suppressing it at another. Some local administrations supported the students in the beginning, involved them in internecine fights in the middle phase, and restored order toward the end. Likewise, the involvement of the People's Liberation Army increased the violence and fighting in 1967, but in 1968, it was the military that restored discipline in the schools. The mass media promoted revolution through inflammatory statements in the early stages and later dampened it by calling for restraint. The thoughts of Mao unified the revolutionaries in 1966, engendered dogmatism in 1967, and then promoted restraint in 1968. In like manner, the Red Guard organization both united and divided the students in the movement. These changing roles of the different factors again point to the difficulty of capturing the dynamics of a revolution within a single and often unavoidably static theoretical framework.

Another interesting observation is that the local administrations, the media, the army, and the thoughts of Mao had been the all-encompassing state apparatus for social control, but at the beginning of the Cultural Revolution, they played a significantly different role by mobilizing the students and later involving them in internecine fights. The soliders could be used to restrain the students, but also to arm them. The media could promote either stability or change, depending on the attitudes of its controlling group. Even the hegemonic ideology of Mao's thoughts could be used to justify mobilization and, at times, to promote violence. The parts these instruments of social control played destroy the usual assumption that the state apparatus necessarily preserves the status quo; an instrument of social control can also be one of social mobilization, depending on how it is used.

Although there are numerous theories that explain the outbreak of revolutions, those explaining the dynamics of revolutionary movements are few and far between. With this consideration in mind, and recognizing the multifaceted developments of revolutions, I have focused on the displacement of goals in this analysis. Barrington Moore offers a plausible explanation for the occurrence of fighting in a revolution.[11] He holds that, with the breakdown of structural controls, there are no institutional channels for settling disputes, and thus the most effective way to do so is through force. This was certainly the case in the Cultural Revolution, but this propensity was further accentuated by the official media's promotion of Mao's thoughts and the students' commitment to his ideology. Each student considered himself or herself the legitimate revolutionary successor to Mao and the ultimate repository of truth in the interpretation of his thoughts. This dogmatism discouraged any compromise, and such convictions legitimized the infliction of punishment on dissenters. Furthermore, the involvement of the soldiers increased the amount of bloodshed, because then military weapons fell into students' hands and the use of physical force became more widespread and lethal.

Fighting for revolutionary goals was not exactly the same as fighting for one's own group interest, but the former led easily to the latter. Given the belief that one's group was the guardian of revolutionary principles, survival of the group was therefore necessary for revolutionary success. The use of force, as the only means of settling disputes, soon became the only safeguard to the security and survival of both the individual and the revolution. Fighting could not always remain on such an idealistic level; it was soon enmeshed with personal pride, and fighting for revolutionary principles became indistinguishable from occasions to settle old scores. A well-meaning revolutionary movement thus degenerated into vendettas and internecine squabbles, and no party involved could afford to be the first to abandon physical force. To do so would expose oneself to the enemies and court destruction: factionalism and internecine fights generated their own momentum, and could not be stopped. In the process, the initial goal of reforming education was delayed and compromised.

Just as there is a dearth of theories explaining the course of a revolution, there is little or no explanation offered about why a revolution comes to an end. In most studies, the question posed is why revolutions succeeded or failed, the unarticulated assumption being that the population was tired and a strong figure had emerged. Yet as the Cultural Revolution in China's schools showed, the last stage of the revolution was equally, if not more, complex than its preceding stages. The tug-of-war between a still relatively strong revolutionary momentum and the growing urge to put an end to it accounted for the Chinese government's prolonged efforts to bring the movement to an end, compared with the ease in initiating it. Like the mobilization to revolt, the demobilization was an intricate interplay of psychological and structural forces. The students' continued fighting alienated the population, which withdrew its material and nonmaterial support, thus weakening and isolating those students bent on continuing the movement. Such developments provided fertile ground for the growing movement for peace. In 1968, as in mid-1966, the government capitalized on this public opinion by encouraging the workers and peasants and providing them with the resources once left at the disposal of the revolutionaries. The conditions that successfully launched the student movement now worked for the workers and peasants' peace efforts. As a result, the revolution came to a close.

This change in the leadership of the movement accounted for the compromising of the students' revolutionary goals, and ironically, also made the movement in the schools a revolution. The touchstone of a revolution is a change in the holders of power, and the unanticipated transfer of authority from the intellectuals and party members to the proletariat made it a revolution. The central leaders who launched the movement had hoped to shake up the bureaucracy and encourage a greater faithfulness in implementing policies congruent with communist ideology. Though the students had no blueprint for educational reforms, they had agitated for shortening the years of education, streamlining the curriculum to give greater relevance to work experience, de-emphasizing grades, and more strongly emphasizing ideological training.

These suggestions and more were carried out by the workers and peasants. They did not dictate these changes, but given their power in the schools and numerical majority in the community in the suffocating social climate that still lingered after the student movement, their voices held sway. The organizational structure and climate in the schools in 1969 were different from what existed before the Cultural Revolution. The school administration was streamlined and run by committees of teachers and administrators under the guidance of the local revolutionary committee of workers, peasants, and soldiers. Thus, there was a greater degree of community initiative and participation in running the schools. The authority of the intellectuals both in pedagogy and administration was undermined, and they had been cowed by the violence and excesses of the movement. But disillusion and silence, as the government was to learn in the 1970s, were not beneficial to the running of the schools. Without cautionary advice from the educated and veteran school administrators, the workers and peasants opted for a pragmatic vocational curriculum that was not entirely beneficial in training the young. The preoccupation with applied knowledge led to the neglect of basic and theoretical studies. The abandonment of the examination system—even with all its pitfalls—and substitution of a system of recommendation for entrance into universities opened the way for corruption and abuse. The classroom climate changed; teachers had lost the respect of students and so became ineffective. The de-emphasis on academic evaluation, together with the lowly status of academics and the inordinate amount of time students spent in production work, undermined the academic climate and quality of the schools. These weaknesses in the new program, as pointed out in Chapter 6, were not evident in the late 1960s, and in any case, its evaluation is not our concern here. These comments, however, highlight the extremes to which the criticisms of education during the Cultural Revolution were taken. Not only were the student revolutionaries disappointed, but also the government's intention to create a flexible and dynamic school administration faithful to communist ideals had failed.

The developments of the Cultural Revolution in China's schools point to the difficulties of implementing radical changes and suggest that factionalism and the displacement of goals are endemic to the revolutionary process. A revolution occurs when the former holders of power are overthrown, usually through the concerted efforts of different groups sharing some general goal. Once the structures of control are dismantled, the rebels can no longer speak in generalities but must attend to their specific sources of dissatisfaction and provide remedies. Differences between the revolutionary allies thus tend to surface. Given the pervasiveness of control of the former dominant group, no one revolutionary group is likely to be able to command the situation. Each group, however, is committed to its own goals, or it would not have taken part in the revolution in the first place. With their recent experience in the efficacy of physical force, the different groups are not slow to resort to this means to assert their views. The initial success of the revolution therefore generates conditions for the outbreak of factionalism. A preoccupation with violence diverts the revolutionaries' attention from implementing and fulfilling their revolutionary programs and promises, however vague these may be. Their fighting alienates their constituents and offers an excellent opportunity for other groups not directly involved in the fighting but generally sympathetic to the revolutionary goals to gain popular support and institute their own programs. Unless the revolutionaries are a homogeneous and organized group, unless they have specific goals and a concrete program of change, or unless one group is strong enough to overpower the others and dominate the situation immediately, factionalism and the displacement of revolutionary ideals seem almost unavoidable.

Appendixes

Glossary of Chinese Names

Bo Yibo 薄一波

Cai Yiou 曹轶欧

Chen Boda 陈伯达

Chen Pixian 陈丕显

Chen Yi 陈　毅

Chi Qun 迟　群

Deng Tuo 邓　拓

Deng Xiaoping 邓小平

Fu Chongbi 傅崇碧

Guan Feng 关　锋

Hai Rui 海　瑞

Han Aijing 韩爱晶

He Long 贺　龙

Jiang Qing 江　青

Kang Sheng 康　生

Kuai Dafu 蒯大富

Kuang Yaming 匡亚明

Lei Feng 雷　锋

Li Da 李　达

Liao Mosha 廖沫沙

Lin Biao 林　彪

Liu Shaoqi 刘少奇

Lu Ping 陆　平

Mao Zedong 毛泽东

Meng He 门　合

Nie Yuanzi 聂元梓

Peng Dehuai 彭德怀

Peng Peiyun 彭佩云

Peng Zhen 彭　真

Qi Benyu 戚本禹

Tan Houlan 谭厚兰

Tao Zhu 陶　铸

Wang Hongwen 王洪文

Wang Li 王　力

Wu De 吴　德

Wu Han 吴　晗

Xia Yan 夏　衍

Xiao Wangdong 肖望东

Xie Fuzhi 谢富治

Yang Chengwu 杨成武

Yang Shangkun 杨尚昆

Yao Wenyuan 姚文元

Zhang Chunqiao 张春桥

Zhang Tixue 张体学

Zhao Ziyang 赵紫阳

Zhou Enlai 周恩来

Zhou Yang 周　扬

Zhu Shoatian 朱劭天

Chronology of the Cultural Revolution in China's Schools

Date	Mobilization	Demobilization/Containment
May 1966	- May 25, Nie Yuanzi and eight other signatories put up wall poster at Beijing University, are criticized by university administration at mass meetings.	
June	- June 2, Nie's wall poster publicized in national media; Lu Ping dismissed as president of Beijing University. Presidents and top administrators of other universities dismissed in the following months.	- June 7, workteams sent to universities.
	- Students write to *People's Daily (PD)* with suggestions for educational reforms.	
	- June 13, examination system suspended.	
	- June 18, university entrance examination stopped.	
July	- July 18, Mao returns to Beijing; workteams are withdrawn from universities the next day.	
	- Central leaders visit campuses to learn from students.	
	- Cultural revolution committees formed on some campuses.	
	- July 26, Mao swims in the Yangtze; students subsequently encouraged to "swim against the tide."	
	- Classes stopped in most schools.	

August

- Aug, 5, Mao's wall poster, "Bombard the Headquarters," put up.

- Aug. 1–12, eleventh plenum of eighth Chinese Communist Party Central Committee (CCPCC) meeting; Aug. 8, CCPCC issues sixteen-point communiqué approving students' actions.

- Aug.–Nov., eight Red Guard rallies held. The first, Aug. 18, significant because of Mao's open support by wearing red arm band. Subsequent rallies held Aug. 31, Sept. 15, Oct. 1, 18, Nov. 3, 10, 26.

- Red Guard organizations emerge across the country, sometimes as many as 70 groups on a campus of 4,000 students.

- Aug. 18, Lin Biao appeals to students to destroy old thoughts, old culture, old customs, and old habits: "Removal of Four Olds" Movement begins and lasts for about two months.

- Aug. 31, Zhou Enlai invites students to Beijing to attend rallies. "Exchange of Revolutionary Experience" begins and lasts throughout 1967.

- Large-scale distribution of Mao's works. Promotion and distribution continue throughout the movement: 80 million copies of *Selected Works*, 35 million copies of *Quotations*, and 57 million copies of *Poetry* distributed in one year.

September

- Students spread movement to farms and factories; they receive mixed reactions.

- *PD* enjoins students to struggle by reasoning, not by coercion or force.

Date	Mobilization	Demobilization/Containment
	- Sept. 7, Mao forbids workers to interfere with student movement.	
	- Sept. 15, First Headquarters (first umbrella organization of Red Guards) is established in Beijing; liaison centers established across the country.	
October–November	- Oct. 22, *PD* promotes "travel on foot, not by train," in exchange of revolutionary experience; Nov. 10, 15, 21, receptions held for those who did so.	
	- "Bloodline theory," which precluded those of nonrevolutionary backgrounds from becoming Red Guards, is denounced; Nov., this pariah group returns to campus. Campuses are further split.	
December	- Dec. 2, Liu Shaoqi denounced on joint Qinghua and Beida poster.	- CCPCC asks People's Liberation Army (PLA) to give students short-term military training, but little action is taken.
	- Dec. 4, Peng Zhen's residence raided by Red Guards. Residences of other leaders also raided.	
January 1967	- Jan. 5, eleven organizations in Shanghai seize power in government and issue "Messages to all Shanghai People." Jan. 11, move approved by government, and seizures of power in government begin. Three of nine state commissions, 30 of 40 ministries, and local government organs transfer power. Chaos ensues.	- Jan. 15, media urges workers, peasants, and cadres to return to their units.
	- Jan. 6, Liu Shaoqi criticized in person; other central leaders (e.g., He Long, Xia Wangdong) also criticized.	- Jan. 16, *PD* urges students to economize and make revolution—i.e., they should not unnecessarily damage public property in carrying out

- Jan. 14, Shanghai universities form "great unity."
- Central government asks PLA to support the left.

- their revolutions. Similar message given Feb. 9, 15, 22, May 15, June 15, 16, July 14, Aug. 26; such repetition reveals the ineffectiveness of the appeal.
- Jan. 28, *PD* emphasizes the importance of great unity—i.e., Red Guard groups should put aside their differences and cooperate with one another.
- Jan. 31, Heilongjiang forms triple-unity revolutionary committee of cadres, soldiers, and revolutionaries; this move subsequently endorsed by central government.

February

- Government calls for unity to increase strength. Red Guard Congress formed in Beijing universities and colleges.
- Students attack government departments and barracks for supplies and weapons. Soldiers told not to use force in their defense.
- Feb. 23, *PD* criticizes those who do not take an active role in the movement. This criticism contradicts other measures taken to contain the movement and again reveals the split at the central level. Conflicting central government policies contribute to factionalism among students.

- Government encourages students to return to school.
- Feb. 2, *PD* urges revolutionaries "to struggle against oneself and criticize revisionism."
- Government urges restraint and later prohibits seizures of power.
- Feb. 20, *PD* appeals to students to help in the harvest; appeal repeated Feb. 3, March 13.

Date	Mobilization	Demobilization/Containment
		- Military Commission forbids attack on the army.
		- Feb. 23, exchange of revolutionary experience outlawed.
		- Because of all these restraints put on the movement, this period often called the February Reversal of Current.
March	- Congress of middle school Red Guards formed in Beijing, augmenting the power and influence of Red Guard organizations.	- March 7, middle and primary schools told to resume classes and make revolution; PLA is sent into schools to provide military training.
		- Repeated appeals to masses not to steal trucks and other supplies or to wantonly destroy public property.
April–May	- Red Guards attack soldiers but PLA is asked by the government not to use force.	- May 22, *PD* asks revolutionaries to stop fighting.
	- More rallies and meetings take place. Life-size statues of Mao appear on campuses.	

	- More alliances are formed among Red Guards.
June	- Messages in media take on more aggressive note. June 2, PD urges revolutionaries to "hound the enemies to the end." - PD publishes Mao's article on correct handling of contradictions among the people. - June 24, five national student leaders express support for great unity.
July	- July 22, Jiang Qing makes statement, "Attack with words, defend with force." - Clashes occur across the country and intensify. Emissaries from central government—Xie Fuzhi and Wang Li—ambushed in Wuhan. The military has to be mobilized to release them. - By July, Red Guards have made peace, albeit short-lived, in four universities in Heilongjiang, seven universities in Shandong, and 130 middle schools in Beijing. - Classes resume in two universities in Mongolia, three in Xian, four in Heilongjiang, and five in Tienjin; probably only one-third of universities in these areas reopened.
August	- Rallies and meetings continue across the country. Commemorations held Aug. 5 for Mao's wall poster "Bombard the Headquarters," and Aug. 18 for the first Red Guard rally. - Red Flag article urges revolutionaries to "completely smash bourgeois headquarters and ferret out enemies in the army," a departure from the official position that civilians should not interfere in army politics.

Date	Mobilization	Demobilization/Containment
September– December		– Sept. 5, Jiang Qing repudiates attacks with force.
		– More newspaper articles urge revolutionaries to help in production (Sept. 17, 24), criticize oneself and combat self-interest (Oct. 6, Dec. 14), resume classes (Oct. 17, 25), and integrate with the cadres to achieve great unity (Oct. 17, Nov. 16).
		– By Sept., most primary schools and some high schools have reopened.
		– Nov., *PD* begins a series on educational reforms that deal with problems faced by the schools that reopened.
		– Media carry messages of Mao encouraging peace. Study sessions of Mao's thoughts are organized in schools and by central government and Red Guards. Activists in the study of Mao's thoughts are honored.

January–February 1968	– Fights continue among Red Guards but become more sporadic.
	– Media continue to urge restraint.
	– Farmers and factory workers return to work; students are isolated.
	– Revolutionary committees begin to be formed.
March	– Rally commemorates March 7 Directive, by which 385 schools and universities in Beijing have received military training.
April–June	– Study of Mao's thoughts further encouraged; May 8, activists in the study of Mao's thoughts meet.
	– Pressure put on rival groups to make peace.
	– By June, 26 revolutionary committees have been formed in the 29 provinces, municipalities, and autonomous regions.

Date	Mobilization	Demobilization/Containment
July		– Appeals made to graduates to go where country needs them most.
		– July 21, *PD* publicizes experience of Shanghai Machine Tools Plant in training technicians and engineers.
		– Proletariat propaganda team sent to Qinghua University on July 27. Similar teams were sent to some schools across the country in the next two months.
August		– Aug. 5, Mao sends gift of mangoes to proletariat propaganda team at Qinghua, thus raising the status of the proletariat. *Red Flag* reiterates that "the working class must exercise leadership in everything."
		– Aug. 27, Mao gives directive that proletariat propaganda teams are to remain in schools.
September 1968– April 1969		– Escalation of educational reforms. Alternatives are discussed and community

opinions sought. New school curricula are drafted and programs experimented with.

October 1968

- Oct. 13–31, twelfth plenum of eighth CCPCC meeting; Liu Shaoqi expelled from party.

December

- By Dec., job assignments given to high school and university classes of 1966, 1967, and 1968.

April 1969

- April 1–24, Ninth Party Congress is held, at which Lin Biao declares that the Cultural Revolution is coming to an end.

Notes

Introduction

1. Ahn Byung-joon, *Chinese Politics and the Cultural Revolution. Dynamics of Policy Processes* (Seattle: University of Washington Press, 1976).

2. Sally Borthwick, *Education and Social Change in China: The Beginning of the Modern Era* (Stanford: Hoover Institution Press, 1983).

3. *Achievement of Education in China, 1949–1983* (Beijing: People's Education Press, 1985), pp. 22–23.

4. *Zhongguo Jiaoyu Nienjian 1949–1981 [Annals of Chinese Education, 1949–1981] (Beijing: Zhongguo Baike Chuanshu Chubanshe, 1984).*

5. The concept was taken from John W. Meyer and W. Richard Scott, *Organizational Environments: Ritual and Rationality* (Beverley Hills, Calif.: Sage Publications, 1983), pp. 39–42.

6. *Achievement of Education*, pp. 30–31.

7. Julia Kwong, *Chinese Education in Transition: Prelude to the Cultural Revolution* (Montreal: McGill-Queen's University Press, 1979), pp. 81–106.

8. Julia Kwong, "The Educational Experiment of the Great Leap Forward, 1958–59: Its Inherent Contradictions," *Comparative Education Review* 23 (1979): 443–55.

9. Harry Harding, *Organizing China: The Problem of Bureaucracy, 1949–1976* (Stanford: Stanford University Press, 1981).

10. Ahn, *Chinese Politics*; Harding, *Organizing China*.

11. Craig Deitrich, *People's China: A Brief History* (New York: Oxford University Press, 1986).

12. Lowell Dittmer, *Lui Shao-chi and the Chinese Cultural Revolution* (Berkeley: University of California Press, 1974).
13. *People's Daily*, November 2, 3, 1968.
14. *Resolution on CPC History (1949–81)* (Beijing: Foreign Languages Press, 1981).
15. *Achievement of Education*, pp. 22–23.

Chapter 1

1. "Resolution on Certain Questions in the History of Our Party Since the Founding of the People's Republic of China," in *Resolution on CPC History (1949–81)* (Beijing: Foreign Languages Press, 1981), p. 35.
2. *People's Daily*, June 2, 1966, p. 1.
3. Victor Nee, *The Cultural Revolution in Peking University* (New York: Monthly Review Press, 1969); *People's Daily*, July 19, 1966, p. 3.
4. Richard Baum and Frederick C. Tiewes, *Ssu-ching: The Socialist Education Movement of 1962–1966* (Berkeley: Center for Chinese Studies, University of California, 1968).
5. Gary T. Marx, "Thoughts on a Neglected Category of Social Movement Participation: The Agent Provocateur and the Informant," *American Journal of Sociology* 80 (1974): 402–42.
6. Merle D. Goldman, *China's Intellectuals: Advise and Dissent* (Cambridge, Mass.: Harvard University Press, 1981), p. 27.
7. *People's Daily*, May 17, 1967, reprinted the directive on its anniversary.
8. *People's Daily*, June 5, 1966.
9. Respondent's account.
10. Stanley Rosen, *Red Guard Factionalism and the Cultural Revolution in Guangzhou* (Boulder: Westview Press, 1982), pp. 119–20.
11. Theda Skocpol, *States and Social Revolutions* (Cambridge, England: Cambridge University Press, 1979).
12. Jacques Ellul, *Autopsy of Revolution* (New York: Knopf, 1971).
13. *Resolution on CPC History (1949–81)* (Beijing: Foreign Languages Press, 1981).
14. Susan Shirk, *Competitive Comrades: Career Incentives and Student Strategies in China* (Berkeley: University of California Press, 1982), chap. 4.
15. James C. Davis, "Towards a Theory of Revolution," *American Sociological Review* 27 (1962): 15–19; Ted Gurr, *Why Men Rebel* (Princeton: Princeton University Press, 1970).
16. *Achievement of Education in China, 1949–1983* (Beijing: People's Education Press, 1985), pp. 22–23.

17. Jonathan Unger, *Education Under Mao: Class and Competition in Canton Schools, 1960–1980* (New York: Columbia University Press, 1982).

18. Jacques Ellul, *Propaganda: The Formation of Men's Attitudes* (New York: Knopf, 1965).

19. Julia Kwong, *Chinese Education in Transition: Prelude to the Cultural Revolution* (Montreal: McGill-Queen's University Press, 1979), p. 126.

20. Shirk, *Competitive Comrades*, p. 55.

21. Ann Thurstone, "Victims of China's Cultural Revolution: The Invisible Wounds," pts. 1 and 2, *Pacific Affairs* 57, no. 4 (1984): 599–620, and 58, no. 1 (1985): 4–27.

22. New China News Agency (NCNA), June 5, 1986.

23. Charles P. Cell, *Revolution at Work—Mobilization Campaign in China* (New York: Academic Press, 1977).

24. Sam Ginsburg, *My First Sixty Years in China* (Beijing: New World Press, 1982), p. 281.

25. *People's Daily*, June 9, 1966; *Yangcheng Wenbao (YCWB)*, July 3, 1966.

26. *People's Daily*, June 6, 19, 20, July 12, 13, 1966, p. 1.

27. Lowell Dittmer, *Liu Shao-chi and the Chinese Cultural Revolution* (Berkeley: University of California Press, 1974), p. 79.

28. *People's Daily*, June 19, 1966, p. 1.

29. Ibid.

30. *Survey of China Mainland Press (SCMP)* 3724 (June 23, 1966): 2–13; *People's Daily*, June 19, 1966.

31. *SCMP* 3724: 2–13.

32. *YCWB*, June 27, 1966; *People's Daily*, June 20.

33. Ahn Byung-joon, *Chinese Politics and the Cultural Revolution. Dynamics of Policy Processes* (Seattle: University of Washington, 1976).

34. Harry Harding, *Organizing China: The Problem of Bureaucracy, 1949–1976* (Stanford: Stanford University Press, 1981), p. 227; Joan Robinson, *The Cultural Revolution in China* (London: Penguin, 1969), p. 96; Ahn, *Chinese Politics*, p. 216; *Red Flag Bulletin*, April 4, 1967, p. 2.

35. *People's Daily*, June 24, 1966.

36. *Red Flag Bulletin*, January 22, 1967.

37. Neale Hunter, *Shanghai Journal: An Eyewitness Account of the Cultural Revolution* (New York: Praeger, 1969), p. 46; J. Unger, *Education Under Mao*, p. 115.

38. *People's Daily*, May 18, 1967.

39. *Middle School War Gazette*, July 12, 1967.

40. *People's Daily*, June 20, 1966.

41. Ibid., March 18, 1967.

Chapter 2

1. *People's Daily*, July 3, 9, 29, 1966.

2. In August, evening newspaper reports carried incendiary messages. For example, an article in the August 12, 1966, *People's Daily* read, "Masses in east, south central, and southwest China courageously carry the great Proletarian Revolution to the end"; another on August 14 read, "Smash the education system"; on August 25, the lead sentence of an article read, "Take the iron broom of the revolution, sweep away all old customs."

3. Theda Skocpol, *States and Social Revolutions* (Cambridge, England: Cambridge University Press, 1979).

4. "CCP Central Committee's Decision on the Great Proletarian Cultural Revolution," in *The Great Cultural Revolution in China* (Hong Kong: Asia Research Centre, 1968), p. 398.

5. *People's Daily*, August 9, 1966.

6. Ibid.

7. Ibid., August 10, 1966.

8. Hong Yung Lee, *The Politics of the Chinese Cultural Revolution: A Case Study* (Berkeley: University of California Press, 1978), p. 85.

9. *People's Daily*, August 12, 1966.

10. Ibid., August 18, 1966.

11. Victor Nee, *The Cultural Revolution in Peking University* (New York: Monthly Review Press, 1969), p. 72.

12. *People's Daily*, August 19, September 1, October 15, 19, November 25, 1966.

13. Ibid., August 20, 1966.

14. Ibid., August 19, 1966.

15. *Yangcheng Wenbao (YCWB)*, September 3, August 26, 1966.

16. Ibid.

17. *Achievement of Education in China, 1949–1983* (Beijing: People's Education Press, 1985), pp. 22–23.

18. Jonathan Unger, *Education Under Mao: Class and Competition in Canton Schools, 1960–1980* (New York: Columbia University Press, 1982), p. 118.

19. Ross Terrill, *Mao: A Biography* (New York: Harper and Row, 1981), p. 326.

20. Jean Esmein, *The Chinese Cultural Revolution* (New York: Anchor, 1973), p. 123.

21. David Milton and Nancy Dale Milton, *The Wind Will Not Subside* (New York: Pantheon, 1976), p. 165.

22. Esmein, *Chinese Cultural Revolution*.

23. Ibid., p. 126.

24. *Survey of China Mainland Press (SCMP)* 3774 (September 6, 1966): 9, 3780 (September 14, 1966): 20; *Red Guard Papers*, September 23, 1966.

25. *Red Guard Bulletin*, n.d.

26. William Hinton, *Hundred Day War: The Cultural Revolution in Tsinghua University* (New York: Monthly Review Press, 1972), p. 126.

27. *People's Daily*, June 8, 1966.

28. Ibid., August 19, 1966; other accounts of Red Guard activities are reported in the August 25 issue.

29. Ibid., August 23, 25, 1966, p. 1.

30. *YCWB*, August 25, 1966.

31. *People's Daily,* August 12, 25, 1966, p. 2; *Wen Hui Bao (WHB)* (Shanghai), September 1966, October 27, p. 2.

32. *Da Gung Bao* (Hong Kong), August 31, 1966; *YCWB*, August 24, 1966.

33. *WHB*, November 19, 21, 1966; New China News Agency (NCNA), September 12, 1966; *People's Daily*, November 4, 1966, p. 6.

34. *WHB*, November 19, 1966.

35. Lowell Dittmer, *Liu Shao-chi and the Chinese Cultural Revolution* (Berkeley: University of California Press, 1974), p. 95.

36. *People's Daily*, October 8, 1966.

37. Ibid., October 10, 1966.

38. Ibid., October 25, 29, 1966.

39. Ibid., September 9, 1966.

40. NCNA, November 24, 1986.

41. *SCMP* 3787 (September 13, 1966): 20.

42. *People's Daily*, October 15, 1966.

43. Ibid., October 22, November 3, 8, 16, 1966.

44. *WHB*, November 19, 1966; *People's Daily*, December 22, 1966, p. 1.

45. *WHB*, November 19, 21, 1966; NCNA, September 12, 1966; *People's Daily*, October 9, November 22, 1966.

46. *People's Daily*, September 7, 1966.

47. Ibid., August 10, 11, 12, 1966.

48. John D. McCarthy and Mayer N. Zald, "Resource Mobilization and Social Movements: A Partial Theory," *American Journal of Sociology* 82 (1977): 1212–41.

49. Tom Bottomore, *Political Sociology* (London: Hutchinson, 1983), p. 95.

Chapter 3

1. Clarence Crane Brinton, *The Anatomy of Revolution* (New York, W. W. Norton, 1938).

2. Susan Shirk, *Competitive Comrades: Career Incentives and Student Strategies in China* (Berkeley: University of California Press, 1982), p. 151.

3. J. Kwong, "Is Everyone Equal Before the System of Grades?" *British Journal of Sociology* 34, no. 1 (1983): 93–108.

4. Hong Yung Lee, *The Politics of the Chinese Cultural Revolution: A Case Study* (Berkeley: University of California Press, 1978), p. 81.

5. Neale Hunter, *Shanghai Journal: An Eyewitness Account of the Cultural Revolution* (New York: Praeger, 1969), p. 23.

6. Jean Daubier, *History of the Chinese Cultural Revolution* (New York: Vintage, 1974), pp. 103–5.

7. Stanley Rosen, *Red Guard Factionalism and the Cultural Revolution in Guangzhou* (Boulder: Westview Press, 1982), pp. 127–28.

8. *Survey of China Mainland Press (SCMP)* 3883 (February 20, 1967): 42–46; *People's Daily*, February 26, 1967.

9. William Hinton, *Hundred Day War: The Cultural Revolution at Tsinghua University* (New York: Monthly Review Press, 1972), p. 239.

10. Ibid.

11. Ken Ling, *The Revenge of Heaven* (New York: G. P. Putnam's Sons, 1972), p. 131.

12. *People's Daily*, December 26, 1967.

13. Ibid., February 2, 1967.

14. Ibid., September 14, 1966; May 2, 3, December 27, 1967.

15. Ibid., September 8, 22, October 22, 24, November 17, 18, December 12, 1966; March 16, December 9, 31, 1967; March 5, May 29, 30, 31; June 1, 2, 3, 1968.

16. Ibid., April 30, 1967.

17. Ibid., December 30, 1967.

18. Ibid., May 17, August 6, 19, 1967.

19. For example, see Helen F. Siu and Zelda Stern, *Mao's Harvest: Voices from China's New Generation* (New York: Oxford University Press, 1983), and Lu Xinhua et al., *The Wounded: New Stories of the Cultural Revolution, 1977–78* (Hong Kong: Joint Publishing Company, 1979).

20. *People's Daily*, October 27, 1966.

21. Daubier, *History*, p. 110; David Milton and Nancy Dale Milton, *The Wind Will Not Subside* (New York: Pantheon, 1976), p. 278.

22. *April 22 Bulletin*, May 29, 1968.

23. Mao Zedong, "Report on an Investigation of the Peasant Movement in Hunan, March 1927," in *Selected Readings from the Work of Mao Tse-tung* (Beijing: Foreign Languages Press, 1967), pp. 20–32; William Hinton, *Fanshen: A Documentary of Revolution in a Chinese Village* (New York: Vintage Books, 1966).

24. Hunter, *Shanghai Journal*, p. 90.

25. Ibid., p. 223.

26. Ling, *Revenge of Heaven*, p. 72.

27. *Red Guard Rebellion*, n.d., p. 88.

28. Ling, *Revenge of Heaven*, p. 94.

Chapter 4

1. *People's Daily*, August 4, 1966; *Survey of China Mainland Press (SCMP)* 3491 (May 18, 1967) 4–9.

2. *People's Daily*, February 8, 1967.

3. *SCMP* 4262 (September 20, 1968): 5.

4. *People's Daily*, November 17, 1966.

5. Julia Kwong, *Chinese Education in Transition: Prelude to the Cultural Revolution* (Montreal: McGill-Queen's University Press, 1979), p. 157.

6. *South Guangdong Survey*, no. 3 (October 1, 1967).

7. Jean Esmein, *The Chinese Cultural Revolution* (New York: Anchor, 1973), p. 119.

8. Ken Ling, *The Revenge of Heaven* (New York: G. P. Putnam's Sons, 1972), p. 141.

9. William Hinton, *Hundred Day War: The Cultural Revolution at Tsinghua University* (New York: Monthly Review Press, 1972); *Jingganshan*, no. 11 (January 1967).

10. Hong Yung Lee, *The Politics of the Chinese Cultural Revolution: A Case Study* (Berkeley: University of California Press, 1978), p. 127.

11. *Zhongda War Gazette*, March 1, 1968, p. 2.

12. *Red Guard Rebellion*, n.d., p. 300.

13. *SCMP* 4008 (August 24, 1967): 15.

14. Thomas W. Robinson, "The Wuhan Incident: Local Strife and Provincial Rebellion During the Cultural Revolution," *China Quarterly* 47 (1971): 413–38.

15. Ibid.

16. *People's Daily*, January 5, 1967.

17. *Canton Red Flag*, no. 2, 1967.

18. Harry Harding, *Organizing China: The Problem of Bureaucracy, 1949–1976* (Stanford: Stanford University Press, 1981), p. 251.

19. *People's Daily*, January 10–15, 20, 1967.

20. Robinson, "Wuhan Incident," p. 213.

21. Lee, *Politics*, pp. 163–66.

22. Stanley Rosen, *Red Guard Factionalism and the Cultural Revolution in Guangzhou* (Boulder: Westview Press, 1982), p. 280.

23. *Steel August 1*, August 8, 1967.

24. *SCMP* 4029 (September 27, 1967), 3941 (May 18, 1967).

25. *People's Daily*, January 20, 1967.

26. Harding, *Organizing China*, p. 269.

27. Esmein, *Chinese Cultural Revolution*, p. 125; Jean Daubier, *History of the Chinese Cultural Revolution* (New York: Vintage, 1974), p. 136.

28. *Steel August 1*, October 15, 1967.

29. *Zhongda Combat News*, no. 63, September 22, 1967.

30. *East Wind Sanshui*, February 16, 1968, pp. 4–8; *Guangzhou Red Guard*, February 10, 1967.

31. Esmein, *Chinese Cultural Revolution*, p. 197.

32. *Liaoning Combat News*, September 6, 1967.

33. Ibid.

34. Hinton, *Hundred Day War*, p. 114.

35. *SCMP* 4043 (October 18, 1967): 15–19.

36. Ibid. 3941: 4–12.

37. Ibid.

38. *SCMP* 4064 (November 21, 1967): 1–9.

39. *SCMP* 4011 (August 29, 1967): 11–13; *Red Flag Workers*, September 29, 1967, pp. 12–14.

40. *SCMP* 4265 (September 25, 1968): 6.

41. Daubier, *History*, p. 190.

42. Esmein, *Chinese Cultural Revolution*, p. 229.

43. An account from a respondent.

44. *SCMP* 4076 (December 8, 1967): pp. 10–16, 4009 (August 25, 1967), 4219 (July 17, 1968): 1–3.

45. Robinson, "Wuhan Incident," p. 423; *People's Daily*, January 28, 1968.

46. *SCMP* 4011: 11–13, 4071 (November 25, 1967): 7; *People's Daily*, February 28, 1967.

47. Livio Maiten, *Party, Army, and Masses in China* (London: New Left Review, 1976), p. 183.

48. Hinton, *Hundred Day War*.

49. *SCMP* 4040 (October 12, 1967): 11.

50. Daubier, *History*, p. 193.

51. *SCMP* 4265: 6.

52. Ibid. 4026 (September 22, 1967): 1.

53. Ibid. 4275 (September 18, 1968): 11.

54. Ibid. 4202 (June 20, 1968): 1–3.

55. Barrington Moore, *Injustice: The Social Bases of Obedience and Revolt* (New York: Pantheon Books, 1978).

Chapter 5

1. *Survey of China Mainland Press (SCMP)* 4262 (September 20, 1968), p. 2.

2. *People's Daily*, January 23, 1967.

3. Alexander Eckstein, *Quantitative Measures of China's Economic Output* (Ann Arbor: University of Michigan Press, 1980), p. 191.

4. Ibid.

5. *SCMP* 4243 (July 10, 1968): 1; Jean Daubier, *History of the Chinese Cultural Revolution* (New York: Vintage, 1974), p. 209; Anthony Grey, *Hostage in Peking* (London: Michael Joseph, 1970).

6. Jules Archer, *Chou En-Lai* (New York: Hawthorn Books, 1973).

7. *Guangming Ribao*, December 1, 1984, p. 3.

8. *People's Daily*, September 5, 1966.

9. Ibid., January 30, 1967.

10. Harry Harding, *Organizing China: The Problem of Bureaucracy, 1949–1976* (Stanford: Stanford University Press, 1981); p. 259.

11. *People's Daily*, January 16, 1967.

12. Ibid., March 16, 1967.

13. Neale Hunter, *Shanghai Journal: An Eyewitness Account of the Cultural Revolution* (New York: Praeger, 1969), p. 206; *People's Daily*, January 30, 1967, p. 3.

14. Hunter, *Shanghai Journal*, p. 214.

15. *SCMP* 4011 (August 29, 1967): 1–6, quoted in Thomas W. Robinson, *The Cultural Revolution in China* (Berkeley: University of California Press, 1971), p. 238. For a detailed analysis of "great unity" campaign, see Hong Yung Lee, *The Politics of the Chinese Cultural Revolution: A Case Study* (Berkeley: University of California Press, 1978), pp. 151–57.

16. Gordon A. Bennett and Ronald N. Montaperto, *Red Guard: The Political Biography of Dai Hsiao-ai* (Garden City, N.Y.: Anchor, 1972), p. 192.

17. Reported in *People's Daily*, August 16, 1967.

18. Stuart Schram, *Mao Tse-tung Unrehearsed: Talks and Letters, 1956–71.* (London: Penguin, 1974), p. 265.

19. Daubier, *History*, p. 146.

20. Ibid.

21. *People's Daily*, June 7, 1968. For another example, see *People's Daily*, April 13, 1967.

22. *People's Daily*, June 24, 1967.

23. Ibid., March 4, 1968.

24. *SCMP* 4108 (January 26, 1968): 4–5.

25. Ken Ling, *The Revenge of Heaven* (New York: G. P. Putnam's Sons, 1972), p. 131.

26. *People's Daily*, January 24, March 3, 27, 1967.

27. Ibid., January 20, 1968.

28. Ibid., April 13, June 15, 19, 1967.

29. Ibid., July 5, October 23, 1967.

30. Ibid., September 22, 1967.

31. *Red Guard Publications*, vol. 20, document no. 6743.

32. *People's Daily*, September 22, 1967. See also *Wen-Hui Bao* (Shanghai), March 2, 1968, for a description of the difficulties the schools encountered.

33. *Spring Thunder* (Beijing), April 13, 1967.

34. *People's Daily*, October 23, 1967.

35. *Red Flag Bulletin*, July 8, 1967. The schedule of Peking Aeronautic Institute reported in *People's Daily*, July 5, 1967, was similar.

36. *People's Daily*, July 19, 1967.

37. Ibid., February 8, 16, April 26, 1967; January 5, 1968.

38. Ibid., January 20, December 15, 1967.

39. Ibid., February 26, December 15, 1967; September 12, 1969.

40. Jean Esmein, *The Chinese Cultural Revolution* (New York: Anchor, 1973), p. 147.

41. *People's Daily*, December 6, 1967.

42. Ling, *Revenge of Heaven*, pp. 179–84.

43. *People's Daily*, September 12, 1967.

44. Ibid., May 10, 1968.

45. William Hinton, *Hundred Day War: The Cultural Revolution at Tsinghua University* (New York: Monthly Review Press, 1972), pp. 226–27.

46. Daubier, *History*, p. 154.

47. *April 22 Bulletin*, no. 6, May 29, 1968.

48. Daubier, *History*, p. 154; Jean Esmein, *Chinese Cultural Revolution*, pp. 234–35; Chien Yu-shen, *China's Fading Revolution: Army Dissent and Military Divisions* (Hong Kong: Centre of Contemporary Chinese Studies, 1969), pp. 148–51.

49. *SCMP* 4009 (August 25, 1967): 1–5.

50. *Jingganshan*, nos. 9, 10, January 11, 1967.

51. *People's Daily*, February 4, 1967.

52. Ibid., November 13, 1967.

53. Ibid. It is interesting to note that the directive was not widely reported until October and November.

54. Ibid., January 24, 1968.
55. Ibid., March 7, 1968.
56. Ibid., March 4, 1968.
57. Esmein, *Chinese Cultural Revolution*, p. 69.
58. *Education Revolution*, March 22, 1967.
59. *Special Bulletin of June 6 Bloodshed.*
60. *People's Daily*, June 21, 1968.
61. *SCMP* 4012 (August 31, 1967): 1–3.
62. Ibid. Similar incidents of attacks on the People's Liberation Army were reported in *SCMP* 4215 (June 25, 1968): 10–11.
63. *People's Daily*, April 28, 29, 1967.
64. Ibid., January 20, 21, 1968.

Chapter 6

1. *People's Daily*, January 20, 23, 1967.
2. Ibid., July 12, 1967.
3. Ibid., November 14, 17, 1967.
4. *People's Daily*, May 9, June 22, 1968; *Wen Hui Bao* (Shanghai), May 6, 1968.
5. For sixteen days, each issue of the *People's Daily* contained a series of articles that addressed the issue of workers and peasants running the schools.
6. According to *Survey of China Mainland Press* (*SCMP*) 4113 (February 7, 1968), revolutionary committees were formed in thirteen provinces, four municipalities, and two autonomous regions.
7. *Guangming Ribao*, January 26, 1981, p. 2.
8. Ellis Joffe, *Party and Army: Professional and Political Control in China, 1949–64* (Cambridge, Mass.: East Asia Research Center, Harvard University, 1965), p. 153.
9. William Hinton, *Hundred Day War: The Cultural Revolution at Tsinghua University* (New York: Monthly Review Press, 1972).
10. *People's Daily*, September 15, 1968.
11. Ibid., August 26, 27, 1968.
12. Hinton, *Hundred Day War*, pp. 226–27.
13. *People's Daily*, July 27, August 21, 1968.
14. Ibid., August 27, October 9, 11, 1968.
15. Ibid.
16. Ibid., September 11, 1968.
17. Hinton, *Hundred Day War*, p. 220.

18. Sam Ginsburg, *My First Sixty Years in China* (Beijing: New World Press, 1982), p. 275.

19. *People's Daily*, September 11, 1968.

20. Ibid., September 4, 1968.

21. Ibid., August 13, 1968.

22. *Frontier War Gazette*, n.d.; see also *SCMP* 4223 (July 23, 1968): 1–3.

23. *The People's Daily* (July 9, 16, 19, 22, 24, August 7, 17, 21, 1968), carried articles lauding students who went to places where their skills were most required. For statistics, see Thomas P. Bernstein, *Up to the Mountains and Down to the Villages: The Transfer of Youth from Urban to Rural China* (New Haven: Yale University Press, 1977), p. 32.

24. *People's Daily*, June 24, September 22, 1969.

25. *Education Revolution*, June 9, 1967; *People's Daily*, October 11, 1969.

26. For details, see Jonathan Unger, *Education Under Mao: Class and Competition in Canton Schools, 1960–1980* (New York: Columbia University Press, 1982), chap. 7.

Chapter 7

1. James C. Davis, "Towards a Theory of Revolution," *American Sociological Review* 27 (1962): 15–19.

2. Kenneth E. Hornback, "Towards a Theory of Involvement Propensity for Collective Behavior," *Sociological Focus* 4 (1971): 61–71.

3. Theda Skocpol, *States and Social Revolutions* (Cambridge, England: Cambridge University Press, 1979).

4. William A. Gamson, *The Strategy of Social Protest* (Homewood, Ill.: The Dorsey Press, 1975): John D. McCarthy and Mayer N. Zald, "Resource Mobilization and Social Movements: A Partial Theory," *American Journal of Sociology* 82 (1977): 1212–41.

5. Davis, "Theory of Revolution."

6. Jacques Ellul, *Propaganda: The Formation of Men's Attitudes* (New York: Knopf, 1965).

7. Skocpol, *States and Social Revolutions*.

8. Ahn Byung-joon. *Chinese Politics and the Cultural Revolution. Dynamics of Policy Processes* (Seattle: University of Washington Press, 1976).

9. Hornback, "Theory of Involvement Propensity."

10. Gamson, *Strategy of Social Protest*; McCarthy and Zald, "Resource Mobilization."

11. Barrington Moore, *Injustice: The Social Bases of Obedience and Revolt* (New York: Pantheon Books: 1978).

Bibliography

I. Education and Social Organization in China

Achievement of Education in China, 1949–1983. Beijing: People's Education Press, 1985.

Baum, Richard, and Frederick C. Tiewes, *Ssu-ching: The Socialist Education Movement of 1962–1966*. Berkeley: Center for Chinese Studies, University of California, 1968.

Bernstein, Thomas P. *Up to the Mountains and Down to the Villages: The Transfer of Youth from Urban to Rural China*. New Haven: Yale University Press, 1977.

Borthwick, Sally. *Education and Social Change in China: The Beginnings of the Modern Era*. Stanford: Hoover Institution Press, 1983.

Cell, Charles P. *Revolution at Work—Mobilization Campaign in China*. New York: Academic Press, 1977.

Ch'en, Theodore. *The Maoist Educational Revolution*. New York: Praeger, 1974.

Cheng, H. *Higher Education in China*. Hong Kong: Union Research Institute, 1972.

Chesneaux, Jean. *China: The People's Republic, 1949–1976*. New York: Pantheon Books, 1979.

Chien, Yu-shen. *China's Fading Revolution: Army Dissent and Military Divisions*. Hong Kong: Centre of Contemporary Chinese Studies, 1969.

Cleverley, John. *The Schooling of China: Tradition and Modernity in Chinese Education*. Sydney: Allen and Unwin, 1985.

Collier, John, and Elsie Collier. *China's Socialist Revolution*. New York: Monthly Review Press, 1974.

Deitrich, Craig. *People's China: A Brief History*. New York: Oxford University Press, 1986.

Eckstein, Alexander. *China's Economic Revolution*. Cambridge, England: Cambridge University Press, 1977.

————. *Quantitative Measures of China's Economic Output*. Ann Arbor: University of Michigan Press, 1980.

Fraser, Stewart E., ed. *Education and Communism in China*. London: Pall Mall, 1971.

Ginsburg, Sam. *My First Sixty Years in China*. Beijing: New World Press, 1982.

Gold, Thomas. "Back to the City: The Return of Shanghai Educated Youth." *China Quarterly* 84 (1980): 755–70.

Goldman, Merle D. *China's Intellectuals: Advise and Dissent*. Cambridge, Mass.: Harvard University Press, 1981.

Harding, Harry. *Organizing China: The Problem of Bureaucracy, 1949–1976*. Stanford: Stanford University Press, 1981.

Hawkins, John N. *Education Theory in the People's Republic of China*. Hawaii: University of Hawaii Press, 1971.

Hinton, William. *Fanshen: A Documentary of Revolution in a Chinese Village*. New York: Vintage Books, 1966.

Jiaoyu Daishiji 1942–1982 [Record of Important Events in Education, 1942–1982]. Beijing: Jiaoyu Kexue Chubanshe, 1984.

Joffe, Ellis. *Party and Army: Professional and Political Control in China, 1949–64*. Cambridge, Mass.: East Asia Research Center, Harvard University, 1965.

Kwong, Julia. *Chinese Education in Transition: Prelude to the Cultural Revolution*. Montreal: McGill-Queen's University Press, 1979.

————. "The Educational Experiment of the Great Leap Forward, 1958–59: Its Inherent Contradictions." *Comparative Education Review* 23 (1979): 433–55.

————. "Is Everyone Equal Before the System of Grades?" *British Journal of Sociology* 34, no.1 (1983): 93–108.

Lofstedt, Jan-Ingvar. *Chinese Educational Policy*. Atlantic Highlands, N.J.: Humanities Press, 1980.

Maiten, Livio. *Party, Army, and Masses in China*. London: New Left Review, 1976.

Orleans, Leo A. *Professional Manpower and Education in Communist China*. Washington: National Science Foundation, 1960.

————. *Every Fifth Child: The Population of China*. Stanford: Stanford University Press, 1972.

Pepper, Suzanne. *China's Universities*. Ann Arbor: Center for Chinese Studies, 1984.

Price, R. F. *Education in Communist China*. New York: Praeger, 1970.

Priestley, K. E. *Education in China*. Hong Kong: Dragon Fly Books, 1961.

Seybolt, Peter. *Revolutionary Education in China*. White Plains, N.Y.: International Arts and Sciences Press, 1973.

Shirk, Susan. *Competitive Comrades: Career Incentive and Student Strategies in China.* Berkeley: University of California Press, 1982.

Siu, Helen F., and Zelda Stern. *Mao's Harvest: Voices from China's New Generation.* New York: Oxford University Press, 1983.

Skinner, G. William, and Edwin Winkler. "Compliance Succession in Rural China," in Amitai Etzioni, ed., *A Sociological Reader of Complex Organizations.* New York: Rinehart and Winston: 1969.

Terrill, Ross. *Mao: A Biography.* New York: Harper and Row, 1981.

Tsang Chiu-sam. *Society, Schools, and Progress in China.* Oxford: Pergamon, 1968.

Unger, Jonathan. *Education Under Mao: Class and Competition in Canton Schools, 1960–1980.* New York: Columbia University Press, 1982.

Zhongguo Jiaoyu Nienjian 1949-81 [Annals of Chinese Education, 1949–1981]. Beijing: Zhongguo Baike Chuanshu Chubanshe, 1984.

II. Works on the Cultural Revolution

Ahn Byung-joon. *Chinese Politics and the Cultural Revolution. Dynamics of Policy Processes.* Seattle: University of Washington Press, 1976.

Archer, Jules. *Chou En-Lai.* New York: Hawthorn Books, 1973.

Baum, Richard, and Louise R. Bennett. *China in Ferment: Perspectives on the Cultural Revolution.* Englewood Cliffs, N.J.: Prentice-Hall, 1971.

Bennett, Gordon A., and Ronald N. Montaperto. *Red Guard: The Political Biography of Dai Hsiao-ai.* Garden City, N.Y.: Anchor, 1972.

Chan, Anita; Stanley Rosen; and Jonathan Unger. "Students and Class Warfare: The Social Roots of the Red Guard Conflict in Guangzhou." *China Quarterly* 83 (1980): 397-446.

Chien Yu-shen. *China's Fading Revolution, Army Dissent, and Military Divisions.* Hong Kong: Centre of Contemporary Chinese Studies, 1969.

Daubier, Jean. *History of the Chinese Cultural Revolution.* New York: Vintage, 1974.

Deshpande, G. P. *China's Cultural Revolution, A View from India.* Bombay: Economic and Political Weekly, 1971.

Dittmer, Lowell. *Liu Shao-chi and the Chinese Cultural Revolution.* Berkeley: University of California Press, 1974.

Dutt, Gargi, and Vidya Prakash Gutt. *China's Cultural Revolution.* New York: Asia Publishing House, 1970.

Elegant, Robert S. *Mao's Great Revolution*. New York: World Publishing Company, 1971.

Esmein, Jean. *The Chinese Cultural Revolution*. Garden City, N.Y.: Anchor, 1973.

Fan, K. H. *The Chinese Cultural Revolution: Selected Documents*. New York: Grove Press, 1968.

Fokkema, D. W. *Report from Peking: Observations of a Western Diplomat on the Cultural Revolution*. London: C. Hurst, 1970.

Grey, Anthony. *Hostage in Peking*. London: Michael Joseph, 1970.

Gudoshnikou, L. M.; R. M. Neronov; and D. P. Barakhta. *China Cultural Revolution and After*. New Delhi: Sterling Publishers, 1978.

Hinton, William. *Hundred Day War: The Cultural Revolution at Tsinghua University*. New York: Monthly Review Press, 1972.

Hsia, Adrian. *The Chinese Cultural Revolution*. London: Orbach G. Chambers, 1972.

Hsin, Chi. *The Case of the Gang of Four*. Hong Kong: Cosmos Books, 1977.

Hunter, Neale. *Shanghai Journal: An Eyewitness Account of the Cultural Revolution*. New York: Praeger, 1969.

Karol, K. S. *The Second Chinese Revolution*. New York: Hill and Wang, 1973.

Lee, Hong Yung. "Mao's Strategy for Revolutionary Change: A Case Study of the Cultural Revolution." *China Quarterly* 77 (1979): 50–73.

———. *The Politics of the Chinese Cultural Revolution: A Case Study*. Berkeley: University of California Press, 1978.

Liang, Hung. *Son of the Revolution*. New York: Knopf, 1983.

Lifton, Robert Jay. *Revolutionary Immortality. Mao Tse-tung and the Chinese Cultural Revolution*. New York: Random House, 1968.

Ling, Ken. *The Revenge of Heaven*. New York: G. P. Putnam's Sons, 1972.

Lotta, Raymond. *And Mao Makes Five: Mao Tsetung's Last Great Battle*. Chicago: Banner Press, 1978.

Lu Xinhua et al. *The Wounded: New Stories of the Cultural Revolution, 1977–78*. Hong Kong: Joint Publishing Company, 1979.

Mehnert, Klaus. *Peking and the New Left: At Home and Abroad*. Berkeley: University of California Center for Chinese Studies, 1969.

Milton, David, and Nancy Dale Milton. *The Wind Will Not Subside*. New York: Pantheon, 1976.

Munro, Robin. "Report from China: Settling Accounts with the Cultural Revolution at Beijing University." *China Quarterly* 83 (1984): 308–33.

Nee, Victor. *The Cultural Revolution in Peking University*. New York: Monthly Review Press, 1969.

Pfeffer, Richard. "Mao Tse-tung and the Cultural Revolution." In Norman Miller and Roderick Aya, eds., *National Liberation*. New York: The Free Press, 1971.

Raddock, David M. "Between Generations: Activist Chinese Youth in Pursuit of a Political Role in the San-fan and in the Cultural Revolution." *China Quarterly* 79 (1979): 511–28.

Red Guard Publications. 20 vols. and supplement. Center for Chinese Research Material. Association of Research Libraries. Washington, D.C., 1975–1980.

Robinson, Joan. *The Cultural Revolution in China.* London: Penguin, 1969.

Robinson, Thomas W. *The Cultural Revolution in China.* Berkeley: University of California Press, 1971.

———. "The Wuhan Incident: Local Strife and Provincial Rebellion During the Cultural Revolution," *China Quarterly* 47 (1971): 413–38.

Rosen, Stanley. *Red Guard Factionalism and the Cultural Revolution in Guangzhou.* Boulder: Westview, 1982.

Schram, Stuart. *Mao Tse-tung Unrehearsed: Talks and Letters, 1956–71.* London: Penguin, 1974.

Solomon, H. Richard. *Revolution Is Not a Dinner Party: A Feast of Images of the Maoist Transformation.* Garden City, N.Y.: Anchor, 1978.

Terrill, Ross. *The White-Boned Demon: A Biography of Mao Zedong's Widow.* New York: William Morrow, 1984.

Thurstone, Ann. "Victims of China's Cultural Revolution: The Invisible Wounds," pts. 1 and 2. *Pacific Affairs* 57, no. 4 (1984): 599–620, and 58, no. 1 (1985): 4–27.

Vogel, E. F. *The Cultural Revolution in the Provinces.* Cambridge, Mass.: Harvard University East Asian Research Center, 1971.

White, Gordon. *The Politics of Class and Class Origin: The Case of the Cultural Revolution.* Paper no. 9, National University Contemporary China Center, Canberra, Australia, 1976.

Wu Tia-wei. *The Great Cultural Revolution in China.* Hong Kong: Asia Research Centre, 1968.

———. *The Great Power Struggle in China.* Hong Kong: Asia Research Centre, 1969.

———. *Lin Biao and The Gang of Four.* Carbondale: Southern Illinois University Press, 1983.

III. General Works on Revolution and Social Organization

Alexander, Yohan; David Carlton; and Paul Wilkinsom. *Terrorism: Theory and Practice.* Boulder: Westview, 1979.

Arendt, Hannah. *On Revolution*. New York: Penguin, 1981.

Aya, Rod. "Theories of Revolution Reconsidered." *Theory and Society* 8 (July 1979): 39–99.

Baechler, Jean. *Revolution*. New York: Harper and Row, 1975.

Bottomore, Tom. *Political Sociology*. London: Hutchinson, 1983.

Brinton, Clarence Crane. *The Anatomy of Revolution*. New York: W. W. Norton, 1938.

Cohn, Steven F., and Markides Kyrioco. "The Location of Ideological Socialization and Age-Based Recruitment into Revolutionary Movements." *Social Science Quarterly* 58 (1977): 462–71.

Crozier, Brian. *A Theory of Conflict*. London: Hamilton, 1974.

Davis, James C. "Towards a Theory of Revolution." *American Sociological Review* 27 (1962): 5–19.

Eisenger, Peter K. "The Conditions of Protest Behavior in American Cities." *American Political Science Review* 67 (1973): 11–28.

Eisenstadt, S. N. *Revolution and the Transformation of Societies*. New York: Free Press, 1978.

Ellul, Jacques. *Autopsy of Revolution*. New York: Knopf, 1971.

———. *Propaganda: The Formation of Men's Attitudes*. New York: Knopf, 1965.

Feinberg, W. E., and Norris R. Johnson. "A Computer Simulation of the Emergence of Consensus in Crowds." *American Sociological Review* 42 (1977): 505–21.

Feuer, Lewis S. *The Conflict of Generations: The Character and Significance of Student Movements*. New York: Basic Books, 1969.

Foss, Daniel A., and Ralph Larkin. *Beyond Revolution: A New Theory of Social Movements*. South Hadley, Mass.: Bergin and Garvey, 1986.

Galtung, John. *A Structural Theory of Revolution*. Rotterdam, Netherlands: Rotterdam University Press, 1974.

Gamson, William A. *The Strategy of Social Protest*. Homewood, Ill.: The Dorsey Press, 1975.

Goldfarb, Walter. "Theories of Revolution and Revolution Without Theory: The Case of Mexico." *Theory and Society* 7 (1979): 135–65.

Gurr, Ted. *Why Men Rebel*. Princeton: Princeton University Press, 1970.

Gusfield, Joseph R. *Protest, Reform, and Revolt: A Reader in Social Movements*. New York: Wiley, 1970.

———. "The Study of Social Movement." In David Sills, ed., *International Encyclopedia of the Social Sciences,* vol. 14. New York: Macmillan, 1968.

Hagopian, Mark N. *The Phenomenon of Revolution*. New York: Dodd, Mead, 1974.

Hobsbawn, E. G. *Revolutionaries*. London: Weidenfeld and Nicholson, 1973.

Hornback, Kenneth E. "Towards a Theory of Involvement Propensity for Collective Behavior." *Sociological Focus* 4 (1971): 61–71.

Jenkins, J. Craig. "Resource Mobilization Theory and the Study of Social Movements." *Annual Review* 9 (1983): 527–53.

Jenkins, J. Craig, and Charles Perrow. "Insurgency of the Powerless: Farm Worker Movements, 1946–1972." *American Sociological Review* 42 (1977): 249–68.

Keniston, Kenneth. "Revolution or Counterrevolution?" In R. J. Lifton and E. Olson, eds., *Explanations in Psycho-history: The Wellfleet Papers.* New York: Simon and Schuster, 1974.

Kornhauser, William. *The Politics of Mass Society.* New York: The Free Press, 1959.

Lang, Kurt V., and Gladys Lang. *Collective Dynamics.* New York: Crowell, 1961.

Lipset, S. M. *Rebellion in the University.* Boston: Little, Brown, 1972.

———. *Student Politics.* New York: Basic Books, 1967.

———. *Consensus and Conflict: Essays in Political Sociology.* New Brunswick: Transaction Books, 1985.

Lo, Clarence Y. H. "Countermovements and Conservative Movements in the Contemporary U.S." *Annual Review of Sociology* 8 (1982): 107–34.

Marx, Gary T. "Thoughts on a Neglected Category of Social Movement Participation: The Agent Provocateur and the Informant." *American Journal of Sociology* 80 (1974): 402–42.

Marx, G., and J. L. Wood. "Strands of Theory and Research in Collective Behavior." *Annual Review of Sociology* 1 (1975).

McAdam, Doug. "Tactical Innovation and the Pace of Insurgency." *American Sociological Review* 48 (1984): 735–53.

McCarthy, John D., and Mayer N. Zald. "Resource Mobilization and Social Movements: A Partial Theory." *American Journal of Sociology* 82 (1977): 1212–41.

Meyer, John, and W. Richard Scott. *Organizational Environment: Ritual and Rationality.* Beverly Hills, Calif.: Sage Publications, 1983.

Moore, Barrington. *Injustice: The Social Bases of Obedience and Revolt.* New York: Pantheon Books, 1978.

———. *Social Origins of Dictatorship and Democracy: Lord and Peasant in the Making of the Modern World.* Boston: Beacon Press, 1966.

Oberchall, A. *Social Conflict and Social Movements.* Englewood, N. J.: Prentice-Hall, 1973.

Olson, Mancur. *The Logic of Collective Action: Public Goods and the Theory of Groups.* New York: Schocken, 1965.

Rude, George. *The Crowd in History: A Study of Popular Disturbances in France and England, 1730–1848.* New York: John Wiley and Sons, 1984.

Scott, James C. "Revolution in Revolution: Peasant and Commissars." *Theory and Society* 7 (1979): 97–134.

Skocpol, Theda. *States and Social Revolutions.* Cambridge, England: Cambridge University Press, 1979.

Skolnick, Jerome H. *The Politics of Protest.* New York: Simon and Schuster, 1969.

Smelser, Neil. *Theory of Collective Behavior.* New York: The Free Press, 1962.

Snow, David A.; Louis A. Zurcher, Jr.; and Sheldon Ekland-Olson. "Social Networks and Social Movements: A Microstructural Approach to Differential Recruitment." *American Sociological Review* 45 (1980): 787–801.

Tilly, Charles. *From Mobilization to Revolution.* Reading, Mass.: Addison-Wesley, 1978.

———. "Revolution and Collective Violence." In F. I. Greenstein and N. Polsky, eds., *Handbook of Political Science.* Reading, Mass.: Addison-Wesley, 1975.

Turner, Ralph, and Lewis Killian. *Collective Behavior.* Englewood Cliffs, N.J.: Prentice-Hall, 1972.

Useem, Michael. *Protest Movements in America.* Indianapolis: Bobbs-Merrill, 1975.

Young, Robert. "Revolutionary Terrorism, Crime, and Mortality." *Social Theory and Practice* 4 (1977): 287–302.

Zald, Mayer N. "Macro Issues in the Theory of Social Movements." Working Paper 204, University of Michigan Center for Research on Social Organization, 1979.

Zald, Mayer N., and Bert Useem. "Movement and Countermovement: Loosely Coupled Conflict." Working Paper 267, University of Michigan Center for Research on Social Organization, 1982.

Index